Taiwan

WORLD BIBLIOGRAPHICAL SERIES
General Editors:
Robert G. Neville (Executive Editor)
John J. Horton

Robert A. Myers   Ian Wallace
Hans H. Wellisch   Ralph Lee Woodward, Jr.

John J. Horton is Deputy Librarian of the University of Bradford and currently Chairman of its Academic Board of Studies in Social Sciences. He has maintained a longstanding interest in the discipline of area studies and its associated bibliographical problems, with special reference to European Studies. In particular he has published in the field of Icelandic and of Yugoslav studies, including the two relevant volumes in the World Bibliographical Series.

Robert A. Myers is Associate Professor of Anthropology in the Division of Social Sciences and Director of Study Abroad Programs at Alfred University, Alfred, New York. He has studied post-colonial island nations of the Caribbean and has spent two years in Nigeria on a Fulbright Lectureship. His interests include international public health, historical anthropology and developing societies. In addition to *Amerindians of the Lesser Antilles: a bibliography* (1981), *A Resource Guide to Dominica, 1493–1986* (1987) and numerous articles, he has compiled the World Bibliographical Series volumes on *Dominica* (1987) and *Nigeria* (1989).

Ian Wallace is Professor of Modern Languages at Loughborough University of Technology. A graduate of Oxford in French and German, he also studied in Tübingen, Heidelberg and Lausanne before taking teaching posts at universities in the USA, Scotland and England. He specializes in East German affairs, especially literature and culture, on which he has published numerous articles and books. In 1979 he founded the journal *GDR Monitor*, which he continues to edit.

Hans H. Wellisch is Professor emeritus at the College of Library and Information Services, University of Maryland. He was President of the American Society of Indexers and was a member of the International Federation for Documentation. He is the author of numerous articles and several books on indexing and abstracting, and has published *The Conversion of Scripts* and *Indexing and Abstracting: an International Bibliography*. He also contributes frequently to *Journal of the American Society for Information Science, The Indexer* and other professional journals.

Ralph Lee Woodward, Jr. is Chairman of the Department of History at Tulane University, New Orleans, where he has been Professor of History since 1970. He is the author of *Central America, a Nation Divided*, 2nd ed. (1985), as well as several monographs and more than sixty scholarly articles on modern Latin America. He has also compiled volumes in the World Bibliographical Series on *Belize* (1980), *Nicaragua* (1983), and *El Salvador* (1988). Dr. Woodward edited the Central American section of the *Research Guide to Central America and the Caribbean* (1985) and is currently editor of the Central American history section of the *Handbook of Latin American Studies*.

VOLUME 113

Taiwan

Wei-chin Lee

Compiler

CLIO PRESS

OXFORD, ENGLAND · SANTA BARBARA, CALIFORNIA
DENVER, COLORADO

British Library Cataloguing in Publication Data

Lee, Wei-chin *1956-*
Taiwan. — (World bibliographical series; v. 113).
1. Taiwan. Bibliographies
I. Title   II. Series
016.951249

ISBN 1–85109–091–6

Clio Press Ltd.,
55 St. Thomas' Street,
Oxford OX1 1JG, England.

ABC-CLIO,
130 Cremona Drive,
Santa Barbara,
CA 93117, USA.

Designed by Bernard Crossland.
Typeset by Columns Design and Production Services Ltd, Reading, England.
Printed and bound in Great Britain by
Billing and Sons Ltd., Worcester.

THE WORLD BIBLIOGRAPHICAL SERIES

This series, which is principally designed for the English speaker, will eventually cover every country in the world, each in a separate volume comprising annotated entries on works dealing with its history, geography, economy and politics; and with its people, their culture, customs, religion and social organization. Attention will also be paid to current living conditions – housing, education, newspapers, clothing, etc.– that are all too often ignored in standard bibliographies; and to those particular aspects relevant to individual countries. Each volume seeks to achieve, by use of careful selectivity and critical assessment of the literature, an expression of the country and an appreciation of its nature and national aspirations, to guide the reader towards an understanding of its importance. The keynote of the series is to provide, in a uniform format, an interpretation of each country that will express its culture, its place in the world, and the qualities and background that make it unique. The views expressed in individual volumes, however, are not necessarily those of the publisher.

VOLUMES IN THE SERIES

Dedicated to
Erica Hovet and Thomas Hovet, Jr.

Contents

Contents

Contents

Introduction

Ilha Formosa: A general profile

Taiwan has for centuries been known to the West as Formosa, a name coined by Portuguese mariners in 1590. As they sailed from Macau to Japan, they sighted the island and exclaimed, 'Ilha Formosa!' ('Beautiful island!').

Taiwan is bound by the Bashi Channel on the south, the Taiwan Strait on the west, the East China Sea on the north, and the Pacific Ocean on the east. The Taiwan Strait, which varies in width from 89 to 124 miles, separates Taiwan from mainland China. Taiwan includes Penghu (a group of sixty-four islands, also called the Pescadores) and thirteen other scattered islands. It is not definitely known where the name Taiwan originated. Some believe that it is a corruption of 'Paiwan', the name of a powerful aboriginal tribe that inhabited the southern part of the island where the Chinese first settled; others believe that the term *Taiwan*, literally 'Terraced bay' in Chinese, was used by the seafarer Cheng Ho during his overseas explorations, around 1430, when a typhoon blew his junks off their course to southern Taiwan. Another explanation is that it is a corruption of 'Tayouan', 'Tayan', 'Tayoun', 'Tyovan', or 'Taivan', different names used during the Dutch occupation of the island for the place that is now the port of Tainan. As time passed, the names used for Tainan, which was an important administrative, economic, and cultural centre prior to the twentieth century, may have been used to identify the whole island.

Shaped roughly like a tobacco leaf, Taiwan proper measures 245 miles from north to south and 89.5 miles from east to west at its broadest point. With an area of 14,000 sq. miles (35,981 sq. km.) in total, Taiwan is about half the size of Scotland, or slightly smaller than Switzerland or Denmark. Yu-shan, or Jade Mountain, at 13,114 ft. (3,997 m.), is the highest peak in Northeast Asia. Mountain ranges, formed like a rugged green spine, run through the island lengthwise and form a watershed; in consequence, most of the rivers in Taiwan flow into the sea in either an easterly or a westerly direction. Moreover, most of the agricultural, commercial, industrial, cultural, and political activities are concentrated in the coastal plains and basin areas. Situated along trade routes between Shanghai, Korea, and Japan to the north, and Hong Kong, Macau, the Philippines, and other Southeast Asian countries to the south, Taiwan constitutes a vital link in the island chain stretching along the east coast of Asia.

Because of its maritime subtropical climate, Taiwan enjoys abundant sunshine and rainfall. These climatic advantages and the island's rich soil provide ideal conditions, making both agriculture and forestry profitable. No wonder Taiwan gained another name from early Chinese settlers – 'Pao-tao' ('Treasure island'). Summers last from May to September, with daytime temperatures often in the 80s and 90s F. (27-35°C.). Winters are short and mild, lasting from December to February. Humidity is high all year, in particular during the summer. Most years, the island is plagued by maritime storms, called typhoons, between June and October.

In 1989, Taiwan's population exceeded twenty million, which is nearly as high as that of Sweden, Norway, and Denmark combined. Taiwanese aborigines, making up one to two per cent of the total population, are believed to be of Malayo-Polynesian origin. The majority of the people in Taiwan came from mainland China at different times, many emigrating from Fukien and Kwangtung before 1945.

As the official language, Mandarin Chinese is the medium of instruction in schools. However, many residents still speak regional dialects such as Hakka, and Taiwanese, which is sometimes referred to as the Min-nan dialect or southern Fukienese dialect. As a result of fifty years of Japanese colonial rule (1895-1945), some of the older inhabitants are also familiar with Japanese, which was taught as the official language.

Religion for most residents of Taiwan, like the traditional Chinese religion practised in other places, is a blend of assorted forms and customs in which the worship of ancestors and that of locally important deities coexist. The exclusive monotheistic nature of Western religions is alien to the traditional polytheistic Chinese approach found in Taiwan. Buddhism and Taoism are sometimes mixed together. Some Chinese deities popular in Taiwan, notably Kuan-yin (goddess of mercy) and Matsu (goddess of the sea and seafarers), originated on the Chinese mainland. One particular feature associated with Taiwanese religions is the ritual festival or pai-pai, which usually involves huge expense and preparation. In addition to Taoism, Buddhism, and other folk religions, Christianity and Islam, although not predominant, are also practised in Taiwan.

History

Pre-1945

Historical records indicate that early Chinese contact with Taiwan was only sporadic. Taiwan was known to southern Sung dynasty historians (AD 1127-1279), whose records describe the islands of Penghu (the Pescadores) and indicate that some Chinese had migrated to these offshore islands to avoid warfare on the mainland. In the fifteenth and sixteenth centuries, Ming dynasty officials visited the island, which had become home to Chinese emigrants from the coastal provinces, as well as a haven for Chinese and Japanese pirates. Although the Portuguese named the island Formosa in 1590, they did not immediately establish a foothold there. By the early 1600s, the Spanish, Japanese, and Dutch were in fierce competition for Taiwan. The Japanese later withdrew when the Shogunate decided to 'close' Japan to the outside world, and the Spaniards were forced out by the Dutch, who eventually gained dominance in 1642 and made Taiwan a base for their trade in Asia. Commercial traffic and migration between the island and the mainland continued to grow during the Dutch period (1624-62). The Chinese settlers, who vastly outnumbered the few hundred Dutch, persistently defied Dutch authority. The Dutch were finally swept from the island in 1662 by invading forces from the mainland led by the Ming dynasty loyalist Cheng Ch'eng-kung, whose latinized name, Koxinga is derived from his ennoblement by the Ming court as Kuo-hsing-yeh, or lord of the imperial surname. Cheng is remembered as a national hero for his expulsion of the 'red-haired barbarians' from Taiwan and for his efforts to retain Taiwan as Chinese territory.

Indeed, the rule of the Cheng family signified a new era in Taiwan's political history. The Chinese system of territorial administration was introduced to the island, implemented by a group of scholars who supervised the civil service. The Chinese stress on education led to the proliferation of schools and academies. During this period the island also enjoyed a remarkable growth in agricultural production. As the immigrant Chinese population increased, aboriginal tribes were Sinicized and assimilated. Although it cannot be claimed that Taiwan was completely Chinese, the institutional and demographic foundations for Sinicization had been well cultivated. Koxinga died in 1662, but his régime survived until 1683, when it surrendered to the Ch'ing dynasty.

Since China was occupied with other pressing national problems, the Ch'ing dynasty ruled Taiwan as a frontier region with a policy that was, at best, passive. The inefficient administration and ineffective control of the early Ch'ing period resulted in frequent rebellions against imperial authority and ceaseless private feuds on the island. Like the coastal regions in mainland China in the nineteenth century, Taiwan was brought within the orbit of the ambitious schemes of Western imperialists. Several ports in Taiwan were forced to open to foreign trade. Europeans and Americans established consulates and trading posts in Taiwan, and at different times, had ideas of colonizing the island. A challenge also came from Japan, which sent a punitive expedition to Taiwan in 1874 after China refused to prosecute in a case involving the massacre of fifty-four members of a Ryukyu vessel by Taiwanese tribesmen.

All these external threats, accompanied by internal chaos, made Peking realize the economic and political significance of Taiwan. In October 1885, Taiwan was proclaimed a separate province of China, and Liu Ming-ch'uan, its first Governor, was entrusted with the task of restoring order to Taiwan and modernizing the new province. Liu moved the capital from Tainan in the south to Taipei in the north; he constructed the first electrical power station; built the first railway system on the island; and redesigned the educational curriculum to include courses on foreign languages and technology. Taiwan came to be regarded as a model province for the whole of China.

Taiwan's promising modernization was unfortunately brought to a halt by the first Sino-Japanese War (1894-95). In the 1895 Treaty of Shimonoseki, China was forced to cede the island to Japan, making Taiwan Japan's first prize in its campaign of imperial expansion. The cession faced vigorous opposition from the Taiwanese people, who, by proclaiming Taiwan an independent republic, made it clear that under no circumstances would the island accept Japanese rule. They pledged that independence was intended to be only temporary and was solely for the purpose of defending the island against a Japanese takeover. Facing the far superior Japanese forces, the resistance of the new republic was bound to fail. The Japanese army, however, did not take the prize without paying a heavy price. Viewed within the context of nineteenth-century China, the Taiwan war of resistance showed another effort on the part of local Chinese defenders to ward off the forces of a formidable foreign nation.

During their fifty years of colonial domination (1895-1945), the

Japanese sought to make the colony into an agricultural supplier for Japan. To improve agricultural production, Japan launched a variety of projects to develop the necessary physical, human, and institutional infrastructures. Hence, the colonial authority established agricultural research stations, organized an island-wide network of farmers' cooperatives, and initiated a large-scale irrigation project. Industry on Taiwan was designed to support agricultural activities. In a manner similar to other colonies during the period of imperialism, Taiwan supplied the colonizing country with primary products, in this case sugar and rice; in return, the colonizing country supplied it with manufactured goods. Although the school system around the island was extensive, education policy was discriminatory, with a sizeable discrepancy between opportunities open to the Japanese and those available to the Taiwanese. Restrictive quotas were imposed on Taiwanese students at certain levels on the educational scale. Despite the efforts to colonize Taiwan, the entire period of occupation witnessed nineteen major uprisings against the Japanese, each brutally suppressed.

'A phoenix from the ashes'

At the end of the Second World War in 1945, Taiwan reverted to Chinese authority. Initially, there was applause from the Taiwanese because the mainland Chinese were regarded as liberators. However, disillusion set in as Taiwan was treated as a potentially wealth-generating but relatively peripheral frontier territory, long exposed to Japanese influence. Things became even worse when 'carpetbaggers' from China began swarming over Taiwan. Assets were seized and made into government monopolies. An anti-Mainlander uprising, later called the 'February 28th Incident' involving the mistreatment of a Taiwanese woman by Mainlander soldiers flared up in 1947. The situation was brought swiftly under control by Nationalist Chinese troops, but estimates of casualties varied from a few thousand to twenty thousand people. This incident has become a lingering scar on the face of Taiwan's modern political development.

At the same time, the Nationalist Party, or Kuomintang (KMT), was suffering defeat at the hands of the Chinese Communist Party in the civil war on the mainland (1947-49). While many former KMT supporters defected to the Communist side in the final months of the war, in 1949, Chiang Kai-shek and his Nationalist Party, along with two million loyalists, retreated to Taiwan. Taipei became the provisional capital of the Republic of China (ROC) in Taiwan. In addition, the Nationalists still held several islands off the mainland, the most important being Quemoy and Matsu. At the end of 1949, the Nationalists beat off a severe attack on Quemoy when the People's Republic of China (PRC) troops advanced southward. Even though this island had never been a direct combat zone, martial law was deemed necessary and was enforced in Taiwan.

While Chiang, like Koxinga, considered Taiwan a temporary base from which to recover mainland China, and viewed the Taipei régime as a legitimate government representing the whole of China, Washington was debating 'who lost China?'. President Truman decided to 'let the dust settle', expecting to see Taiwan go down before Mao's troops. The start of the 1950-53 Korean War, accompanied by other changes in international politics, shifted US foreign policy towards Taiwan and away from a 'hands off' approach to active support. The US Seventh Fleet started to patrol the Taiwan Strait, and military and economic aid to Taiwan was greatly expanded. The 1954 Mutual Defense Treaty between the United States and the ROC made Taiwan part of US global strategy for containing Communist expansion. Until the 1970s, the United States formally endorsed the ROC in Taiwan as the legitimate government of China and supported Taiwan as the holder of China's seat in international organizations, including the United Nations (UN). To some extent, US aid and protection allowed the ROC to consolidate and to survive Peking's constant military threats, including the heavy bombardment of Quemoy in 1958.

Mourning the tragic loss of the mainland and realizing that Taiwan would be the last refuge for them, the Nationalists implemented land reform programmes on the island. Large landowners were compensated for loss of land with commodities certificates and shares of stocks in government enterprises. The majority of landlords took advantage of the land reform to start new commercial and industrial enterprises. These new native entrepreneurs, collaborating with refugee businessmen from the mainland, successfully managed Taiwan's transition from an agricultural to a commercial and industrial economy.

While agricultural improvement was given first priority in the development policies of the 1950s, the emphasis shifted to the growth of light industry in the next decade. During the 1970s, the construction of heavy industry and the enhancement of welfare throughout the island became major policy priorities. The 1980s witnessed a more capital oriented and high technology intensive stage of development in Taiwan. The ROC has grown steadily into a major trading power in both the American market and the world economy; it has also shown a remarkable ability to adjust in the face of new domestic demands and international challenges. It survived, for instance, the marked rise of oil prices in 1973 and rebounded from the global economic recession in the early 1980s.

How did a nation with such a small territory and virtually no major natural resources manage to achieve economic prosperity so rapidly? How did it boost its per capita Gross National Product (GNP) to over $7,500 (£4,600) in 1989? Several factors have made great contributions to the island's impressive economic performance, including: agricultural land reforms; high savings and investment rates; export-oriented growth; excellent educational attainment; population growth restraint; abundant reserves of low-cost labour; and US economic aid (1949-65). Today, Taiwan is in the front rank of the newly industrialized countries, due to its rapid economic growth, low inflation and unemployment rates, healthy balance of payments, and near-universal literacy. Worthy of note is its simultaneous achievement of economic growth and equal income distribution. This indicates that the long and widely accepted notion of the incompatibility of growth and equality in the process of economic development has to be reevaluated. The letters 'MIT' could be described as having changed their meaning from 'Made in Taiwan', which once represented shoddy goods, to 'Miracle in Taiwan'.

The light of democracy never faded

Since the ROC claims to be the government of all of China, it still retains the full array of central administrative bodies set up on the mainland before 1949. The governments of Taiwan province and of the special municipalities of Taipei and Kaohsiung are separately constituted local bodies distinct from the central administration. In addition to the National Assembly, which has the power to select the president and vice-president, there are five administrative branches ('Yuan'): Executive, Legislative, Judicial, Examination and Control. The Executive Yuan constitutes the cabinet and is responsible for policy making and implementation, while the Legislative Yuan is the main lawmaking body. The Judicial Yuan functions like the US Supreme Court to interpret the constitution; the Examination Yuan performs the functions of a civil service commission. The Control Yuan monitors the efficiency of the civil service and investigates cases of corruption. Members elected to national parliamentary bodies before 1949 are still in the majority and hold their seats 'indefinitely' because general elections to select new representatives from constituencies on the mainland cannot be held. Yet the percentage of younger legislators elected in Taiwan is gradually increasing as older members resign or die.

Introduction

In terms of party structure and party-state relations, the political system dominated by the KMT could be called a quasi-Leninist régime. Party organizations closely parallel the administrative structure of the government. The KMT controls the military and employs mass communication as well as community organizations to mobilize support from the populace.

Unlike other Leninist régimes, however, the KMT does not advocate the principle of proletarian dictatorship. On the contrary, it endorses a free, capitalist economy. Until 1986, the whole political structure was virtually a one-party system; a few established opposition parties were allowed to play only marginal rôles and new parties were banned. Incidents involving the violation of human rights have occurred. For example, in 1960, Lei Chen was arrested because of his attempt to form an opposition party. Those who have expressed political views supporting independence for Taiwan or those who have strongly challenged KMT political authority have been considered seditious. Nevertheless, over the years a considerable number of personal freedoms have existed.

Meanwhile, an emerging group of independents or 'nonpartisans' ('tang-wai') have achieved increasing successes in several elections, and finally, in 1986, in defiance of the martial law ban on new political parties, established Taiwan's first new party: the Democratic Progressive Party (DPP). In the early 1980s, the KMT began to loosen restrictions on political competition, and the scope of political discourse in the public domain widened. The KMT also promoted gradual 'Taiwanization' of the national government by appointing more natives to high-level positions in the party and the administration. The thirty-eight-year-old decrees of martial law were dismantled in 1987. Political dissidents may still be harassed or even arrested, but the use of severe legal sanctions has become rare and exceptional. The process of gradually expanding individual freedoms and human rights seems unlikely to be reversed.

Taiwan's 'strongman' politics came to an end in early 1988, when President Chiang Ching-kuo died. Chiang Kai-shek had dominated the island from 1949 to 1975; his son ruled from 1978 until his death ten years later. Both Chiangs were credited for their undisputed contribution to maintaining Taiwan's stability as well as security against Communist threats. Beyond respect for his authority as his father's heir, Chiang Ching-kuo's far-reaching political reforms, begun during his later years, and his long-standing attention to Taiwan's economic modernization earned him widespread support. Lee Teng-hui, a Taiwanese US-educated agricultural economist, succeeded Chiang Ching-kuo in a smooth transition of power and represents part of the 'Taiwanization' effort of the KMT, which aims to increase the status of the Taiwanese in the political decision making process and thus maintain stability on the island.

A solitary island?

Over the years, several storms have broken Taiwan's diplomatic calm, but none was comparable to the loss of China's seat in the UN to the PRC in 1971. This loss cast doubt on Taiwan's continuing viability as an independent state. Secretary of State Kissinger's secret mission to Peking in 1971, followed by President Nixon's visit in 1972, indicated a change in US foreign policy. An informal relationship was established between the US and the PRC for the first time since the Communists took power in 1949. Since then, Taiwan has suffered a series of diplomatic setbacks, as more and more countries shift their official recognition from Taipei to Peking, and fewer and fewer international organizations recognize ROC membership.

Another blow came in 1979 when the US decided to recognize the government of the PRC as the sole legal government of China and to view Taiwan as part of China, terminating the 1954 Mutual Defense Treaty. This blow was softened by the Taiwan Relations Act of 1979, which continued the sale of carefully selected defensive military equipment to Taiwan to ensure a peaceful resolution of the Taiwan question. A non-governmental agency, the American Institute in Taiwan (AIT), was created to oversee US interests in Taiwan and to continue cultural and commercial interaction with the Taiwanese people. Its counterpart, the Coordination Council for North American Affairs (CCNAA), was designated to represent Taiwan in Washington.

Taiwan's adherence to the dogmatic principle of 'no coexistence with the Communists', and its claim of legitimacy in representing all of China, has resulted in Taiwan's increasing diplomatic isolation from the international community. Only approximately twenty countries still maintain relations with the ROC and, with the exception of a few like South Korea, South Africa, and the Holy See, most of them do not possess significant international status.

Taiwan's strategy for ending its diplomatic isolation involves the cultivation of informal ties with many countries by expanding economic relations. In 1989, an ROC International Economic Cooperation Development Fund of $1.2 billion (£736 million) was established to assist nations friendly to the ROC through investment or technology transfer. Taiwan's growing global economic stature has made many nations see it as convenient, or even necessary, to exchange unofficial representatives with Taipei. Indeed, a few have even upgraded their relations with Taiwan to proper diplomatic levels in order to gain full economic cooperation. Even with strong protests from the PRC, Grenada, Liberia, and Belize for example, established diplomatic ties with Taipei in 1989. Taiwan's long-standing principle of 'non-coexistence' has been softened to allow coexistence with the PRC in terms of dual membership in international organizations and jointly courting third countries for dual diplomatic recognition. An apparently more flexible and innovative foreign policy has been initiated and implemented, though the future remains uncertain.

No easy solution for unification

The Chinese civil war ended on the mainland in 1949, but hostility continues and the rift between the ROC and the PRC remains. In the late 1970s, when Teng Hsiao-ping (Deng Xiaoping) scored a victory against the Maoists and economic modernization held high priority among domestic policies, the PRC started to emphasize peaceful means for unification. Since 1979, there have been several unification proposals to reintegrate Taiwan into the PRC. One is the formula of 'one country, two systems', which would grant Taiwan a high degree of autonomy as a special administrative region of the PRC: Taiwan could keep its own armed forces, could retain its socioeconomic system, and could have the final say over its local affairs. Peking has also encouraged trade, cultural exchanges, travel and communications between Taiwan and the mainland. The 1984 Sino-British Accords on the Future of Hong Kong, which will be turned over to the PRC in 1997, have often been described as the model of 'one country, two systems' for the peaceful resolution of the Taiwan question. These 'peace offensives', however, met with a cold response from Taiwan. To the KMT, the Chinese Communists have a record of duplicity, of making and breaking promises easily. The example of Tibet is usually cited to refute the PRC's credibility since its promise of autonomy in Tibet has never materialized. The reliability of the 'one country, two systems' scheme is also open to question due to the endless political turmoil within the PRC.

While governmental contacts and official negotiations between both sides appear unlikely to materialize soon, exchanges in trade and communication have proceeded in both direct and indirect ways, planting the seeds of greater cooperation for both sides. In 1987, Taiwan lifted its ban on residents visiting the Chinese mainland, but so far many who have visited the mainland have returned with total disillusion with the PRC, and a new feeling of confidence in Taiwan.

Nevertheless, distrust of the PRC and dissent from the KMT's long-term political dominance in Taiwan have prompted a number of Taiwanese intellectuals, businesspeople, and politicians at home and abroad to proclaim the principle of 'self-determination'. For the advocate of moderation, this term implies greater political power for the majority of Taiwanese, open elections, and rules for fair play in social and economic interaction. For the radical, it means the establishment of Taiwan as a separate, independent state. The feasibility of Taiwan's independence will continue to occupy the political forum on the island, even though PRC leaders have repeatedly indicated their intention to resort to force if Taiwan declares independence.

The path to new challenges

Between 1962 and 1987, the average economic growth rate for the ROC was 9.3 per cent, which far exceeds the 3.5 per cent of the industrialized nations and the 4.7 per cent rate for developing countries. It was the leading rate among Asia's four 'little dragons', which include Hong Kong, Singapore, and South Korea. Achievements aside, there are challenges lying ahead for Taiwan. Domestically, national parliamentary bodies must be restructured to make them more representative and respect for the rule of law in party competition must be nurtured. If Taiwan is to rank as an economically developed country, it must solve labour shortage problems, ensure the stability of its currency's value at a realistic level, and harmonize labour-management relationships in the industrial sector. Rapid growth has been heedless of environmental concerns, and the question of how to redress long-term ecological neglect on the island must be a major concern in economic planning. The agricultural sector also requires another land reform to consolidate small holdings, a consequence of the 'tiller to the land' programme implemented by a previous land reform, in order to facilitate large-scale mechanical production of crops.

For the near future, Taiwan will continue to be a province of China, functioning as an independent political entity in the global community. A more active and pragmatic foreign policy, however, would enhance Taiwan's international standing and would be expedient for Taiwan in responding to the PRC's overtures toward peaceful reunification.

In the area of international economy, cash-rich Taiwan has become the target of international protectionism because of its foreign reserves of US $75 billion, earned mainly from export. Overdependence on US markets for its manufactured exports has created a substantial trade surplus with the United States and has left Taiwan highly vulnerable to the demands of the US administration. Although Taiwan has revalued its currency and opened its markets substantially, it still exposes its export sector to the vagaries of American economic decisions. Apart from the continuation of economic liberalization to reduce import tariffs on an ever larger list of products, the diversification of risks and the maximization of opportunities are necessary adjustments for Taiwan's export market, given rising wages and the more than thirty per cent appreciation of the New Taiwan dollar against the US dollar since 1985.

Taiwan studies: a neglected focus

While the world market today has been flooded with a variety of Taiwanese products, a surprising number of internationally aware people in the West still have a vague idea of Taiwan. Quite a few Americans, for example, confuse Taiwan with Thailand. As an accidental tourist, I sat beside a middle-aged lady on a domestic flight in the US. 'Oh, you are from Taiwan', she said, 'my husband was stationed there during the Vietnam War and he got along very well with the Thai people'.

If there is little understanding of Taiwan among the public, there is also neglect of the island in the academic community. Certainly before the 1970s, Taiwan was a 'substitute China' for Western scholars barred from field trips in the PRC. Economists and anthropologists examined Taiwan's complicated ethnic differences, social customs, folk religions, and economic development. Despite this early interest, since the American normalization of relations with the PRC in the early 1970s, little research has been done on Taiwan in academic circles. Taiwan came to be considered a backwater, not representative of mainland China and not of sufficient historical, political, and cultural importance on its own. In comparison with China, Taiwan was judged to be too small to merit attention and research. After all, it was constantly under the threat of Communist China and would soon be unified. Therefore, the current overwhelming emphasis on the PRC catches some academics, consciously or unconsciously, looking the other way when it comes to Taiwan.

Academic neglect of Taiwan, is, however, no longer justifiable given Taiwan's economic and international importance. The rapid rise of the country poses challenges not only to policy makers, who are compelled to seek information pertinent to their critical decisions, but also to scholars, who have made strenuous efforts to establish satisfactory explanations for the economic prosperity of East Asia. The current 'East Asian query enterprise' being pursued by academics must include an investigation of Taiwan. The results of such an investigation may offer the PRC and other developing countries many valuable lessons. For this very reason, it is vital that academics readjust their attitudes towards the PRC and ROC by providing a balanced treatment of the two areas, thus deepening our understanding of both sides.

The abundance of research materials in Taiwan is an advantage for extensive and in-depth study of this island. Most documentary sources are carefully shelved in the libraries and archives of individual research institutes or official agencies, such as the Taiwan Museum and the National Central Library, including its Taiwanese Branch. These house materials regarding Japanese colonial administration, Ch'ing dynasty frontier policy, and the like. Statistical surveys on almost every aspect of Taiwan's society are collected, published, and updated regularly in a wide range of yearbooks, journals, and magazines. For example, the Taiwanese government has maintained a system of household and land registration records over the years, following the Japanese colonial government's practice. This wealth of primary sources enables scholars to apply approaches and ideas developed by social scientists outside the field of China studies.

Many questions about Taiwan have only been partially explored, still wait to be answered, or are in need of reexamination. Should the US encourage Taiwan to assert greater international identity, distinct from the PRC? Taiwan's efforts in rejuvenating its national parliament and holding multi-party competitions are viewed positively for democratization, but how stable would such a democracy be? How can we interpret the movement toward democratization without large-scale political violence in Taiwan? Unlike most developing countries, Taiwan seems to be relatively unafraid of extensive military engagement in politics. What are the dynamics of Taiwan's civil-military relations? While many agree that Taiwan should be a model for China, there is less consensus on what the PRC can learn from the Taiwan experience. How did Taiwan achieve socioeconomic equality in its rapid economic development and how can others learn from the experience of the ROC? What were the settlement patterns, lineage networks, land tenure rules, and interactions between aborigines and colonizers in different periods of Taiwan's history, and how did they compare with those in other regions of China? Would a comparison between the development of mainland China in the Republican period and the development of Taiwan since 1949 yield significant findings as to why the KMT failed in the former period and succeeded in the latter? It is apparent that more research and fresh perspectives are needed for Taiwan studies.

About the bibliography

The items included in this bibliography are intended to represent the most judicious assessments available of various aspects of Taiwan including geography, history, religion, society, population, law, politics, foreign relations, economic development, trade, agriculture, language, the arts and information resources. Entry items are arranged alphabetically by author within each broad subject, except within sections on periodicals and newspapers, where they are arranged by title. Where appropriate, sections are subdivided into more specific categories to allow readers easy access to subject matter. Since some entries concern more than one specific category, cross-references have been added at the end of some sections.

There are literally thousands of English-language publications on Taiwan. In this volume, the vast majority of entries are books and journal articles, with a small number of doctoral dissertations and official reports included to cover unusual subjects. In general, recent materials have been selected, in particular those which appeared after 1980. However, older works have not been excluded, if they are deemed to be valuable classics, or if new publications are scarce. In some cases, older materials are included to offer the opportunity of 'looking back', and help further the reader's understanding of Taiwan. The items included in this volume have been selected from a huge pool of about 1,500 entries.

It cannot be said, therefore, that this bibliography is comprehensive because virtually no bibliography is ever complete. Moreover, the decision regarding the inclusion or exclusion of certain entries no doubt reflects my own speciality in international and Chinese politics.

Acknowledgements

The preparation of a project of this magnitude would not have been possible without the help of a number of people. At the recommendation of Dr. Gerald Fry, Dr. Robert Neville, the Executive Editor of the Clio Press *World Bibliographical Series*, suggested that I should undertake this study. I am grateful for Dr. Fry's confidence and Dr. Neville's patient editorial guidance and wise advice. Ms. Rachel Houghton, Senior Assistant Editor, also deserves much of the credit for offering many helpful suggestions.

This project has been financially supported by the William C. Archie Fund and a research and publication grant from the Wake Forest Graduate School. The former made possible a short summer trip to Taiwan and the latter eased the burden of preparation costs.

I would like to express my appreciation to my colleagues in the Department of Politics at Wake Forest University. Collectively, they provided support and lightened my work pressures. Dr. Jack Fleer, Department Chair, and Ms. Elide Vargas, Department Secretary, were very helpful in fulfilling many of my requests for this project. Dr. Richard Sears, Director of the International Studies Office of Wake Forest University, allowed me to use his office printing facilities. Ms. Margaret Backenheimer, a longstanding family friend, has been a patient reader and critic. To all of them I owe a debt of gratitude. I would also like to record my appreciation of the efforts of the staff, in particular, Mrs. Carrie Thomas, in the interlibrary loan section of Wake Forest University Main Library for their unfailing assistance in locating and obtaining the materials I needed. My parents, sisters, and brothers deserve my sincere gratitude for their perennial support and understanding. Even during my visit to Taiwan, they provided me with all that they could, but received so little in return, as my long stays in the library left me little time with them. Above all, I feel particularly indebted to my wife, Cristina, for her encouragement and emotional support. Cristina also painstakingly typed the first draft of these detailed entry items in the warm and humid months of the South and took over many family chores.

The late Dr. Thomas Hovet, Jr., guided my intellectual growth during my graduate study at the University of Oregon. Both he and his wife, Erica, were always willing to offer their friendship and help, whenever needed. To them this book is dedicated.

Since the book was completed in just over a year, readers may notice some shortcomings and errors. I am solely responsible for these. I hope that I have conveyed enough of the complexity and excitement of the people and places of Taiwan so that readers will find them interesting and will continue their own journey of inquiry into Taiwan.

Wei-chin Lee
Winston-Salem, North Carolina
October 1989

Romanization of Chinese Names and Terms

In this bibliography, the Wade-Giles romanization system, the system most prevalent in Taiwan, has been used to transliterate Chinese names and phrases, with the exception of names that are widely used and known to foreign readers, for example, the name of 'Chiang Kai-shek'. If the names and phrases in the titles have already been transliterated and printed in the Pinyin system, they are left intact for convenience of retrieval. This policy requires familiarity with two romanization systems, but it is adopted in order to cause the least confusion in identification of people, places, and literary works. Several examples are listed below to show the difference between the two systems.

Wade-Giles	*Pinyin*
Chou En-lai	Zhou Enlai
Hua Kuo-feng	Hua Guofeng
Kuomintang	Guomindang
Mao Tse-tung	Mao Zedong
Nanking	Nanjing
Peking	Beijing
Taipei	Taibei
Teng Hsiao-ping	Deng Xiaoping

Abbreviations

Below are some frequently used terms appearing in this volume.

AIT	American Institute in Taiwan
CCNAA	Coordination Council for North American Affairs
CCP	The Chinese Communist Party
DPP	Democratic Progressive Party
JCRR	Joint Commission for Rural Reconstruction
KMT	The Kuomintang or the Nationalist Party
PLA	People's Liberation Army
PRC	People's Republic of China
ROC	Republic of China
TIM	Taiwan Independence Movement
TRA	The Taiwan Relations Act of 1979

Selected Resources
and Research
Institutes in Taiwan

Academia Sinica (Nan-kang, Taipei)
As the highest academic institution in Taiwan, the academy has fourteen institutes: American Culture, Biological Chemistry, Botany, Chemistry, Earth Sciences, Economics, Ethnology, History and Philology, Information Science, Mathematics, Modern History, Physics, Three Principles of the People, and Zoology. Each institute houses invaluable collections in its field and has conducted extensive research on Taiwan.

Asia and World Institute (Taipei)
This institute studies issues and events affecting Taiwan for the purpose of informing and advising government and private agencies on foreign policy matters.

Chung-hua Institution for Economic Research (Taipei)
Founded for advanced research on both domestic and international economics concerning Taiwan, this institute has a library housing selected materials on international economics and the economics of Taiwan and mainland China.

The Historical Research Commission of Taiwan (Taichung)
The importance of this commission lies in its collection of over 12,000 volumes of documents from the office of Government-General during the Japanese occupation period.

Institute of International Relations, National Chengchi University (Mucha, Taipei)
This institute focuses on the study of international relations with emphasis on Taiwan and mainland China. It also houses numerous materials dealing with Chinese communism.

National Central Library (Taipei)
A copy of most publications printed in Taiwan must be submitted to

this library, which houses the Resource and Information Center for Chinese Studies. The Library's Taiwan Branch, located separately in Taipei, is well known for its special collection of publications from the colonial period.

National Palace Museum (Taipei)
This museum houses some 640,000 pieces of the most priceless of Chinese art treasures from China's fabled dynasties. Its library possesses some 173,475 volumes of rare and old books. Invaluable Ch'ing dynasty palace archives and documents are kept here.

National Taiwan University Library (Taipei)
Its precursor was the Imperial Taihoku University Library established by the Japanese government in 1928. Among its special collections, the Archives of the Dutch East India Company on Taiwan are useful for the study of early Taiwanese history.

Taipei Documents Committee Library (Taipei)
This library publishes many collections of historical documents relating to Taipei.

The Country and its People

1 **Background notes: Taiwan.**
Bureau of Public Affairs.   Washington, DC: Bureau of Public Affairs,
Department of State, 1988. 9p.
Provides concise background information on Taiwan, beginning with a profile of its
people, geography, political establishment, and economy. This is followed by more
detailed material on Taiwan's defence capabilities, political conditions, and foreign
relations. Principal officials in the government are listed. The piece includes helpful
travel notes, with a discussion of climate and clothing, immigration regulations, health
concerns, and the transportation system.

2 **Area handbook for the Republic of China.**
Frederick H. Chaffee, George E. Aurell, Helen A. Barth, Ann S. Cort,
John H. Dombrowski, Vincent J. Fasano, John O. Weaver.
Washington, DC: Government Printing Office, 1969. 435p. bibliog.
(Foreign Area Studies Handbook Series, no. DA Pam 550-63).
This volume is one of a series of handbooks prepared by the Foreign Area Studies
group (FAS) of the American University, Washington, DC. It is designed to provide
readers with a convenient compilation of basic facts about the social, economic,
political and military institutions and practices of Taiwan.

3 **Reflections of Taiwan.**
Derek A. C. Davies, Daniel P. Reid, translated by Y. S. Yang
Singapore: R. Ian Lloyd Productions; Taipei: Caves Books, 1987. 207p.
Taiwan reflects an eclectic blend of East and West, modern and traditional. Beneath
the modern cosmetics, however, beats a traditional heart. Relying on R. Ian Lloyd's
beautiful photographs and a compelling introduction, this volume offers its readers a
brief but in-depth view of Taiwan. In the introduction, the cultural heritage and social
norms of Taiwan are compared to those of the West.

The Country and its People

4 New image of Taipei.
Department of Information. Taipei: Department of Information, Taipei
City Government, 1985. 5th ed. 204p.

Taipei has experienced great changes, brought about by Taiwan's rapid economic growth. This bilingual volume is a pictorial presentation of the various aspects of this modern, dynamic city. A general description of Taipei, is followed by four sections on its political, economic, social, and cultural development.

5 Taiwan in a time of transition.
Edited by Harvey Feldman, Ilpyong J. Kim.   New York: Paragon
House, 1988. 285p.

How Taiwan, an erstwhile pariah, became a model for successful development, a widely-courted aid and trade partner, and a growing force in international politics is the subject of this skilfully edited volume. It provides well-coordinated analyses of the factors responsible for Taiwan's internal and external transformation, and a valuable set of guidelines to help readers follow future developments. Its nine essays, written by American and Asian experts, deal with US-Taiwan relations, Taiwan and the regional economy of East Asia, social change and the political development of the island, Taiwan and the unification campaign launched by the PRC, and prospects for the ROC's politics in the 1990s.

6 China.
Michael Freeberne, Christopher Howe, Ramon H. Myers.   In: *The Far
East and Australia, 1982-83*. London: Europa, 1982, p. 325-404.

This section covers a vast spectrum of topics concerning both Taiwan and mainland China. It includes essays on Taiwan's geography, history and economy, and gives detailed information on its constitution, government, legislature and other political, economic and commercial institutions. It also provides a particularly useful statistical survey which covers agriculture, forestry, history, mining, finance, industry, transport, communication media, and other areas in detail.

7 Taiwan.
Noel Grove.   *National Geographic*, vol. 161, no. 1 (1982), p. 92-119.

The author describes how Taiwan, born in the defeat of civil war and united by diplomatic isolation, survives on economic stamina and patriotic zeal. Although mainland China has continuously stepped up its diplomatic drive for reunification by promising Taiwan economic autonomy, the Nationalist government in Taiwan remains steadfast in rejecting such proposals.

8 Taiwan today.
Lih-wu Han.   Taipei: Cheng Chung, 1986. 310p. map.

A wide-ranging discussion of important elements in Taiwan's society, this volume covers political and social conditions, military defence, foreign relations, external trade, finance, agriculture, industry, communications, and education. It also offers a brief comparison of similar aspects in mainland China and Hong Kong.

9 **Taiwan.**
Bob King. In: *The Asia and Pacific review, 1988*. Saffron Walden,
England: World of Information, 1987, 9th ed., p. 232-36.
Shows that the Nationalist government in Taiwan has begun to see the world in new
terms. During 1987, Taiwan ended thirty-eight years of martial law and decades of
control over foreign-exchange movements and the media. This essay describes
Taiwan's domestic economy and foreign investment, as well as its industrial
development, with the focus on the economy rather than politics. It also includes a
useful business guide and directory.

10 **The Republic of China under Chiang Kai-shek: Taiwan today.**
F. A. Lumley. London: Barrie & Jenkins, 1976. 167p. bibliog.
This book, started in 1973, provides a general description of Taiwan's history and
political development. It also gives details of the ROC's successful land reforms,
educational labyrinth, foreign aid, economic infrastructure and environmental
problems.

11 **Formosa today.**
Edited by Mark Mancall. New York: Praeger, 1964. 171p.
The essays in this volume, mostly written by specialists with diverse backgrounds and
qualifications, first appeared in *China Quarterly* (no. 15, 1963). Topics covered include
intellectuals, military forces, foreign relations, economic growth, and political
movements. Mancall's introduction provides a conceptual framework for these essays.
He argues that the Nationalist Party maintained the entire panoply of political methods
and institutions that characterized totalitarian and near-totalitarian states in the 1950s
and 1960s. These essays provide the background necessary to understand Taiwan's
current efforts at political reforms.

12 **Taiwan.**
Daniel P. Reid, edited by Paul Zach. Hong Kong: APA, 1984. 2nd ed.
355p. maps
The brilliant colour photographs, accurate maps, and excellent text of this volume
present the natural beauty of Taiwan's mountain peaks and golden beaches and offer
evidence of the ROC's modern economic miracle as well. Reid describes Chinese art,
culture, and religion as they have been preserved in Taiwan's museums, folk temples,
and local communities. This is a book not only for tourists but also for general readers
who want to further their understanding of a unique island.

13 **Through Formosa: an account of Japan's island colony.**
Owen Rutter. London: Adelphi Terrace, 1923. 288p. bibliog.
This is an account of the author's journey through Taiwan some seventy years ago.
Although Rutter acknowledges that he lacks intimate and exhaustive knowledge of the
island, he nevertheless provides a brief introduction to Taiwan's history, its natural
resources, and Japan's colonial administration. He is particularly interested in Taiwan's
aborigines and Japan's policy toward them. The volume includes photographic
illustrations of the aborigines and the places that the author visited, a selected
bibliography, and several appendices outlining details of colonial revenue and
expenditure.

3

14 **Taiwan: the watchful dragon.**
    Helen Schreider, Frank Schreider.   *National Geographic*, vol. 135, no. 1
    (1969), p. 1-45.

This essay paints a particularly vivid portrait of all aspects of life in Taiwan in the 1960s. The authors describe the daily life of the people, their religious beliefs, economic expectations and living standards. They also cover industrial development and military defence. Colour illustrations are included.

15 **Republic of China 1988: a Reference Book.**
    Edited by Dixon D. S. Sung.   Taipei: Hilit; New York: Highlight
    International, 1988. annual.

Presents a compendium of detailed information on Taiwan. Using graphs and diagrams, it supplies information and statistics on national trends in economy, politics, culture and society. An alphabetical listing of important personalities and an annotated chronology of annual events in the Republic of China are included. Provides fascinating browsing for the casual reader and solid background material for the businessperson and scholar.

Tourism and Travellers' Accounts

16 **Old hundred-names, pictures of the people of Taiwan.**
Frederick Andrews. Taipei: Mei-ya, 1968. 95p.
The title is taken from the Chinese expression for the common people (Lao-pai-hsing, in Chinese, or 'Old hundred-names'). This collection of photographs is assembled from many taken by the author while he worked in Taiwan for the *New York Times* and the Times-Life News Service. His photographs illustrate life in Taiwan in the 1960s, which presents quite a contrast to contemporary society in the ROC.

17 **Official Guidebook 1984-85: Taiwan, Republic of China.**
China Travel and Trade. Taipei: China Travel and Trade, 1984.
annual.
This guidebook, published under the authority of the Tourism Bureau of the Republic of China, offers a wide range of information about Taiwan, including maps of major cities and colour illustrations. It is updated regularly and provides a very convenient guide for tourists planning to visit Taiwan.

18 **Quest for the best in Taiwan: a complete guide for visitors and residents.**
Dorothy Orr Cole. Taipei: The Author, 1985. 227p.
An in-depth guide to getting the best out of visiting or living in Taiwan, this book contains useful information and interesting suggestions, such as handy household hints and advice on special shopping areas in Taipei. Since the author has resided in Taiwan more than thirteen years, she is eminently qualified to guide the newly-arrived through the details of daily life.

19 **Living in Taiwan: a handbook for housewives.**
Helen Freytag. Taipei: Mei-ya, 1970. 289p.
Materials are presented chronologically from the preparatory and packing stages of the
move to unpacking and settling down in Taiwan. Although specific information, such
as addresses of doctors and travel agents is now out of date, Freytag's description of
social customs and cultural values in Taiwan is still very useful.

20 **'As others see us': views of the Republic of China.**
Pacific Cultural Foundation. Taipei: Pacific Cultural Foundation, 1984.
96p.
The result of an English essay contest for foreign students living in Taiwan, this volume
presents the eleven winning entries. These enlightening essays cover various aspects of
the nation. Readers who plan to visit Taiwan but dislike the usual tourist books will
enjoy reading this slim volume.

21 **Taiwan: a travel survival kit.**
Robert Storey. Oakland, California: Lonely Planet, 1987. 256p.
Provides tips on cheap accommodation, meals and transportation, as well as extensive
notes on history and customs. This excellent guide, with thirty-two colour photographs
and forty-nine maps, is designed for the independent traveller on a limited budget.

22 **Taiwan on-your-own.**
Robert Storey. Tainan, Taiwan: Chiu Yo, 1985. 298p. maps.
The first part of this book deals with information for the independent traveller, such as
postal services, hiking hints, clothing requirements, and driver's licence regulations.
These essentials are interspersed with the author's personal observations and
experience. For example, he notes that fruit is usually served at the end of the meal
and that a Chinese host will often indicate that the food and service are inadequate for
his honoured guest. The second portion of the book describes the different cities and
tourist attractions of Taiwan. A brief essay on Taiwanese customs is appended. Some
illustrations and hand-drawn maps are provided.

Reflections of Taiwan.
See item no. 3.

Through Formosa: an account of Japan's island colony.
See item no. 13.

From far Formosa: the island, its people and missions.
See item no. 88.

Japanese rule in Formosa.
See item no. 114.

**Mountains and streams of inexhaustible splendor: Taiwan's favorite new
scenic spots.**
See item no. 736.

The realm of jade mountain: the ten top scenic spots of Taiwan, the Republic of China
See item no. 737.

The beauty of Yushan.
See item no. 738.

Tourism, hot spring resorts and sexual entertainment, observations from northern Taiwan: a study in social geography.
See item no. 739.

Beer houses: an indicator of cultural change in Taiwan.
See item no. 740.

Geography

23 **East China Sea: boundary problems relating to the Tiao-yu-tai Islands.**
     K. T. Chao.   *Chinese Yearbook of International Law and Affairs*, vol. 2
     (1982), p. 45-97.

The Tiao-yu-tai (Senkaku) Islands are situated on the edge of the continental shelf in the East China Sea extending from mainland China. This article focuses attention on the territorial dispute between Japan and China (both the PRC and the ROC) over the Islands and on the effect of these Islands on the delimitation of continental shelf boundaries in the East China Sea.

24 **Atlas of land utilization in Taiwan.**
     Cheng-siang Chen.   Taipei: National Taiwan University, 1950. 154p.

This atlas contains vital data on Taiwan's agricultural geography. It consists of eight aerial photographs of various parts of Taiwan and 164 maps showing, for example: distribution of water buffaloes; crop area of tobacco; land settlement of early migrants; population density of cultivated land; distribution of poor farmers; areas under irrigation; and many other topics related to agricultural geography. Students of Taiwan's agriculture, economic development, and geography of the 1940s and 1950s will find this book invaluable.

25 **Geo-essays on Taiwan.**
     Cheng-siang Chen.   Hong Kong: Commercial Press, 1982. 524p.

Twenty papers written by the author and published in different places are collected in this volume. Covering a variety of topics related to Taiwan's geography, he discusses such subjects as the sugar industry, marine and aquatic resources, industrial development, land use and cropping systems and geographical regions.

26 **Taiwan: an economic and social geography.**
Cheng-siang Chen. Taipei: Fu-min Geographical Institute of Economic Development, 1963. 653p. (Fu-min Geographical Institute of Economic Development, Research Report, no. 96).
Discusses every aspect of Taiwan's geography. In addition to describing the physical setting of the island, its chapters cover: water resources and hydroelectric power, land utilization, the rice economy, the sugar industry, forests, marine and aquatic products, livestock raising, coal mining, power supply, and foreign trade. Generous illustrations and detailed descriptions make this an excellent source for students of Taiwan's economic and social development.

27 **Surnames in Taiwan: interpretations based on geography and history.**
Kuang-ho Chen, L. L. Cavallis-Sforza. *Human Biology*, vol. 55, no. 2 (1983), p. 367-74.
The author describes a survey of surnames in Taiwan. The geographic distribution of these surnames was studied as a potential source of information on the migration history of the Taiwanese population.

28 **Land constraints and development planning in Taiwan.**
Roland J. Fuchs, John M. Street. *Journal of Developing Areas*, vol. 14, no. 3 (1980), p. 313-26.
Following a discussion of environmental and land resource constraints as related to economic development in Taiwan, the authors identify land use conflicts and trade-offs in current economic development goals and policies.

29 **Taiwan-Ilha Formosa: a geography in perspective.**
Chiao-min Hsieh. Washington, DC: Butterworths, 1964. 372p.
Divided into three parts for the natural setting, historical settlement. and present cultural landscape of Taiwan, despite a few typographical errors and misinterpretations, this volume should be useful for general reference.

30 **The geographer and Taiwan.**
Ronald G. Knapp. *China Quarterly*, no. 74 (June 1978), p. 356-68.
Knapp examines the contributions made by geographers to Taiwan studies and argues that Taiwan offers a particularly satisfactory area for the study of frontiers and their historical development, and a well-documented area of interest in geography.

31 **The East Asian seabed controversy revisited: relevance (or irrelevance) of the Tiao-yu-tai (Senkaku) Islands territorial dispute.**
Ying-jeou Ma. *Chinese Yearbook of International Law and Affairs*, vol. 2 (1982), p. 1-44.
The Tiao-yu-tais are a group of eight uninhabitable islets scattered in the East China Sea between Taiwan and Japan. Since these islands sit right on top of an oil reservoir and since they themselves may be used, under existing international law, in measuring continental shelf entitlements, sovereignty over them has become a bitter point of friction between Japan and Taiwan. This article focuses primarily on the relevance of the islands in the delimitation of maritime boundaries. with special reference to the

implications of relevant provisions of the third United Nations convention on the Law of the Sea of 1982 and the Tunisian-Libyan continental shelf case decided by the International Court of Justice in 1982.

32 Development and the middle city in Taiwan.
Clifton W. Pannell. *Growth and Change*, vol. 5, no. 3 (1974), p. 21-29.

Examines the rôle of the middle-sized city in the evolution of the urban system in Taiwan. The author shows that most of these cities, even in the face of official neglect, are closely linked to the process of economic growth and other facets of national development in Taiwan. The middle-sized cities function as transition centres for rural dwellers making their initial entry into the urban scene, yet permit them to retain in part their residential and social attachment to their native homes.

33 China: the geography of development and modernization.
Clifton W. Pannell, Lawrence J. C. Ma. London: Edward Arnold, 1983. 342p.

The authors claim that most of the topics and issues involved in the modernization of both Taiwan and mainland China are related to the geography of the country. Good geographical analysis can provide the basis for better planning and policy and can contribute significantly to more rapid modernization. This volume offers details and insights into the rôle of geography in China's recent modernization efforts. One section (p. 259-300) deals with land use in Taiwan and the geographical aspects of its economic development.

34 Agricultural use of slopelands in Taiwan.
Jack F. Williams. *China Geographer*, no. 11 (1981), p. 89-111.

The slopelands in Taiwan constitute an extremely vulnerable region that has been under massive attack, both legal and illegal, especially in the past thirty years. Both private parties and government agencies have gradually invaded these formerly untapped land resources. This paper offers an overview of the slopelands in terms of physical environmental conditions, land use patterns and practices, and government land policies. It indicates some of the problems associated with the use of slopelands for agricultural purposes.

35 Land settlement and development: a case study from Taiwan.
Jack F. Williams, Chang-yi Chang, Chiu-yuan Wang. *Journal of Development Areas*, vol. 18, no. 1 (1983), p. 35-52.

Taiwan's upper Ta-chia River basin has been the focus of both planned and spontaneous land settlement and land development for over twenty years. This study uses the Ta-chia River basin to illustrates many facets of resource development in Taiwan, including the question of who is to decide what the use of land should be.

China's island frontier: studies in the historical geography of Taiwan
See item no. 69.

The law of the sea and the delimitation of maritime boundaries in the East China Sea.
See item no. 493.

Some problems concerning the delimitation of the maritime boundaries between the Republic of China (Taiwan) and the Philippines.
See item no. 494.

South China Sea islands: implications for delimiting the seabed and future shipping routes.
See item no. 495.

The Republic of China's claims relating to territorial sea, continental shelf, and exclusive economic zones: legal and economic aspects.
See item no. 497.

Flora and Fauna

36 **List of common names of the fishes of Taiwan.**
Johnson T. F. Chen.   Taipei: Taiwan Fishing Bureau, 1954. 126p.
741 fish of Taiwan are listed in English, Japanese, and Chinese. Indexes of Chinese and English scientific names are included.

37 **Chinese medical herbs of Taiwan.**
Taipei: Hao-hsiung-ti Press, 1987. 5 vols.
These five volumes provide an illustrated and descriptive guide to medicinal plants indigenous to and naturalized in Taiwan. Descriptions are in Chinese and English. Each volume contains about 200 pages and includes colour plates and an index.

38 **T'ai-wan je tai chih wu ts'ai se t'u chien.** (Tropical plants of Taiwan in colour.)
Feng-chi Ho.   Ping-tung, Taiwan: Heng-chun Tropical Botanical Garden, 1977, 1979, 1981. 3 vols.
Both native and introduced species are covered. Although the description is in Chinese, the scientific names are in Latin, with full citations and the common names. A sixteen-page glossary provides illustrations of botanical terms, with English inscriptions, as well as an index of Latin names.

39 **Nomenclature of plants in Taiwan.**
A-tsai Hsieh, Tsai-i Yang.   Taipei: College of Agriculture, National Taiwan University, 1969. 1,082p.
Taiwan is sometimes described as a giant, natural, botanical garden characterized by an unusual variety of vegetation and great fertility for plant growth. However, much confusion in the nomenclature of plants prevails all over the island. The present work was undertaken in an attempt to compile a list of plant names and so minimize the confusion. For each plant, Chinese, English and Japanese scientific names are provided, along with its geographical distribution on Taiwan.

40   **The illustrated edible wild plants of Taiwan.**
      Chiao-mu Hsu, Nien-yung Chiu.   Taipei: Southern Materials Center,
      1986. 2nd ed. 283p.

Introduces Taiwan's edible plants, both wild and cultivated, covering 256 species in
eighty-six families. For each plant, the authors provide a colour photograph,
description, scientific name, Japanese name, alternative name, and an analysis of
geographical distribution, physical appearance, edible parts, method of preparation,
and medicinal uses.

41   **Illustrations of common plants of Taiwan; vol. 1: weeds.**
      Chien-chang Hsu.   Taipei: Taiwan Provincial Education Association,
      1975. 2nd ed. 557p.

Deals with 200 herbaceous plants that are commonly seen along roadsides, in fields, or
on waste ground. Each entry is accompanied by a drawing made from a living plant, as
well as descriptions in English and Chinese. The author cites where and when each
plant was collected.

42   **A list of plants of Formosa.**
      Takiya Kawakami.   Taipei: Cheng-wen Publishing Company, 1971.
      119p.

This volume was first published in 1910 by the Bureau of Productive Industry,
Formosan Government. It contains 2,368 species, with both scientific names and
Japanese names. Formosan names are provided where available. An index of genera is
appended.

43   **Flora of Taiwan.**
      Edited by Hui-lin Li, Tang-shui Liu, Tseng-chieng Huang, Tetsuo
      Koyama, Charles E. Devol.   Taipei: Epoch, 1980. 2nd ed. 6 vols.

This set of books provides a systematic account of the vast range of flora on Taiwan.
Volumes one to five cover all native vascular plants. Volume six contains the
bibliography, the general index, and a checklist for the flora of Taiwan. It is of great
reference value not only to botanists but also to general readers.

44   **A new guide to the birds of Taiwan.**
      Sheldon Severinghaus, Kenneth T. Blackshaw.   Taipei: Mei-ya, 1976.
      222p.

Describes 201 species of birds found in Taiwan. Most of the information on the birds'
status, distribution, habitat and behaviour is based on direct field research and
observation. The descriptions are written in both Chinese and English. Some colour
illustrations are provided.

45   **Coastal fishes of Taiwan.**
      Shih-chieh Shen.   Taipei: Taiwan Provincial Museum, 1984. 190p.

This book presents 1,051 species of fish belonging to 153 families. Most of these species
are found either along the coast of Taiwan or near the adjacent islands. There are
numerous color plates to illustrate the differences in patterning that occur with growth
or sexual differentiation.

46 **Synopsis of fishes of Taiwan.**
Shih-chieh Shen. Taipei: Southern Materials Center, 1984. 533p.

Categorizes the fish of Taiwan. Although the main text is written in Chinese, English names are attached. Descriptions and illustrations are presented side by side. An index of English scientific names is appended.

47 **The illustrated plants of special uses in Taiwan.**
Edited by Chen-tsung Tsai. Taipei: Taiwan Provincial Museum, 1985. 218p.

Describes 203 plants with special uses found in Taiwan. Some are used for perfume; some are for human consumption. Scientific names, distribution, and usage are detailed for each plant. Written descriptions are accompanied by colour illustrations.

48 **A list of plants in Taiwan.**
Tsai-i Yang. Taipei: National Publisher, 1982. 1,632p.

Lists the accepted scientific names of plants and the synonyms previously used for reference. Misused Chinese names have been removed to avoid confusion. The plant names used by the aboriginal people are described in Roman phonetics with the tribal names or the locality of use given in parentheses. For each plant, Japanese and English scientific names are also indicated.

49 **The illustrated Chinese materia medica: prepared drugs.**
Kun-ying Yen. Taipei: Southern Materials Center, 1986. 210p.

With the exception of some seeds and roots, the medicinal substances used in the preparation of prescriptions for Chinese medicine must be either chopped up or pounded into powder. This illustrated guide presents information on how drugs are refined, and how medicinal substances are processed to insure maximum efficacy in treatment. There are 162 colour photographs included in this volume.

50 **Alpine plants of Taiwan in color.**
Shao-shun Ying. Taipei: Department of Forestry, National Taiwan University, 1975, 1978. 2 vols.

Colourful illustrations and concise descriptions in both Chinese and English are provided for Taiwan's numerous alpine plants. In addition, this volume contains essays on the ecology, cultivation, and morphology of alpine plants.

51 **The illustrated penaeoid prawns of Taiwan.**
Hsiang-ping Yu, Tin-yam Chan. Taipei: Southern Materials Center, 1986. 183p.

The aim of this publication is to aid readers in identifying the Taiwan penaeoid prawn. A series of colour photographs and distribution maps for each species are presented. In total fifty-four species in fifteen genera and four families are described, including all the common penaeoid species.

Prehistory and Archaeology

52 **Prehistoric archaeology of Taiwan.**
Kwang-chih Chang. *Asian Perspectives*, vol. 13 (1970), p. 59-77.
Evidence suggests that human occupation on Taiwan might have begun around 2,500 BC, a time of destruction of primeval forests and the rise of subtropical and warm temperate vegetation. This paper analyses different ethnological and archaeological data for Taiwan. The author tries to place Taiwan in the larger context of prehistoric East and Southeast Asia in order to explore fully its archaeological potential.

53 **Prehistoric ceramic horizons in southeastern China and their extension into Formosa.**
Kwang-chih Chang. *Asian Perspectives*, vol. 7 (1963), p. 243-50.
Evaluates the argument that much of the prehistoric culture of Taiwan was essentially an offshoot of that on the Chinese mainland to the west. In this article, prehistoric ceramics of the southeastern coastal provinces of China are described and characterized, and a comparison of the archaeological evidence from southeastern China and Taiwan reaffirms the long-held view that the bulk of prehistoric cultures on Taiwan arrived from mainland China during different chronological periods.

54 **Fengpitou, Tapenkeng, and the prehistory of Taiwan.**
Kwang-chih Chang, with the collaboration of Ch'ao-ch'i Lin, Minze Stuiver, Hsin-yuan Tu, Matsuo Tsukada, Richard J. Pearson, Tse-min Hsu. New Haven, Connecticut: Yale University Press, 1969. 279p. bibliog. (Publications in Anthropology, no. 73).
Two site reports and a summary of Taiwan's prehistory are followed by a discussion of the island's relationship to the prehistory of surrounding areas and an analysis of possible relationships between prehistoric cultures and present day ethnic groups on Taiwan. Taiwan is viewed as an archaeological laboratory in which the cultural history of East Asia may be studied, providing a means of understanding the diffusion and migration of peoples and cultures between China and Southeast Asia. During 1964-65,

Prehistory and Archaeology

Chang and Wen-hsun Sung carried out excavations at various sites. Here, the site of Fengpitou in southwestern Taiwan and the site of Tapenkeng in the Taipei area are analysed.

55 Man in the Choshui and Tatu River valleys in central Taiwan.
Kwang-chih Chang, et al. *Asian Perspectives*, vol. 17, no. 1 (1974), p. 36-55.

Describes research into Taiwan's prehistory, using the area of the Choshui and the Tatu River valleys in central Taiwan. The Choshui is the longest river in Taiwan, and the total area of these two river systems is vast, about a seventh of the total area of the island. The overall objective of this project is to study cultural variation and change in relation to both diversity and changes in the natural environment and to the adaptive capabilities of human groups.

56 Jar burial on Botel Tobago island.
Inez De Beauclair. *Asian Perspectives*, vol. 15, no. 2 (1973), p. 166-76.

Botel Tobago, an offshore island near Taiwan, has long been a place for prisoners. In August 1969, while a school building was being constructed, a broken jar was found not far from the shore, together with other artefacts. The author describes the site and the significance of the buried objects.

57 Ecological context and the prehistory of the west central Taiwan coast.
Robert Dewar. *Asian Perspectives*, vol. 11, no. 2 (1981), p. 207-41.

Provides a general, simplified description of the palaeoecology of the west central Taiwan coast area. This study attempts to define the important characteristics of the territory of the neolithic settlers in this area and discusses the local developmental sequence of their culture.

58 The prehistoric southern islands and East China Sea islands.
Naoichi Kokubu. *Asian Perspectives*, vol. 7 (1963), p. 224-42.

Studies the pattern of cultural distribution and stratification in an area of the East China Sea as derived from archaeological evidence of such cultural contacts and movements. In particular, the paper shows the prehistoric contact between Taiwan and the Ryukyu Islands.

59 K'en-ting: an archaeological natural laboratory near southern tip of Taiwan.
Kuang-chou Li. PhD thesis, State University of New York, Binghamton, New York, 1982. 398p. (Available from University Microfilms, Ann Arbor, Michigan, order no. 8202788).

This study tests the hypothesis that the prehistoric K'en-ting people may have had a highly structured dwelling pattern, i.e., related females were normally restricted to living on the same site through several generations, while male spouses moved to the site from different communities. The prehistoric site of K'en-ting near the southern tip of Taiwan was excavated in 1977, and the remains found therein, along with other relevant data, support the author's theory of structured behaviour. Moreover, the K'en-ting excavation has brought to light several other concerns, such as the origin of agriculture in prehistoric China, and overall methodological problems encountered in Chinese archaeological research.

60 **Geology and ecology of Taiwan prehistory.**
C. C. Lin. *Asian Perspectives*, vol. 7 (1963), p. 203-13.
Discusses findings which show that during the several regressive periods of the Pleistocene, Taiwan was a part of the Chinese mainland and must have formed part of the Pacific coast. There were abundant forests and rich fauna and flora on the coastal plains and hills. It is probable that Taiwan was habitable during the Pleistocene.

61 **Archaeological investigations in eastern Taiwan.**
Richard Pearson. *Asian Perspectives*, vol. 11 (1968), p. 137-56.
Recent advances in the archaeology of Taiwan have taken place primarily on the west coast, where prehistoric cultures are clearly related to those of southern mainland China. This paper, however, provides information concerning archaeology on the east coast of Taiwan. It offers a survey of pertinent literature and describes various unpublished reports and lesser-known excavations.

62 **New light on Taiwan's prehistory.**
Richard B. Stamps. *Asian Perspectives*, vol. 20, no. 2 (1977), p. 183-90.
Explanations for the cultural diversity of Taiwan, in both ethnographic and archaeological terms, have been one of the key issues for anthropologists studying the island over the past seventy years. This paper examines several explanations presented by K. C. Chang, Judith Treistman, and other Chinese historians.

63 **Prehistory of the Formosan uplands.**
Judith M. Treistman. *Science*, vol. 175 (1972), p. 74-76.
Discusses archaeological surveys in the central mountain ranges of Taiwan which show human occupation dating back to more than 1,000 years ago. The pattern of ecological adaptation between uplands and plains which is typical of Southeast Asia is also a feature of prehistoric Taiwanese settlement.

Burial patterns of prehistoric Taiwan (part I).
See item no. 133.

Bibliography of Taiwan archaeology from 1950-1968.
See item no. 824.

History

General

64 Beautiful island.
Parris H. Chang. *Wilson Quarterly*, vol. 3, no 4 (1979), p. 57-68.
Chang looks at Taiwan's neglected early history until 1949, when the Nationalists set up a temporary wartime capital in Taipei, despite the Pentagon's prediction that the Nationalists could not hold out on their island fortress for more than a year.

65 Taiwan under Chiang Kai-shek's era: 1945-1976.
Peter P. C. Cheng. *Asian Profile*, vol. 16, no. 4 (1988), p. 299-316.
Describes Taiwan's economic and social conditions, government and politics, and foreign relations during Chiang Kai-shek's era. In particular, the author presents a detailed analysis of the change in US attitudes toward Taiwan. Eventually, the Chiang Kai-shek régime ceased to be an ideological symbol of the worldwide struggle against Communism. Once the People's Republic of China became regarded as the sole government representing China, the US had to acknowledge that its ties with Taiwan posed obstacles to the normalization of relations with China.

66 Taipei: history of growth and problems of development.
Lan-hung Nora Chiang, Hsin-huang Michael Hsiao. *National Taiwan University Journal of Sociology*, vol. 17 (1985), p. 93-120.
Traces Taipei's history through three periods: the Ching dynasty (1683-1895), the Japanese colonial period (1895-1945), and the postwar years. Once Taipei became the capital city of Taiwan, it experienced rapid growth and the problems which accompany such urban development. The authors offer several suggestions for addressing these problems.

67 **China, seventy years after the 1911 Hsin-hai revolution.**
Edited by Hungdah Chiu, Shao-chuan Leng. Charlottesville, Virginia:
University Press of Virginia, 1985. 589p.
The majority of essays collected here describe how the path of political, economic,
social, and legal development has varied in mainland China and Taiwan since 1949.
Clear and informative, these essays on Taiwan constitute the best general introductory
text on society in the ROC.

68 **A pictorial history of the Republic of China: its founding and
development.**
Compilation Committee. Taipei: Modern China Press, 1981. 2 vols.
Presents an account of the Republic of China from the start of Dr. Sun Yat-sen's
revolutionary endeavours in 1894 up to 1981. The historical data are grouped into
sixteen chapters, each dealing with a specific subject or particular period. Illustrations
have been taken from various sources, some of them rare. Preceding each section of
pictures is a synoptic description of what it is about. Charts and tables accompany
factual accounts, maps show where and how military operations were conducted.
Matters or events related to Taiwan are mostly covered in volume two. In particular,
chapter eleven provides a historical sketch of the relationship between Taiwan and
mainland China.

69 **China's island frontier: studies in the historical geography of Taiwan.**
Edited by Ronald G. Knapp. Honolulu: University Press of Hawaii,
1980. 312p.
Focuses on the patterns and processes of Taiwan's historical geography. Knapp divides
this book into two parts. Part one, 'Migration and rural settlement', includes
discussions of Taiwan's historical development before 1683, cultural contact and
migration of Taiwan's aborigines, the land tenure system, social organization and social
disorder during the Ch'ing Dynasty, and the relationship between place names and
sequent occupancy. The second part, 'Urbanization and economic integration', looks
at the walled cities and towns as outposts of imperial authority, the trading system in
Lukang which was once Taiwan's major centre for trade, the development and
structure of transportation networks in Taiwan, the contribution to Taiwan's economic
development of the so-called push car railway, and an analysis of Taiwan's principal
cash crop industry – sugar cane. Overall, this is an interesting and varied collection of
essays, tackling different aspects of Taiwan's social, political, and economic
development in terms of historical geography.

70 **Taiwan in modern times.**
Edited by Paul K. T. Sih. New York: St. John's University Press, 1973.
521p.
This volume contains eleven articles which are divided into two sections. The first deals
with the history of Taiwan as a backdrop to the question of how and when Taiwan
became Chinese. In the second section, the focus turns to the modern period with a
comparison between the Japanese and the Nationalist Government's modernization
programmes in Taiwan in order to determine which government brought the island's
society and economy further along the path of modernization. Although one may take
exception to conclusions presented in some of the essays, this book enhances our
understanding of the place of Taiwan in Chinese history.

Surnames in Taiwan: interpretations based on geography and history.
See item no. 27.

The anthropology of Taiwanese society.
See tem no. 125.

City temples in Taipei under three regimes.
See item no. 127.

History and magical power in a Chinese community.
See item no. 141.

Christianity in Taiwan: a history.
See item no. 157.

Mass political incorporation, 1500-2000.
See item no. 360.

Pre-twentieth century

71 **Commercial contract law in late nineteenth-century Taiwan.**
Rosser H. Brockman. In: *Essays on China's legal tradition*. Edited by
Jerome A. Cohen, R. Randle Edwards, Fu-mei C. Chen. Princeton,
New Jersey: Princeton University Press, 1980, p. 76-136.
In this fine study of Taiwan's traditional legal system, Brockman draws upon the
valuable research of Japanese colonial authorities into the customary law that had
evolved in Taiwan, prior to Japan's annexation of the island in 1895. He shows that the
magistrate's tribunal was an infrequent last resort for businessmen, although this
reluctance to go to court did not reflect a lack of appreciation for the importance of
contracts. The commercial community managed to develop the requisite norms and
forms into an unofficial, yet binding, customary law of contracts. Brockman analyses
the types of contracts in use for different business transactions.

72 **Foreigners in Formosa, 1841-1874.**
George Williams Carrington. San Francisco, California: Chinese
Materials Center, 1977. 308p.
This volume is an account of the British, Americans, and Japanese in Taiwan from the
time of the Opium War to 1974. In addition to describing foreign interests on Taiwan,
it analyses several spheres of activity, such as scientific expeditions, coal mining,
trading, and missionary work. Unfortunately, Carrington failed to consult extensively
the primary or secondary sources in Chinese and thus mistakes occur. Nevertheless,
the account is a welcome addition to the knowledge of Western understanding and
misunderstanding concerning Taiwan during the nineteenth century.

73 **Liu Ming-chuan and modernization of Taiwan.**
Samuel C. Chu. *Journal of Asian Studies*, vol. 23, no. 1 (1963) p. 37-53.
In the course of his seven-year administration of Taiwan during the Ch'ing dynasty, Liu acted as a modernizing force to make the island an integral part of the Chinese Empire. Because of Liu's energy, independence of mind, and drive for change, Taiwan underwent a systematic scheme of reform on a province-wide basis. Chu evaluates Liu's efforts to modernize Taiwan in the late nineteenth century.

74 **Koxinga and Chinese nationalism: history, myth, and the hero.**
Ralph C. Croizier. Cambridge, Massachusetts: Harvard University Press, 1977. 116p.
Croizier illustrates how various groups have, over several centuries, created their own image of Koxinga, the hero who expelled the Dutch from Taiwan in 1662. Honoured by both Nationalist and Communist China, Koxinga also became the symbol of the Taiwanese Independence Movement.

75 **The island of Formosa: historical view from 1430 to 1900.**
James W. Davidson. London; New York: Macmillan, 1903. Reprinted, Taipei: Wen-hsing Book, 1964. 646p.
Davidson deals with Taiwan's history during the Dutch period, the era of Chinese sovereignty, and the first years of Japanese occupation. In addition, the inhabitants, cash crops, natural resources, and socioeconomic situation of the island are all covered. This is a very complete work because Davidson consulted many ancient Japanese and Chinese writings, as well as original works by Dutch authors, in the preparation of his manuscript. Numerous illustrations, maps, and diagrams are enclosed. Appendices include a comparative vocabulary of nine aboriginal groups, and data on Formosa's land, mammalia, climate, and earthquakes. The book contains a detailed and extensive index for the reader's reference.

76 **Neglected Formosa.**
Edited by Inez De Beauclair. San Francisco, California: Chinese Materials and Research Aids Service Center, 1975. 207p.
In 1675, Frederic Coyett published a defence of his decision, as Governor, to surrender Dutch Taiwan to Koxinga in 1662. This is a complete English version of that defence. Coyett explains why surrender was his only course, given the enemy's strength and Dutch policy errors in Batavia. De Beauclair also includes the Dutch version of the 1662 treaty between Coyett and Koxinga.

77 **Social structure in a nineteenth-century Taiwanese port city.**
Donald R. DeGlopper. In: *The city in late imperial China.* Edited by G. William Skinner, Stanford, California: Stanford University Press, 1977, p. 633-50.
Basing his findings on a field study undertaken in Lu-kang, which lies halfway down the west coast of Taiwan, DeGlopper explores the social structure of this nineteenth-century port city. The author observes that although Lu-kang consisted of overlapping groups, which each recruit members on a different principle and each act in a different

sphere, its social structure presents a symmetrical set of balanced oppositions and exchanges.

78   The cession of Taiwan: a second look.
      Leonard H. D. Gordon. *Pacific Historical Review*, vol. 45, no. 4 (1976), p. 539-68.

When peace was negotiated immediately after the Sino-Japanese War in 1895, the Japanese insisted that the island of Taiwan be ceded to them. Gordon examines the cession, which was not an isolated development but resulted from several long-standing policy differences involving both China and Japan. One explanation for the transfer of Taiwan is based on conflicting views about China's claim to sovereignty, a demand which became a constant source of friction between China and other powers.

79   Taiwan and the limits of British power, 1868.
      Leonard H. D. Gordon. *Modern Asian Studies*, vol. 22, no. 2 (1988), p. 225-35.

After the treaty system between the Western powers and China had been firmly established in 1860, a new 'cooperative' approach emerged to replace a previously arbitrary and often combative relationship. However, some British diplomats, in concert with military personnel, continued to take an independent course and a hostile stand toward China. The study examines the result of this hostile approach to China, as illustrated by two incidents on Taiwan in 1868, involving the Chinese camphor monopoly and missionary activities.

80   Taiwan: studies in Chinese local history.
      Edited by Leonard H. D. Gordon. New York: Columbia University Press, 1970. 124p.

Presents a collection of four articles about Taiwan in the latter half of the nineteenth century. The articles comprise: a discussion of the Lin family of Wufeng, which took advantage of weak Manchu control to increase its own power; a description of the 1895 Taiwan war of resistance against Japanese takeover; an examination of the conditions of land tenure under the Chinese rule; and a review of the major powers' policy toward Taiwan from 1840 to 1895. These articles show that a careful study of Taiwan's history can broaden knowledge of China studies.

81   Taiwan under the Cheng family 1662-1683: sinicization after Dutch rule.
      Chien-chao Hung. PhD thesis, Georgetown University, Washington, DC, 1981. 354p. (Available from University Microfilms, Ann Arbor, Michigan, order no. 8203928).

Examines the complicated process of Sinicization. After Cheng Ch'eng-kung (Koxinga) defeated the Dutch in 1662, the flow of immigrants increased. As a result, the Chinese population was double that of the natives by the time Cheng K'o-shuang surrendered to the Ch'ing dynasty. This numerical majority was the first step toward Taiwan's complete Sinicization. Ch'eng-kung's claim of Taiwan for China, the Confucian educational system, and the institution of a Chinese form of government all advanced the process of Sinicization on Taiwan.

82 **Chinese frontier settlement in Taiwan.**
Ronald G. Knapp. *Annals of the Association of American Geographers*, vol. 66, no. 1 (1976), p. 43-59.
Describes how the eighteenth-century immigrants from China settled in Tao-yuan county where they duplicated the land tenure patterns and social conditions of their mother country.

83 **Drilling oil in Taiwan: a case study of two American technicians' contribution to modernization in late nineteenth-century China.**
Sampson Hsiang-chang Kuo. PhD thesis, Georgetown University, Washington, DC, 1981. 502p. (Available from University Microfilms, Ann Arbor, Michigan, order no. 8302772).
Through a critical evaluation of the experiences of two Americans hired to drill oil in Taiwan in 1877-78, the author explains the difficulties and hardships encountered during the drilling process, and the motivation for the project as well as the reasons for its failure. He concludes that, although the drilling attempt made by A. Port Karns and Robert D. Locke was not a success, it did bring more advanced techniques and newly invented machinery to Taiwan.

84 **The formation of cities: initiative and motivation in building three walled cities in Taiwan.**
Harry J. Lamley. In: *The city in late imperial China*. Edited by G. William Skinner. Stanford, California: Stanford University Press, 1977, p. 155-209.
The Chinese walled city has long been cited as evidence of continuity within China's long historical tradition. Lamley's contribution is to show the city-building process as the interaction between local and imperial goals and expectations, reflecting joint efforts on the part of officials and the inhabitants. The cities discussed in this study are Hsin-chu, T'ai-pei-fu and I-lan, all situated in northern Taiwan.

85 **Gideon Nye and the Formosa annexation scheme.**
Harold D. Langley. *Pacific Historical Review*, vol. 34, no. 4 (1965), p. 397-420.
Gideon Nye, Jr. (1833-88) made a fortune in the China trade. As an American merchant in Canton, he was involved in a conspiracy, in 1857, to persuade the US to seize Formosa, when he used his personal contacts to influence powerful US officials. As the author explains, annexation was justified on the grounds of commercial expansion and protection of US national interests, as well as the advancement of civilization on Taiwan.

86 **Social change in China's frontier areas during the Ching dynasty.**
Kuo-chi Lee. *Chinese Studies in History*, vol. 17, no. 3 (1984), p. 29-49.
Studies the process of Sinicization in Manchuria, Taiwan, and Sinkiang (or Hsin-chiang), with special reference to the differences in social change between the frontier areas and China proper. Social change on Taiwan is discussed in great detail.

87 **The quasi-war in East Asia: Japan's expedition to Taiwan and the Ryukyu controversy.**
Edwin Pak-wah Leung. *Modern Asian Studies*, vol. 17, no. 2 (1983), p. 257-81.

In 1874, Japan sent an expeditionary force to Taiwan to punish the aborigines there, who had killed fifty-four shipwrecked Ryukyuans three years earlier. According to many scholars, the result of this incident put an end to the controversy over the ambiguous political status of the Ryukyu Islands. Leung disagrees, and reassesses this episode in the 'quasi-war' in East Asia. As this study shows, no clear statement concerning Ryukyu status had been made in the 1874 Sino-Japanese Treaty. His conclusion refutes the customary view held by many scholars that in 1874 China renounced her claim over Ryukyu and yielded to the Japanese claim she had earlier disputed. As a result, in Leung's judgment, the Ryukyu issue continued to trouble Peking and Tokyo in the years that immediately followed.

88 **From far Formosa: the island, its people and missions.**
George Leslie MacKay, edited by J. A. MacDonald. New York; Chicago, Illinois: Fleming H. Revell, 1895. 346p.

After twenty-three years as a missionary in Formosa, Dr. MacKay describes his life and travels on the island. In addition, this book provides a brief introduction to Taiwan's geography, geology, plants, animals, and aborigines. This is a very interesting and valuable source for readers interested in Taiwan's religious development, early history, and society.

89 **A Chinese pioneer family: the Lins of Wu-feng, Taiwan 1729-1985.**
Johanna Menzel Meskill. Princeton, New Jersey: Princeton University Press, 1979. 375p. maps.

In this work, Meskill highlights the importance of Taiwanese history for a better understanding of China's past, and demonstrates the advantages of field-work in the study of Chinese history. Drawing on an extensive range of sources, including Lin family records, government archives, folktales, and interviews, the author introduces the reader to a family history as well as to the social history of late imperial China. This is an absorbing account of a frontier family's rise to local eminence, from its pioneer days in the eighteenth century to its attainment of gentry status a century later. Meskill's analysis of the rôle of local strongmen – men of private armed power – provides an antidote to earlier studies which have focused on the local leadership rôle of the scholar-gentry. The book represents a milestone in the study of Chinese local history. Numerous illustrations, maps, figures and photographs accompany the text.

90 **Taiwan under Ch'ing imperial rule, 1684-1895: the traditional economy.**
Ramon H. Myers. *Journal of the Chinese Studies of the Chinese University of Hong Kong*, vol. 5, no. 2 (1972), p. 373-411.

This study of Taiwan's economy makes clear that prior to 1858, population growth, settlement of new land, and slowly expanding commerce determined Taiwan's economic growth. After 1858 new trade opportunities encouraged more specialization and greater production in agriculture for export. The author argues that the food grain supply and yield gradually rose over time.

91 **Taiwan under Ch'ing imperial rule, 1684-1895: the traditional order.**
Ramon H. Myers. *Journal of the Institute of Chinese Studies of the Chinese University of Hong Kong*, vol. 4, no. 2 (1971), p. 495-522.
Examines how the Ch'ing government ruled Taiwan, using formal and informal organizations to preserve peace and order, indoctrinating the populace, and maintaining imperial authority and power.

92 **Taiwan under Ch'ing imperial rule, 1684-1895: the traditional society.**
Ramon H. Myers. *Journal of the Institute of Chinese Studies of the Chinese University of Hong Kong*, vol. 5, no. 2 (1972), p. 413-53.
Describes the community, its process of formation, its social classes, and the quality of life in Taiwanese society during the late Ch'ing period.

93 **Preserving the dragon seeds: the evolution of Ch'ing emigration policy.**
Shih-shan H. Tsai. *Asian Profile*, vol. 7, no. 6 (1979), p. 497-506.
Before 1859 the Ch'ing government prohibited Chinese subjects from emigrating to foreign lands. It then altered its policy and legalized Chinese emigration. This essay deals in part with the Ch'ing emigration policy toward Taiwan.

94 **Taiwan in China's foreign relations, 1836-1874.**
Sophia Su-fei Yen. Hamden, Connecticut: Shoe String, 1965. 404p. bibliog.
In this comprehensive study of the rôle played by Taiwan in China's foreign relations during the period 1836-1874, the author covers Taiwan's involvement in the first Anglo-Chinese war, the opening of the ports in the western part of Taiwan by the Treaties of Tientsin in 1858, Japan's policy and action toward Taiwan after the Meiji restoration in 1868, and the final settlement of China's sovereignty over all of Taiwan in 1874. The book makes an important contribution to the study of a period of Taiwanese history which has not been widely explored.

City gods, filiality, and hegemony in late imperial China.
See item no. 153.

Aboriginal peoples of the southwestern Taiwan plain.
See item no. 266.

Plains aborigines and Chinese settlers on the Taiwan frontier in the seventeenth and eighteenth centuries.
See item no. 268.

Colonial period (1895-1945)

95 Colonial development and population in Taiwan.

George Watson Barclay. Princeton, New Jersey: Princeton University Press, 1954. 274p.

When the Japanese decided to examine the quality of life in Taiwan, they collected valuable population statistics in a series of seven censuses, the first one in 1905, the next in 1915, and one every five years thereafter until 1940. Based on these materials, Barclay indicates that the Japanese occupation inaugurated a period of population increase so rapid that if it had long continued, it could have resulted in disaster. Despite Barclay's Malthusian vision, this book would be of great interest to demographers and others concerned with problems of economic development.

96 Impact of Japanese colonial rule on Taiwanese elites.

Ching-chih Chen. *Journal of Asian History*, vol. 22, no. 1 (1988), p. 25-51.

Studies the changing nature of Taiwanese élites during the Japanese period. The emergence, composition, and sociopolitical status of the new élites are all analysed and comparisons are made with élites in Korea under Japanese colonial rule and with Asian indigenous élites under Western colonialism.

97 The Japanese adaptation of the Pao-chia system in Taiwan, 1895-1945.

Ching-chih Chen. *Journal of Asian Studies*, vol. 34, no. 2 (1975), p. 391-416.

The imperial administration of the Ch'ing dynasty (1664-1912) relied on a bureaucratically organized rural police system, known as the Pao-chia, for the purpose of local control. Japan found the Pao-chia system necessary in order to maintain its colonial rule, following its takeover of Taiwan from China in 1895. Chen discusses the features and functions of the Pao-chia system during the period of Japanese occupation and the Taiwanese attitude toward the system. In their employment of the system, the Japanese utilized it shrewdly both as an instrument of local control and as a valuable auxiliary administrative organ.

98 Police and community control systems in the empire.

Ching-chih Chen. In: *The Japanese colonial empire, 1895-1945*. Edited by Ramon H. Myers, Mark R. Peattie. Princeton, New Jersey: Princeton University Press, 1984, p. 213-39.

In the Japanese view, management of colonial peoples resembled management of society in the early Meiji period. Therefore, the colonial police played a rôle similar to that of the Japanese police at home. It was in Taiwan that the first colonial police apparatus was installed. Chen examines how the Japanese created a new police force and how the colonial police carried out the tasks assigned to it.

99 **Formosan political movements under Japanese colonial rule, 1914-1937.**
Edward I-te Chen. *Journal of Asian Studies*, vol. 31, no. 3 (1972),
p. 477-97.

Thoroughly convinced of the futility of armed resistance, Taiwanese leaders decided to adopt different tactics by creating political organizations and proclaiming legitimate goals such as racial equality and popular elections in order to resist Japanese colonial rule. This study describes the goals, leadership, and principal activities of six political organizations active during the period of 1914-37. It also assesses to what extent Japanese liberalism and Chinese nationalism influenced the formation and activities of these organizations.

100 **Japan's decision to annex Taiwan: a study of Ito-Mutsu diplomacy, 1894-95.**
Edward I-te Chen. *Journal of Asian Studies*, vol. 37, no. 1 (1977),
p. 61-72.

The conventional wisdom has been that Japan annexed Taiwan in order to acquire the island's raw materials and potential as a new market in the rapidly expanding Japanese Empire. In addition, it is argued that Japan saw Taiwan as a stepping stone for further expansion into Southeast Asia. Chen contends that Japan did not have a long-range plan for the annexation of Taiwan. It is even doubtful that the notion of annexation ever entered the minds of Premier Ito Hirobumi and Foreign Minister Mutsu Munemitsu at the time of the outbreak of Sino-Japanese War (1894-95).

101 **Japan's abortive colonial venture in Taiwan, 1874.**
Leonard Gordon. *Journal of Modern History*, vol. 37, no. 2 (1965),
p. 171-85.

This examination of the source materials in the Japanese Ministry of Foreign Affairs and the Japanese Army and Navy archives suggests that the expedition to Taiwan in 1874 was more than a mere diversionary move by the Japanese government to deter the samurai of Kagoshima from launching an adventurous plan of aggression against Korea. The lengthy period of planning and preparation, the impact of a growing national consciousness, and the need for a favourable settlement of the Ryukyu question in Japan all lend credence to Gordon's contention that the expedition was a serious colonization effort.

102 **Formosa today: an analysis of the economic development and strategic importance of Japan's tropical colony.**
Andrew Jonah Grajdanzev. New York: Institute of Pacific Relations,
1942. 193p.

Relying upon official Japanese sources, Grajdanzev presents a picture of Japanese colonial exploitation. Taiwan bore the costs of development by itself, instead of depending on monetary aid from Japan. Moreover, Taiwan was ruled by the governor-general with the help of the military and police, and the Taiwanese had no political voice whatsoever under Japanese rule. This book provides a welcome addition to the understanding of the Japanese colonial régime.

103 **Agricultural transformation under colonialism: the case of Taiwan.**
Samuel P. S. Ho. *Journal of Economic History*, vol. 8, no. 3 (1968),
p. 313-40.

The transformation of Taiwan's agriculture was the major accomplishment of the Japanese colonial administration. To enable Taiwan to make a contribution to Japanese efforts at industrialization, the colonial government was given the task of modernizing and streamlining Taiwan's agriculture. Taiwan helped Japanese labourers convert from agricultural to industrial activities by providing surplus food. Ho studies how Taiwan's agriculture was transformed and squeezed to help Japan's economic development.

104 **The Chinese Communist Party and the status of Taiwan, 1928-1943.**
Frank S. T. Hsiao, Lawrence R. Sullivan. *Pacific Affairs*, vol. 52,
no. 3 (1979), p. 446-67.

Examines the position of the Chinese Communists towards the Taiwanese people and the political movements on Taiwan during the period 1928-43. It also discusses the impact of the 1943 Cairo Conference on the Chinese Communist Party's unification policies, which called for the return of Taiwan to Chinese sovereignty.

105 **A political history of the Taiwanese Communist Party, 1928-1931.**
Frank S. T. Hsiao, Lawrence R. Sullivan. *Journal of Asian Studies*,
vol. 42, no. 2 (1983), p. 269-89.

After its establishment in April 1928, the Taiwanese Communist Party (TCP), which was founded by a small group of intellectuals educated in Japan and China, and was a 'Nationality Branch of the Japanese Communist Party' (JCP), confronted numerous difficulties in organizing a communist-led movement in Taiwan. In 1931, there were mass arrests of Taiwanese communists by Japanese colonial police. This study examines the history and internal politics of the TCP and shows that the failure of the TCP reflected more than just the efficiency of the Japanese police. An incessant factionalism within the party and the often contradictory influence of Communist International (Comintern), the JCP, and the Chinese Communist Party policies contributed to the destruction of the TCP.

106 **Formosa: licensed revolution and the home rule movement, 1895-1945.**
George H. Kerr. Honolulu, Hawaii: University Press of Hawaii,
1974. 284p. bibliog.

The author states that Taiwan experienced a remarkable technological, social, and economic revolution under the Japanese administration and calls it 'the licensed revolution'. He then argues that the Taiwanese have a historical tradition of separatism that is apparent from the rebellions and uprisings against the Ching imperial rule. When their armed resistance against the Japanese takeover failed, the Taiwanese demanded 'home rule' through political means. Their request for Japanese recognition of a distinct Formosan identity within the Japanese Empire was rejected by the Japanese. Although flawed by inadequate sources and confusing romanization of Chinese and Japanese names, this book provides readers with an overview of the Japanese period of Taiwan's history.

107 **Civilization over savagery: the Japanese, the Formosan frontier, and United States Indian policy, 1895-1915.**
Ronald G. Knapp, Lawrence M. Hauptman. *Pacific Historical Review*, vol. 49, no. 4 (1980), p. 647-52.
After Japan acquired Taiwan as a result of the Sino-Japanese War of 1895, Japanese policies mimicked those set up by the Americans in dealing with their Indian problems. The Japanese used a moving line of frontier posts and punitive expeditions to wrest control of the Formosan interior from hostile aborigines. This study is based on the records in the National Archives and other primary sources.

108 **The evolution of Japanese colonialism.**
Hyman Kublin. *Comparative Studies in Society and History*, vol. 2, no. 1 (1959-60), p. 67-84.
Traces the development of Japan's colonialism from the opening of Japan in 1854 to the First World War. Colonial policy, first formulated in Taiwan and then applied to Korea, was devoted to economic exploitation. The author describes Japan's colonial control in Taiwan, where local institutions were never fully developed and natives were made to conform to Japanese customs.

109 **The 1895 Taiwan Republic.**
Harry J. Lamley. *Journal of Asian Studies*, vol. 27, no. 4 (1968), p. 739-62.
In a desperate scheme to keep Taiwan from being ceded to Japan after the Sino-Japanese War of 1894-95, Taiwan was declared a republic. The author provides a detailed description of the short-lived republic of Taiwan, known as 'Asia's first republic', and considers its significance in the recent history of China.

110 **Taiwan's agrarian economy under Japanese rule.**
Ramon H. Myers. *Journal of the Institute of Chinese Studies of the Chinese University of Hong Kong*, vol. 7, no. 2 (1974), p. 451-75.
Describes Taiwan's agrarian economy during the Japanese colonial period, as the island's countryside began to experience gradual but profound change. In 1900 agriculture accounted for the largest source of income and employment, and, by the 1930s, a prospering agriculture supported a small industrial base and a large export trade. The author studies how the State created favourable conditions in which farmers found it profitable to supply more to the market.

111 **Agricultural development in the empire.**
Ramon H. Myers, Yamada Saburo. In: *The Japanese colonial empire, 1895-1945.* Edited by Ramon H. Myers, Mark R. Peattie. Princeton, New Jersey: Princeton University Press, 1984, p. 420-52.
This study compares the development of agrarian systems in Korea and Taiwan with those in Japan. In Taiwan rural wages rose more slowly than urban wages, so that the gap in living standards between countryside and town widened. Stated differently, in Taiwan as well as in Korea, Japanese colonial administrations paid little attention to agricultural development until the 1930s.

History. Colonial period (1895-1945)

112 **Incentives, productivity gaps, and agricultural growth rates in prewar Japan, Taiwan, and Korea.**
James I. Nakamura. In: *Japan in crisis: essays in Taisho democracy.* Edited by Bernard S. Silberman, Harry D. Harootunian. Princeton, New Jersey: Princeton University Press, 1974, p. 329-73.

The colonial period, lasting from 1895 to 1945, was remarkable for rapid economic growth in Japan itself, and for even more vigorous expansion in the Japanese Empire. This paper shows that at the onset of their period of modern agricultural development, Taiwan and Korea had lower incentives and productivity than Japan. It examines the policies with which the Japanese government attempted to raise productivity and the response of the colonial agricultural system to these policies.

113 **Imperial China and international law: a case study of the 1895 Treaty of Shimonoseki.**
Mitchell A. Silk. *Chinese Yearbook of International Law and Affairs,* vol. 2 (1982), p. 121-51.

Basing his work upon examination of a vast number of Chinese and Western sources, the author studies the 1895 Treaty of Shimonoseki, which included the cession of Taiwan to Japan.

114 **Japanese rule in Formosa.**
Yosaburo Takekoshi, preface by Baron Shimpei Goto, translated by George Braithwaite. London; New York: Longmans, Green, 1907. 342p.

This book was the outcome of an extensive tour of the island, in which the author had ample opportunity to observe the manners and customs of the Taiwanese people. Moreover, Takekoshi's observations are supplemented by information found in the archives in the Governor-General's Office. Various aspects of socioeconomic development are discussed, including: the opium monopoly; aborigines; foreign trade; police administration; real estate and tenant's rights; judicial systems; geography and history; and education. Although glorifying Japan's colonial policy and administration in Taiwan, this volume offers a valuable insight into colonial administration and socioeconomic conditions. This is essential reading for anyone interested in Japan's colonial policy in Taiwan.

115 **Capital formation in Taiwan and Korea.**
Mizoguchi Toshiyuki, Yamamoto Yuzo. In: *The Japanese colonial empire, 1895-1945.* Edited by Ramon H. Myers, Mark R. Peattie. Princeton, New Jersey: Princeton University Press, 1984, p. 399-419.

Examines capital formation in Taiwan and Korea before the Second World War in terms of its structure and impact on the economy of these two countries, within the context of their general economic growth.

116 **Colonial education in Korea and Taiwan.**
E. Patricia Tsurumi. In: *The Japanese colonial empire, 1895-1945.*
Edited by Ramon H. Myers, Mark R. Peattie. Princeton, New Jersey:
Princeton University Press, 1984, p. 275-311.
Examines Japan's colonial education in Korea and Taiwan and compares the differing
response of the two peoples. By the end of the colonial period, the Japanese-educated
Taiwanese of the middle and upper classes had absorbed a whole spectrum of Japanese
tastes and attitudes. In Korea, these same classes were seething with militant
nationalism.

117 **Japanese colonial education in Taiwan, 1895-1945.**
E. Patricia Tsurumi. Cambridge, Massachusetts: Harvard University
Press, 1977. 334p.
The purpose of the Japanese educational system in Taiwan, in Tsurumi's opinion, was
to pacify the Taiwanese, cultivate their loyalty to Japan, and, as a result, integrate
them into modern Japanese society. The author examines how Japan used the
educational system as an instrument of colonial development and assesses its impact on
Taiwanese life. Comparisons with other colonial educational policies enhance the value
of this study. Sources are carefully evaluated and documented in this solid work of
scholarship.

118 **Mental captivity and resistance: lessons from Taiwanese anti-
colonialism.**
E. Patricia Tsurumi. *Bulletin of Concerned Asian Scholars*, vol. 12,
no. 2 (1980), p. 2-13.
Imperialism is not just a matter of mines and plantations from which economic benefits
are extracted, Tsurumi argues. It is also the imposition of cultures, values, ethics,
attitudes, and modes of reasoning. Such cultural imperialism is part of the story of anti-
colonialism in Taiwan during the fifty years of Japanese rule. Tsurumi's paper vividly
illustrates the damage that colonialism does to minds. The captive mind becomes a
grave impediment to the anti-colonial movement.

Through Formosa: an account of Japan's island colony.
See item no. 13.

Marriage and adoption in China, 1845-1945.
See item no. 214.

Colonial origins of Taiwanese capitalism.
See item no. 513.

The evolution of the Taiwanese new literature movement from 1920 to 1937.
See iem no. 704.

**China watching by the Japanese: reports and investigations from the first
Sino-Japanese War to the unification of China under the Communist party: a
checklist of holdings in the East Asian collection, Hoover Institution.**
See item no. 812.

The Chiangs (Chiang Kai-shek and Chiang Ching-kuo)

119 The man who lost China: the first full biography of Chiang Kai-shek.
Brian Crozier, Eric Chou. New York: Scribner, 1976. 430p.

Although this book fails to break new ground in exploring Chiang's life and career, it provides a fuller and more balanced portrait than previous biographies. In Crozier's sketch, Chiang is a flawed and tragic hero whose personality defects and errors of judgement were largely responsible for the loss of China to the Communists.

120 Chiang Ching-kuo and Taiwan: a profile.
Tillman Durdin. *Orbis*, vol. 18, no. 4 (winter 1975), p. 1023-42.

In a fashion different from his famous father, Chiang Kai-shek, Chiang Ching-kuo tempers sternness with a man-of-the-masses approach to the people of Taiwan. Durdin describes Chiang Ching-kuo's experiences in the Soviet Union and China, and examines his leadership style and policies during his period as new ruler, after his father's death.

121 Perspectives: selected statements of President Chiang Ching-kuo, 1978-1983.
Government Information Office. Taipei: Government Information Office, 1984. 2nd ed. 275p.

Contains Chiang's addresses, remarks, interviews with foreign newspapers and magazines, and essays concerning both his father's policies and his own rulings in Taiwan.

122 Jiang Jie-shi (1887-1975).
John Stradbroke Gregory. St. Lucia; London, New York: University of Queensland Press, 1982. 41p.

Through an examination of the career of Chiang Kai-shek (Jiang Jie-shi), this brief but stimulating book is aimed at enriching our awareness of China. In this short biography, Chiang's life from 1887 to its end in Taiwan in 1975 is traced against the background of Chinese society and Chinese history. While Chiang is praised for his strong leadership in the first half-century, he failed to move far beyond a political-military objective towards the new social order necessary for the later decades of his rule.

123 Chiang Kai-shek.
Hollington K. Tong. Taipei: China Publishing, 1953. 562p.

Although the author does not view his book as a definitive biography, it is in fact an important study of Chiang. Tong, a newspaperman for forty years, had access to Chiang's personal documents and to lifelong associates of the 'Generalissimo'. His close relationship with Chiang has made this biography more authoritative than others.

The Republic of China under Chiang Kai-shek: Taiwan today.
See item no. 10.

Taiwan under Chiang Kai-shek's era: 1945-1976.
See item no. 65.

Religion

Buddhism, Taoism, and other folk religions

124 **The cult of the dead in a Chinese village.**
Emily Martin Ahern.   Stanford, California: Stanford University Press, 1973. 280p. bibliog.

In this sociological analysis of the village belief system, Ahern first presents the social organization of the village, focusing on Ch'inan, located on the southern edge of the Taipei basin, showing the variations between lineages. She then provides a detailed study of ancestor tablets and geomancy (*feng-shui*). Intricate variations in ancestor worship are illustrated. For example, a disinherited son is allowed to leave the care of his father's grave to his luckier brothers. Future field-workers should benefit from Ahern's lead in this well-written and perceptive study.

125 **The anthropology of Taiwanese society.**
Edited by Emily Martin Ahern, Hill Gates.   Stanford, California: Stanford University Press, 1981. 491p. map.

Based on a conference held in 1976, this volume brings together essays by many anthropologists (and a few historians) with field research experience in Taiwan. Their purpose was to explore the state of anthropological work in Taiwan and to criticize its findings in order to draw lessons for future research. The fifteen essays are grouped under six topics: political organizations, local organization, economic organization, ethnicity, the family, and religion and ritual. For example, Gary Seaman explores the meaning of the ceremony of 'breaking the blood bowls', where a son symbolically drinks the polluting blood of his birth as an act of filial piety for his deceased mother. Ahern argues that the Thai-ti-kong or 'slaughter of honourable pig' festival reveals the conflict between local communities and central government in Taiwan. Essays contributed by Arthur Wolf, Burton Pasternak, Stevan Harrell, Hill Gates, Lawrence W. Crissman, Alexander Chien-chung Yin, and others provide an excellent guide to

Religion. Buddhism, Taoism, and other folk religions

the understanding of Taiwanese society. One paper in each section (except the section on religion and ritual) provides a summary and synthesis of that section.

126 Religion and ritual in Lukang.
Donald R. DeGlopper. In: *Religion and ritual in Chinese society*. Edited by Arthur P. Wolf. Stanford, California: Stanford University Press, 1974, p. 43-69.

Lukang, a city in western Taiwan, has many temples. This study explores why its inhabitants need or want so many temples, when most of their compatriots manage with far fewer. In addition, the author notes that public ritual in Lukang is characterized by a restricted range of activity and expression.

127 City temples in Taipei under three regimes.
Stephan Feuchtwang. In: *The Chinese city between two worlds*. Edited by Mark Elvin, G. William Skinner. Stanford, California: Stanford University Press, 1974, p. 263-301.

The author has done an excellent job of combining historical research with anthropological field-work to describe the major temples of popular religion in Taipei. The main theme of this essay is the relationship between these religious institutions and the successive governments that have ruled Taiwan since the nineteenth century.

128 Domestic and communal worship in Taiwan.
Stephan Feuchtwang. In: *Religion and ritual in Chinese society*. Edited by Arthur P. Wolf. Stanford, California: Stanford University Press, 1974, p. 105-29.

Describes the religious life of a Taiwanese town, which is called Mountainstreet in this paper. Feuchtwang explores the meaning of the annual round of domestic and communal rituals and discusses three major categories of spiritual beings – gods, ghosts, and ancestors.

129 Money for the gods.
Hill Gates. *Modern China*, vol. 13, no. 3 (1987), p. 259-77.

Shows that money deeply penetrates Chinese folk culture: in gift giving, as a means of acquiring rights over other people; and especially in ritual. For example, money is used in funeral and marriage practices. The author suggests that these rituals imply that the market should govern transactions of all sorts, and that capitalist relations should exist between 'people' and 'gods' or between common individuals and authorities. The author focuses on the class culture of Taiwan's numerous petty capitalists, who include the highly market-orientated rural population, the urban shopkeepers, craftspeople and small-scale industrial producers.

130 **The ancestors at home: domestic worship in a land-poor Taiwanese village.**
Stevan Harrell. In: *Ancestors.* Edited by William H. Newell. The Hague: Mouton, 1976, p. 373-85.

What happens to ancestor worship in a Taiwanese community where there are no lineages, where almost nobody owned land until recently, and where an unusually large proportion of households contains members with two or more lines of descent? Such a community is Ploughshare village in Taiwan. The author finds that the absence of any lineage organization means that ancestral rites are reduced to the domestic cult. Rites get simpler, not more elaborate, as ancestors recede farther from memory.

131 **The concept of soul in Chinese folk religion.**
Stevan Harrell. *Journal of Asian Studies,* vol. 38, no. 3 (1979), p. 519-28.

Folk religious behaviour reveals much about the nature of the 'soul' (ling-hun). Using evidence drawn from his own field-work on Taiwan and from published sources dealing with Taiwan and other parts of China, Harrell seeks to answer such questions as: how many souls does each person have, and how do souls help to make up a person?

132 **Modes of belief in Chinese folk religion.**
Stevan Harrell. *Journal for the Scientific Study of Religion,* vol. 16, no. 1 (1977), p. 55-65.

Interviews with sixty-six residents of a Taiwanese village about their folk religion indicate that there is no simple division between believers and nonbelievers, but rather that people's faith can be categorized into four types or modes: intellectual belief, which tries to make sense out of reality; true belief, which accepts everything with total credulity; practical belief, which evaluates religious tenets on the basis of evidence; and non-belief, which declares that folk religion is irrelevant.

133 **Burial patterns of prehistoric Taiwan (part I).**
Chuan-kun Ho. *Journal of the Institute of Chinese Studies of the Chinese University of Hong Kong,* vol. 19 (1988), p. 433-70.

Examines prehistoric burial patterns in Taiwan both spatially and sequentially. The author then analyses how the data collected may shed light on sociocultural change in Taiwan during prehistoric periods.

134 **Gods, ghosts, and ancestors: the folk religion of a Taiwanese village.**
David K. Jordan. Berkeley, California: University of California Press, 1972. 197p.

Taking the case of a southwestern Taiwanese village, Jordan presents a vivid and perceptive account of the beliefs and practices which play a part in Taiwanese community and family life. This investigation makes a significant contribution to Chinese studies.

Religion. Buddhism, Taoism, and other folk religions

135 **The recent history of the Celestial Way: a Chinese pietistic association.**
David K. Jordan. *Modern China*, vol. 8, no. 4 (1982), p. 45-62.

'Celestial Way' is the modern esoteric name of the Chinese religious society formerly known as the 'United Way' or Yi-kuan Tao in Taiwan. Jordan describes the historical development of the Celestial Way and the competition among its many branches.

136 **Taiwanese poe divination: statistical awareness and religious belief.**
David K. Jordan. *Journal for the Scientific Study of Religion*, vol. 21, no. 2 (1982), p. 114-18.

In temples and homes, the Taiwanese perform simple divination by means of *poe*, two half-moon-shaped wooden or bamboo blocks, each of which is flat on one side and rounded on the other. The poe are thrown on the floor to see whether they land rounded-side-up or flat-side-up. This paper explores the statistical properties of poe as they are used by the Taiwanese. It suggests that the Taiwanese are aware of the statistical likelihoods in divination by use of poe, and deliberately manipulate the outcome, even though they simultaneously believe that the gall of the poe is governed by divine will.

137 **The flying phoenix: aspects of Chinese sectarianism in Taiwan.**
David K. Jordan, Daniel L. Overmyer. Princeton, New Jersey: Princeton University Press, 1986. 329p.

Chapters on the history of religious sects and spirit writing in China are followed by discussions of three 'pai-luan' groups. Pai-luan literally means 'phoenix worship', 'phoenix' here indicating the large stylus used to write the god's or spirit's message. The groups studied – the Hall of the Wondrous Dharma, the Compassion Society, and the Unity Sect – were all formed in the present century and are all flourishing in Taiwan today. Especially noteworthy is the treatment of the Unity Sect (I-kuan Tao), which has received scant study. Jordan, an anthropologist, and Overmyer, a historian of religion, have made a major contribution to our understanding of Chinese religion, one that combines an anthropologist's extensive field-work with a historian's research in premodern documents.

138 **Chinese geomancy and ancestor worship: a further discussion.**
Yih-yuan Li. In: *Ancestors*. Edited by William H. Newell. The Hague: Mouton, 1976, p. 329-38.

Li points out that the relationship between the ancestors in the tomb and their living descendants is a reciprocal one. A good grave site, or feng-shui, may benefit the descendants of the one who has been buried, but the prosperity of the descendants will in turn ensure the continuous worship of the ancestors. The data from Taiwan seems convincing in support of this argument.

139 **The parting of the ways: a study of innovation in ritual.**
John L. McCreery. *Bulletin of the Institute of Ethnology, Academia Sinica*, no. 46 (1978), p. 121-38.

Ritual by definition is the repetition of set forms which are unchanging. This article examines the rituals of Taoist priests in Taiwan. Here, Taoist priests are entrepreneurs competing in a market for ritual services, and hence the rituals they perform actually vary from individual to individual. Masters hoard their knowledge of rituals as businesspeople hoard their trade secrets. Wherever similar social and economic conditions affect ritual, innovation in ritual should be expected.

140 **Religions of China: the world as a living system.**
     Daniel L. Overmyer. San Francisco: Harper & Row, 1986, 125p.
Presents clearly the religious beliefs and values found in China. Overmyer covers early ancestor cults and nature worship, shamanism, Buddhism, Taoism, and Confucianism. He traces the development of Chinese religious traditions, with their recurrent patterns and themes, practices, organizational structures, impact on evolving Chinese society and culture, and vitality and diversity today. The development of religious practices in Taiwan is also described and examined. This brief yet comprehensive introduction is an excellent work for readers with no prior knowledge of Chinese religions.

141 **History and magical power in a Chinese community.**
     P. Steven Sangren. Stanford, California: Stanford University Press, 1987. 268p. illus.
The scope of this case study, which considers history and popular culture in a northern Taiwanese marketing region, is larger than that of most other community studies. Sangren argues that our understanding is significantly increased by taking into account the structure of regional economic systems. Moreover, he claims that the connection between Chinese social institutions and religious ideas is even more intimate than has been supposed in conventional scholarly treatments. The author's holistic analysis of rituals in a particular locality provides a particularly valuable insight into Chinese culture.

142 **Orthodoxy, heterodoxy, and structure of value in Chinese rituals.**
     P. Steven Sangren. *Modern China*, vol. 13, no. 1 (1987), p. 63-89.
Argues forcefully for an encompassing, nearly unassailable hegemony in China. The traditional concepts of Yang and Yin, order and disorder, essential to élite and folk cosmology, are hierarchically ordered: Hegemonic Yang must always encompass and subsume Yin heterodoxies. The case of Taiwan is examined in Sangran's paper.

143 **Lu shan, ling shan, and mao shan: Taoist fraternities and rivalries in north Taiwan.**
     Michael Saso. *Bulletin of the Institute of Ethnology, Academia Sinica*, no. 34 (1972), p. 119-51.
Three separate Taoist groups, Lu-shan, Lung-hu shan, and Mao-shan, are described and discussed. Saso argues that a study of these three is helpful in understanding the practices and profession of religious Taoism. Sets of documents used by these groups are listed in the appendix.

144 **Neighborhood cult associations in traditional Taiwan.**
     Kristofer M. Schipper. In: *The city in late imperial China*. Edited by G. William Skinner. Stanford, California: Stanford University Press, 1977, p. 651-76.
Old Taiwan is said to have been a place of a hundred temples. By discussing various types of neighbourhood cult associations, Schipper explores their socioreligious functions in the community.

145   **Religious organization in the history of a Taiwanese town.**
Shih-ching Wang.   In: *Religion and ritual in Chinese society*. Edited by
Arthur P. Wolf. Stanford, California: Stanford University Press, 1974,
p. 71-91.

Describes the development of religious groups in Shu-lin township, which is located on
the southwestern side of the Taipei Basin. The author argues that shortly after the turn
of this century, place of residence became the primary criterion for defining
membership in religious organizations. He describes the criteria employed to define
membership and the way these criteria change as the town grows, commercializes, and
finally becomes an industrial suburb. Wang maintains that the religious organization of
a Taiwanese town is best understood as an aspect of its social history.

146   **Ancestors proper and peripheral.**
Sung-hsing Wang.   In: *Ancestors*. Edited by William H. Newell. The
Hague: Mouton, 1976, p. 365-72.

According to Wang, the Chinese in Taiwan divide ancestors into two categories: those
who are patrilineal forebears and those who are nonpatrilineal kin. The former are
called 'proper ancestors' and the latter 'peripheral ancestors'. While many studies have
been concerned with proper ancestors, this article emphasizes that the worship of
peripheral ancestors is also very important.

147   **Wine for the gods; an account of the religious traditions and beliefs of
Taiwan.**
Henry Yi-min Wei, Suzanne Coutanceau.   Taipei: Cheng-wen, 1976.
234p.

Describes the customs, folklore, and livelihood of the Taiwanese people. The book
consists of four sections: 'festivals', 'dreams', 'omens and tabus', and 'fortune-telling'.
Part one is a step-by-step account of religious festivals; part two describes the
interpretation of dreams; part three lists numerous dos and don'ts still to be observed
in Taiwanese society; part four delineates fortune-telling methods. Readers interested
in folk religions in Taiwan will find this book a fascinating resource.

148   **Bandits, beggars, and ghosts: the failure of state control over religious
interpretation in Taiwan.**
Robert P. Weller.   *American Ethnologist*, vol. 12, no. 1 (1985), p. 46-
61.

Throughout the last century, Taiwan's local temples propitiated socially lonely ghosts
in the Pu-du (universal salvation festival). The State tried several times to manipulate
these ghost cults in order to enhance its control over the people, but these efforts
largely failed. Weller explains why these attempts by officials and élites were
unsuccessful.

Religion. Buddhism, Taoism, and other folk religions

149 **The politics of ritual disguise: repression and response in Taiwanese popular religion.**
Robert P. Weller. *Modern China*, vol. 13, no. 1 (1987), p. 17-39.
Addresses state attempts to control folk religious ideologies, and considers the ways in which people adapt to resist such control. Several disguised rituals developed under both the Japanese and Nationalist régimes are discussed to show how difficult it is for governments to establish effective ideological control.

150 **Sectarian religion and political action in China.**
Robert P. Weller. *Modern China*, vol. 8, no. 4 (1982), p. 463-83.
Concentrates on Taiwan's heterodox sects, which contrasts with the 'orthodoxy' of Buddhism and Taoism. The orthodox religions possess established priesthoods and long textual traditions recognized both by Western scholars and by the Chinese government. Weller argues that the heterodox sects or sectarian ideologies provide an alternative world view that is potentially in conflict with official desires, but is not inherently rebellious.

151 **Unities and diversities in Chinese religion.**
Robert P. Weller. Seattle, Washington: University of Washington Press, 1987. 215p. bibliog.
Examines Chinese religion in Taiwan as a whole, covering both the popular religious traditions and the established religions like Buddhism and Taoism. Several questions are addressed in this book. To what extent does more than one religious tradition exist in China? How do people use and interpret religion in different situations? How much does religion unify this complex society, and how much does it rather divide one group from another? What are the political implication of such religious unity or diversity? Weller shows that Chinese religion is neither simply unified nor simply diverse. The varying social relations of religious believers foster interpretation and reinterpretation of religious symbols, creating both unities and diversities. Readers will find this book interesting and challenging. The appendix illustrates some of the complexities of geomancy.

152 **Aspects of ancestor worship in northern Taiwan.**
Arthur P. Wolf. In: *Ancestors*. Edited by William H. Newell. The Hague: Mouton, 1976, p. 339-64.
Presents much information about ancestor worship, obtained in the course of studying problems related to family organization, marriage and adoption practices, and inheritance. Eight examples are offered to show the complexity of the relationship between the living and the dead in ancestor worship.

153 **City gods, filiality, and hegemony in late imperial China.**
A. R. Zito. *Modern China*, vol. 13, no. 3 (1987), p. 333-71.
Introduces a popular deity, the city god, who was paired with the local district magistrate as his counterpart in the invisible world. Recognition by the populace of the partnership of city god and district magistrate was part of a recurrent political practice intended to underpin the power to govern. Zito discusses the Taiwanese folk legend about the city god and shows how the State has achieved successful domination of folk ideology by making use of the legend.

The concept of fate in Chinese folk ideology.
See item no. 164.

Christianity

154 **Christianity and animism in Taiwan.**
Alan Frederick Gates. San Francisco, California: Chinese Materials Center, 1979. 262p.
In a study based largely on library research, the author argues that the Christian church in Taiwan is still a slow-growing, alien institution within Chinese society. Taiwanese animism, which includes a mixture of Confucianism, Buddhism, and Taoism, has proved to be a rather resistant opponent of Christianity.

155 **American evangelicalism in Chinese environment: Southern Baptist convention missionaries in Taiwan, 1949-1981.**
Murray A. Rubinstein. *American Baptist Quarterly*, vol. 2, no. 3 (1983), p. 269-89.
The author describes the work of Southern Baptist missions among the Chinese on Taiwan, which stemmed both from their long-term involvement in China and from their commitment to the Nationalist government. Personal and mass evangelism were used to establish the Church, as was the mass media. Church growth was slowed from 1962-71 because changes in politics and society reduced the importance of Christianity and also because mission personnel changed frequently. Since 1970 mission growth has increased because missionaries are now willing to learn more about Chinese culture, language, and religion.

156 **Taiwan's churches of the holy spirit.**
Murray A. Rubinstein. *The American Asian Review*, vol. 6, no. 3 (1988), p. 23-58.
Studies Charismatic/Pentecostal Christianity as it exists on Taiwan. The author examines how the churches that make up the community began. This essay can be seen as a brief introduction to a complex aspect of Taiwanese religious life.

157 **Christianity in Taiwan: a history.**
Hollington K. Tong. Taipei: China Post, 1961. 249p.
Chronicles the history of the Christian experience in Taiwan. Tong includes the beginnings of Christianity on Taiwan in the early sixteenth century, the 200-year eclipse which followed, the fifty-year era under the Japanese, and post-war development. His findings show that more than seventy different sects were established, with beliefs ranging from the imminent second coming of Christ to the establishment of one kingdom on earth, and from the Trinity to the separate existence of three divine personalities. This study is based on the author's two tours of the island, visiting churches of many denominations, Christian institutes of education, mission hospitals and clinics, theological seminaries, and missionary headquarters.

Although somewhat outdated, this book is very informative. However, no index or list of references are included.

158 **Christians and the Taiwanese Independence Movement: a commentary.**
James Tyson. *Asian Affairs*, vol. 14, no. 3 (1987), p. 163-70.

By supporting the native Taiwanese movement for independence from the Nationalist government, several local Christian organizations find themselves endorsing radical approaches to Taiwan's political future. This essay details the complex relations between the State and the Church in Taiwan.

Far from Formosa: the island, its people and missions.
See item no. 88.

Society and Social Structure

General

159   **A comparison of the quality of life between the Taiwan area and mainland China.**
Chien-hsun Chen.   *Issues and Studies*, vol. 24, no. 5 (1988), p. 106-25.
Investigates whether or not the recent economic reforms on the Chinese mainland have helped to improve the welfare of the mainland people. Chen also uses various indicators to show differences in quality of life between Taiwan and mainland China from 1979 to 1986, and to probe into the causes of these differences.

160   **Gender, culture, and geography: a comparison of seating arrangements in the United States and Taiwan.**
Rebecca J. Cline, Carol A. Puhl.   *International Journal of Intercultural Relations*, vol. 8, no. 2 (1984), p. 199-219.
Seating preferences among Taiwanese and Americans are described and compared. In general, results show that the Taiwanese are more likely to prefer side seating and less likely to prefer corner seating than the Americans. Culture and sex of the interaction partner are both shown to influence preferences.

161   **Social loafing in cross-cultural perspective: Chinese on Taiwan.**
William K. Gabrenya, Jr., Bibb Latane, Yue-eng Wang.   *Journal of Cross-Cultural Psychology*, vol. 14, no. 3 (1983), p. 368-84.
Research indicates that people exert greater effort at a variety of tasks when they perform individually than they do when they perform in a group. Groups tend to obscure the identity of members' individual outputs, and encourage a phenomenon called 'social loafing'. The author reports that Taiwanese school children (in grades two to nine) demonstrated levels of social loafing similar to those observed in the US.

162 **The integration of village migrants in Taipei.**
Bernard Gallin, Rita S. Gallin. In: *The Chinese city between two worlds*. Edited by G. William Skinner, Mark Elvin. Stanford, California: Stanford University Press, 1974, p. 331-58.

The authors distinguish between people who move from villages to nearby urban areas and those who move to larger and more distant cities. Their findings show that short-distance migrants are better off financially and better educated; long-distance migrants are poorer and less well educated. This study illustrates how the economic characteristics of city life have subtly subverted the kinship- and village-based relationships from which the migrants have been accustomed to seek support.

163 **State and society in the Taiwan miracle.**
Thomas B. Gold. Armonk, New York: M. E. Sharpe, 1986. 176p. bibliog.

Relying upon data collected from archives, official sources, and interviews, Gold chronicles Taiwan's rapid progress in economic growth, structural change, improved standard of living, and political democratization. He examines the characteristics of the economy and polity before Japan's colonization, during Japanese rule, and afterwards, when Taiwan adopted a policy of export promotion under the control of the Nationalist Party. In Gold's view, Taiwan's experience is too unusual to be a model for development, although it can still offer valuable lessons for other developing countries.

164 **The concept of fate in Chinese folk ideology.**
Stevan Harrell. *Modern China*, vol. 13, no. 1 (1987), p. 90-109.

Explores the concept of fate as understood by a particular segment of the petty-capitalist class in Taiwan, the inhabitants of Ploughshare village, in the southern Taipei Basin, where Harrell conducted field-work in the 1970s.

165 **Growing old in rural Taiwan.**
Stevan Harrell. In: *Other ways of growing old: anthropological perspectives*. Edited by Pamela T. Amoss, Stevan Harrell. Stanford, California: Stanford University Press, 1981, p. 193-210.

Examines the position of old people in Chinese society in terms of two factors: cultural ideas about how old people should behave and be treated, and the ways in which they actually behave and are treated. The study shows that treatment of the aged is a compromise between the dictates of cultural values and practical exigencies.

166 **Normal and deviant drinking in rural Taiwan.**
Stevan Harrell. In: *Normal and abnormal behavior in Chinese culture*. Edited by Arthur Kleinman, Tsung-yi Lin. Boston, Massachusetts: D. Reidel, 1981, p. 49-59.

Examines both the nature and the context of normal and deviant drinking. This essay provides a clear idea of the ways in which Chinese society has achieved moderate success in controlling alcohol, and an analysis of what happens when that society fails in its task.

167 **Ploughshare village: culture and context in Taiwan.**
Stevan Harrell. Seattle, Washington: University of Washington Press,
1982. 234p. bibliog.
Ploughshare village and its surrounding communities are situated in a marginal upland
area south of the market town of San-hsia, an area where good farmland is almost nonexistent. Ploughshare is therefore a 'workers' village' where residents earn a living
from coal-mining and coal-cart pushing. Because of the lack of land for growing rice as
a suitable endowment for a lineage trust, it has become a non-lineage village. Using
the interaction of environment and culture as a mode of behavioural explanation,
Harrell gives us an ethnography of a rural locality in northern Taiwan. This book is
informative, thoughtful, original, and interesting.

168 **Assessing police cynicism in Taiwan.**
Charles Hou, Andrew Miracle, Eric D. Poole, Robert M. Regoli.
Police Studies, vol. 5, no. 4 (1983), p. 3-7.
Indicates that low-ranking police are more cynical than high-ranking ones, rural police
are less cynical than urban police, and that career stage is only slightly related to
cynicism.

169 **Urban deconcentration in developing countries: an analysis of the
processes of population dispersion in Taiwan and South Korea.**
You-wen Hsieh. PhD thesis, Rutgers University, New Brunswick,
New Jersey, 1985. 456p. (Available from University Microfilms, Ann
Arbor, Michigan, order no. 8520367).
Analyses both socioeconomic growth and government development policies in the
cities of Taiwan and South Korea. The findings of this study verify that urban
deconcentration is significantly influenced by socioeconomic growth and government
development policies. Institutional reform and increasing coordination of all government agencies are indispensable requirements for the implementation of national
urban and regional development plans.

170 **Contemporary Republic of China: the Taiwan experience 1950-1980.**
Edited by James C. Hsiung, et al. New York: American Association
for Chinese Studies, 1981. 518p. bibliog.
This book deals with various aspects of the island's developmental experience in the
period 1950 to 1980. Its eight sections cover cultural values and cultural continuity, the
educational system, economic development, social conditions and social change, law
and justice, domestic politics, foreign relations, and security and defence capabilities.
These sections, edited by a team of respected scholars, highlight Taiwan's sociopolitical
development, and economic achievement. This is an invaluable volume for those
interested in Taiwanese society and politics.

171 **Chinese studies, cross-cultural studies and Taiwan.**
J. Bruce Jacobs. *Pacific Affairs*, vol. 54, no. 4 (1981-82), p. 688-98.
Through a review of two relevant books, Jacobs argues that Taiwan studies is a
significant new field with important implications both for China studies and for cross-
cultural research in a wide range of disciplines.

Society and Social Structure. General

172 **Socioeconomic advance in the Republic of China (Taiwan).**
Charles H. C. Kao, Ben-chieh Liu. *American Journal of Economics and Sociology*, vol. 43, no. 4 (1984), p. 399-412.
The significance of economic development in Taiwan cannot be recognized adequately without a concomitant evaluation of social changes. This essay shows that Taiwan has achieved remarkable progress in every aspect of social development.

173 **Itinerant merchants in Taiwan.**
Ronald G. Knapp. *Journal of Geography*, vol. 69, no. 6 (1970), p. 344-47.
This paper shows that the itinerant merchant in Taiwan, whether working in a densely populated urban area or purveying his goods in the country where farmhouses are separated from one another by paddy fields, offers an alternative source of supply for the consumer and a profitable outlet for the small entrepreneur.

174 **Entrepreneurial role and societal development in Taiwan.**
Wen-lang Li. In: *Confucianism and economic development*. Edited by Hung-chao Tai. Washington, DC: The Washington Institute for Values in Public Policy, 1989, p. 128-48.
Taiwan serves as an ideal social laboratory for the study of entrepreneurship. The author assesses the determinants of entrepreneurial rôles and the success of entrepreneurial business enterprises. Li refutes the psychological school of thought which generally regards entrepreneurship as a reflection of nonconformist, nontraditional characteristics. He also takes issue with the Schumpeter school, which claims entrepreneurship as a unique characteristic of capitalism. The author argues that entrepreneurial traits can be discovered in traditional, noncapitalistic societies.

175 **Social change on mainland China and Taiwan, 1949-1980.**
Alan P. L. Liu. Baltimore, Maryland: School of Law, University of Maryland, 1982. 55p. (Occasional Papers/Reprints Series in Contemporary Asian Studies, no. 3).
The author argues for the intrinsic value of a comparative study of social change on Taiwan and mainland China. The PRC and the ROC have adopted different approaches to the government of their socioeconomic programmes. Liu contrasts the most fundamental differences in their strategies and describes specific areas of social change in Taiwan and mainland China: occupational promotion, education, social stratification and social mobility, the status of women, public health, the communications media, and social consensus and integration. Liu's intention is that these comparisons may shed light on the relative efficacy of different approaches to social change that are of major concern to Third World countries.

176 **Economic growth and quality of life: a comparative indicator analysis between China (Taiwan), USA and other developed countries.**
Ben-chieh Liu. *American Journal of Economics and Sociology*, vol. 39, no. 1 (1980), p. 1-21.

A composite model indicating quality of life and containing five major components – social, economic, energy and environmental, health and education, and national vitality and security – was developed to conduct this comparative study. Based on cross-national data assembled in 1975, thirty-two developed countries in addition to Taiwan were ranked according to the five components and their overall quality of life was measured. Taiwan ranked thirtieth overall.

177 **Sociology in Taiwan.**
Minako K. Maykovich. *International Review of Modern Sociology*, vol. 17, no. 1 (1987), p. 139-62.

Describes how the relatively new field of sociology has developed in Taiwan. A small number of sociologists, social workers, social affairs administrators, and social and cultural anthropologists established the discipline of sociology during the early 1950s. In the initial stages of its development, sociology was not a purely academic discipline but was often combined with social work. In part, this reflects Chinese pragmatism, which emphasizes the applied side of social studies rather than its theoretical aspects. In addition to this pragmatism, financial constraints limited pure research, the build-up of theory, and the study of methodology, making it difficult for this new field in Taiwan to meet international standards.

178 **Taiwanese images of Americans and their government.**
Minako K. Maykovich. *Asian Survey*, vol. 22, no. 4 (1982), p. 385-98.

This survey shows that among variables such as sex, age, region, occupation, exposure to mass media, contact with the US, and attitudes toward the Nationalist government, occupation has the greatest influence on the ways in which the Taiwanese respond to Americans and their government. In particular, farmers and industrial workers tend to hold a negative view of Americans, seeing them as indolent, hypocritical, and warlike.

179 **Youth change in Taiwan, 1975 to 1985.**
Gerald A. McBeath. *Asian Survey*, vol. 26, no. 9 (1986), p. 1020-36.

Argues that Taiwanese young people today are unlike their parents due to the different nature of the socialization agencies and the altered emphases within them, as well as because of the different temporal events to which they have been exposed.

180 **Value dimensions in American counseling: a Taiwanese-American comparison.**
Lichia Saner-yiu, Raymond Saner-yiu. *International Journal for the Advancement of Counseling*, vol. 8, no. 2 (1985), p. 137-46.

Discusses prevailing American values in counselling theory and practice and compares these values of those of the Taiwanese-Chinese. The paper concludes that the difference between the US and Taiwan lies in the polar opposition of American individualism and Taiwanese collectivism.

181   Socioeconomic mobility and the urban poor in Taiwan.
      David C. Schak.   *Modern China*, vol. 15, no. 3 (1989), p. 346-73.

Discusses two low-income populations in Taiwan and the progress that they have made towards improving their lives. This essay is based on longitudinal studies of two groups of poor people: the residents of a beggars' den located in a suburb of Taipei, and a sample of welfare recipients who, in 1973, lived in a low-income housing estate in Taipei itself. The study indicates that the majority of households in the two samples have improved their socioeconomic position, both in absolute terms and in relation to the wider society. The finding is significant in that what has happened to these sample households paints a more optimistic picture than that depicted by much of the literature on the urban poor in the US and in developing countries other than Taiwan.

182   Sex roles and the subjective: a cross-cultural test.
      Gertrude Schmeidler, George Windholz.   *Signs*, vol. 2, no. 1 (1976),
      p. 207-12.

Subjective perceptions of sex rôles among college students in Korea, Japan, Okinawa, Taiwan, Thailand, and New York city are described. Although there is consensus on the association of female sex rôles with happiness and love, and male rôles with pride and strength, there are cross-cultural differences with respect to other sex-rôle terms and aspects.

183   Urbanization and development: the rural-urban transition in Taiwan.
      Alden Speare, Jr., Paul K. C. Liu, Ching-lung Tsay.   Boulder,
      Colorado: Westview, 1988. 217p.

Surveys the historical development of cities in Taiwan and examines the relationship between urbanization and economic development. One chapter focuses on the growth of the Taipei metropolitan area since the 1950s. The authors explain specifically what causes people to immigrate to the city, basing their conclusions, in large part, on a detailed field survey carried out in 1973. They discuss how migrants adapt economically to life in Taipei and evaluate the living conditions and social life of migrants in the city. This volume serves as a useful reference in understanding the migration process in Taiwan within a historical context.

184   Migrants and cities in Japan, Taiwan, and Northeast China.
      Irene B. Taeuber.   In: *The Chinese city between two worlds*. Edited by
      Mark Elvin, G. William Skinner. Stanford, California: Stanford
      University Press, 1974, p. 359-84.

The relationship between migration patterns and urban growth is the theme of Taeuber's study, in which Taiwan is compared with Japan and Manchuria. Taeuber explores the links between the rate of increase in city populations and the size and maturity of the cities in Taiwan.

185   Modernization and crimes: the Taiwan case.
      Wen-hui Tsai.   *Journal of Chinese Studies*, vol. 1, no. 3 (1984), p. 261-
      79.

The economic success of Taiwan has not been without cost. Crime has become a threat to social stability on the island. Tsai's study reveals, however, that crime rates have remained impressively stable during the years of economic prosperity. The general pattern of criminality in Taiwan shows that there is a roughly inverse relation between the crime rate and the economic growth rate.

The anthropology of Taiwanese society.
See item no. 125.

The recruitment of elites in the Republic of China: a case study in the social utility of education.
See item no. 276.

Law and social change in a Chinese community: a case study from rural Taiwan.
See item no. 309.

The great transition: political and social change in the Republic of China.
See item no. 355.

Language choice and interethnic relations in Taiwan.
See item no. 678.

Language planning and language use in Taiwan: social identity, language accommodation, and language choice behavior.
See item no. 686.

Attitudinal and sociocultural factors influencing language maintenance, language shift, and language usage among the Chinese on Taiwan.
See item no. 687.

Social organizations and classes

186 **'Fang' and 'chia-tsu': the Chinese kinship system in rural Taiwan.**
Chi-nan Chen. PhD thesis, Yale University, New Haven, Connecticut, 1984. 283p. (Available from University Microfilms, Ann Arbor, Michigan, order no. 8509694).

Basing his thesis on a field study undertaken in central Taiwan, the author formulates a paradigm of the Chinese kinship system from the analysis of the key concepts of *fang* and *chia-tsu*, and discusses how the genealogical *fang/chia-tsu* system operates in the formulation of domestic groups and lineage groups. The underlying concept behind this genealogical system is father-son filiation: a son constitutes a *fang* in relation to his father's *chia-tsu*. Chen shows how such a system operates to regulate a man or a woman's kinship status, property ownership, domestic organization, agnatic adoption, and other elements of social interaction.

Society and Social Structure. Social organizations and classes

187   **Sociopolitical power and sworn brother groups in Chinese society: a Taiwanese case.**
Bernard Gallin, Rita S. Gallin.   In: *The anthropology of power.*
Edited by Raymond D. Fogelson, Richard N. Adams. New York:
Academic Press, 1977, p. 89-97.

Groups of 'sworn brothers' (Chieh-pai Hsiung-ti) were organized among small numbers of men in order to increase their economic and sociopolitical manoeuvrability and to maximize their potential as a source of mutual aid. These alliance groups are active in Taiwan. The authors examine the nature and function of sworn brotherhoods and discuss the conditions contributing to their proliferation in Taiwan today.

188   **Networks and their nodes: urban society on Taiwan.**
Susan Greenhalgh.   *China Quarterly*, no. 99 (1984), p. 529-52.

After sketching the history of urban society in Taiwan, Greenhalgh outlines the nature of social and economic organization in, and extending from, Taiwan's cities. This is followed by a discussion of the social and economic differentiation among groups of differing ethnic, class and spatial backgrounds.

189   **Development strategies and class transformation in Taiwan and South Korea: origins and consequences.**
Hsin-huang Michael Hsiao.   *Bulletin of the Institute of Ethnology, Academic Sinica*, no. 61 (1986), p. 183-217.

Explores the relationship between state development strategies and class transformation in Taiwan and South Korea. For example, the initial period of land reforms created a class of small landowners and diminished the old landlord class. The later period of industrialization created industrial capitalists.

190   **Changes in class structure and reward distribution in postwar Taiwan.**
Wey Hsiao.   *Research in Social Stratification and Mobility*, vol. 6 (1987), p. 257-78.

Relying on government statistics, Hsiao examines the change in social class structure and the distribution of material rewards in post-war Taiwan. In a historically specific context with rapid economic growth and high economic dependency, the social classes in Taiwan have become more equal in terms of income distribution, wage differentials, and capital-labour income ratio.

191   **The development of regionalism in Ta-chia, Taiwan: a non-kinship view of Chinese rural social organization.**
Shu-min Huang.   *Ethnohistory*, vol. 27, no. 3 (1980), p. 243-65.

Family groups and kinship organizations tend to be used as key factors in understanding the dynamics and changes in rural Chinese social organizations. Ethnographical data gathered in Ta-chia, central Taiwan, suggests that kinship organizations have not functioned as important social mechanisms there and that alternative models must be pursued.

192 **Social class and rural-urban patterning of socialization in Taiwan.**
Nancy J. Olsen. *Journal of Asian Studies*, vol. 34, no. 3 (1975), p. 659-74.

Demonstrates that the patterns of social class and rural-urban differences that exist in Taiwan are similar to those found in other countries. For instance, educational level has been a crucial determinant of social class in Taiwanese patterns of socialization.

193 **Kinship and community in two Chinese villages.**
Burton Pasternak. Stanford, California: Stanford University Press. 1972. 174p.

The villages of Tatieh and Chungshe in southern Taiwan are similar physically, demographically, and in their distance from an industrial urban centre, but they differ in social organization. Pasternak argues that access to critical resources – land, manpower, water – largely determines the character of sociocultural adaptation and thus affects various community structures in these two villages. This volume should be welcomed by specialists in Chinese social organization.

194 **Property and lineage of the Chinese in northern Taiwan.**
Lung-sheng Sung. *Bulletin of the Institute of Ethnology, Academia Sinica*, no. 54 (1982), p. 25-45.

Sung examines the interrelationship of forms of ownership, family, line of descent, and lineage among the Chinese living in the Taipei Basin in northern Taiwan. His main thesis is that certain aspects of kinship relations and lineage organization are associated with different forms of property ownership, which are established by Chinese customary laws. Arguments are supported by an examination of land records and field research.

The recent history of the Celestial Way: a Chinese pietistic association.
See item no. 135.

The flying phoenix: aspects of Chinese sectarianism in Taiwan.
See item no. 137.

Lu shan, ling shan, and mao shan: Taoist fraternities and rivalries in north Taiwan.
See item no. 143.

Neighborhood cult associations in traditional Taiwan.
See item no. 144.

Religious organizations in the history of a Taiwanese town.
See item no. 145.

The interplay of state, social class, and world system in East Asian development: the case of South Korea and Taiwan.
See item no. 523.

Family

195 The distribution of family names in Taiwan.
Shao-hsing Chen, Morton H. Fried. Taipei: Department of Sociology, National Taiwan University; New York: Department of Anthropology and East Asian Institute, Columbia University, 1968, 1970. 3 vols.

The focus of this research is on the primary records of the 1956 census of Taiwan. Raw data were recorded on cards of two types, household cards (1,638,673) and individual cards (9,311,312). Relying on this data, the study shows the number, identity, and frequency of surnames in Taiwan, and describes demographically, by region, changes in the composition of village or regional population. The information provides a baseline against which any future census data of a similar kind may be compared. This extensive treatise is in three volumes. Volume one presents in full the data on which the study is based. The second volume comprises fifty-one maps covering a variety of aspects related to the distribution of population and surnames. General pertinent discussion and evaluation of the data are in the third volume.

196 House united, house divided: the Chinese family in Taiwan.
Myron L. Cohen. New York: Columbia University Press, 1976. 267p. map.

The subject of this volume is a village of Hakka people (who are believed to be one of the earliest immigrants from Mainland China) in which the proportion of traditional extended families is large, even by Chinese standards. By examining the economic basis of this group of traditional families, Cohen notes that the economic requirements of tobacco farming and several other interdependent family enterprises have made this family structure particularly advantageous.

197 Structural considerations in the contemporary Taiwanese farm family: survival of the large family ideal.
Pamela A. Devoe. *International Journal of Sociology of the Family*, vol. 17, no. 1 (1987), p. 57-65.

Devoe uses structured interview data to examine the nature of ninety-six farm families in a rural area of the Hsiu-shui district in west-central Taiwan which is becoming industrialized. Her findings indicate that industrialization has caused significant technological and social changes. With these changes, however, there has not been a move away from the traditional extended family toward a nuclear family structure.

198 Families and networks in Taiwan's economic development.
Susan Greenhalgh. In: *Contending approaches to the political economy of Taiwan*. Edited by Edwin A. Winckler, Susan Greenhalgh. Armonk, New York: M. E. Sharpe, 1988, p. 224-45.

Discusses the rôles of two microsocial institutions – families and networks – in Taiwan's macro-economic performance. Greenhalgh describes the family enterprise and examines the reasons for its promotion of rapid growth and integration into the global economy. The conclusion spells out implications for Taiwan's economic development and outlines areas for future research.

199 **The Chinese family and its ritual behavior.**
Edited by Jin-chang Hsieh, Ying-chang Chuang. Taipei, Taiwan:
Academia Sinica, 1985. 323p. (Institute of Ethology Monograph Series
B, no. 15).

This collection of essays addresses a central subject: the Chinese family and its rôle in
ritual, inheritance, kinship, and related areas. The theoretical findings challenge many
long-held assumptions. For instance, one study suggests that the distinctions among
'family', 'lineage', and 'clan' – defined as distinct social entities in anthropology – may
not apply in the Chinese context. The possibility that anthropologists operating under
different cultural premises may look at realities differently is further explored in
Francis Hsu's essay 'Field work, cultural differences, and interpretation'. Overall the
books provide a valuable reader for anthropologists interested in conducting research
in Chinese and Taiwanese societies and for general readers wanting to learn more
about the Chinese family system.

200 **Bibliography of studies of the Chinese family.**
Edited by Yih-yuan Li, Ying-chang Chuang. Taipei: Center for
Chinese Studies, 1987. 86p.

Includes Chinese and English publications on the Chinese family. In total there are
1,069 entry items, which are divided into fourteen categories. These include family
education, family planning, the Chinese family overseas, marriage, women's status,
family structure, and others. The entries are unannotated.

201 **Changing family attitudes of Taiwanese youth.**
Nancy J. Olsen. In: *Value change in Chinese society*. Edited by R. W.
Wilson, A. A. Wilson, S. L. Greenblatt. New York: Praeger, 1979,
p. 171-84.

Taiwan is a nation engaged in the process of industrialization and urbanization. This
study is an attempt to discern the extent to which industrialization and urbanization
have affected the family attitudes of Taiwanese youth, and in particular to determine
whether the forces of modernization have influenced the sexes equally.

202 **The role of grandmothers in Taiwanese family socialization.**
Nancy J. Olsen. *Journal of Marriage and the Family*, vol. 38, no. 2
(1976), p. 363-72.

Interviews were conducted with mothers and grandmothers in forty-nine carefully
selected Taiwanese families. When compared with their daughters-in-law, Taiwanese
grandmothers are more concerned with aggression control and behavioural conformity,
but are less punitive and less demanding of obedience and self-reliance in their
grandchildren.

203 **The effect of family pathology on Taipei's juvenile delinquents.**
Hsien Rin. In: *Normal and abnormal behavior in Chinese culture.*
Edited by Arthur Kleinman, Tsung-yi Lin. Boston, Massachusetts: D.
Reidel, 1981, p. 213-29.
This study was carried out under the sponsorship of the ROC's National Science
Council as part of its analysis of the youth problem in Taiwan's rapidly changing
society. Rin analyses family backgrounds of juvenile delinquents to determine how
family pathology affected their deviance as well as their work and school performance.

204 **The timing of family formation: structural and societal factors in the Asian context.**
Ronald R. Rindfuss, Charles Hirschman. *Journal of Marriage and the Family,* vol. 46, no. 1 (1984), p. 205-14.
The timing of family formation affects the potential rôles that a woman may occupy
during her life. This is a comparative study of four Asian countries: Taiwan, Korea,
Thailand, and Malaysia. The findings indicate that such factors as education and rural-
urban origins have the same effect on the timing of family formation in each of these
countries. Moreover, three Confucian heritage groups – Taiwanese, Koreans, and the
Malaysian Chinese – are essentially identical with respect to the timing of family
formation, suggesting the importance of a shared heritage.

205 **Family structure and industrialization in Taiwan.**
Ramsay Leung-hay Shu, Chung-cheng Lin. *California Sociologist,* vol. 7, no. 2 (1984), p. 197-212.
Tests the generalization that, as a society becomes more industrialized, its family
structure tends to converge toward the nuclear family model. Empirical data is
examined for evidence of an increase in nuclear families corresponding to increasing
industrialization.

206 **Social and economic change, intergenerational relationships, and family formations in Taiwan.**
Arland Thornton, Ming-cheng Chang, Te-hsiung Sun. *Demography,* vol. 21, no. 4 (1984), p. 475-99.
Using data drawn from two island-wide surveys in 1973 and 1980, this study indicates
that social changes, such as the spread of schooling and the employment of young
people outside the family, have been accompanied by rapid changes in family structure
and relationships, such as the increasing separation of the residence of parents and
children before and after marriage.

207 **The house of Lim: a study of a Chinese farm family.**
Margery Wolf. New York: Appleton-Century-Crofts, 1968. 147p.
Based on her experience of living in the home of a Chinese family named Lim in a
village in northern Taiwan during 1959, Wolf provides a case study of a Chinese
extended family and an account of village life. She devotes a chapter to each of seven
of the most important figures in the Lim family. The value of this book lies in its
appreciation of the workings, customs, and tensions of a Chinese family as exemplified
in the lives of the main characters. No serious student of Chinese culture can afford to
ignore the data presented in this book, which is one of the most popular ethnographic
texts available on Chinese culture.

208 **The changing Chinese family pattern in Taiwan.**
Joseph Chun-kit Wong. Taipei: Southern Materials Center, 1981.
328p.

Examines the relationship between modernization and Chinese family structure in Taiwan over the past thirty years in order to determine the extent to which 'nuclearization' of the family has taken place. Wang notes the differences between the family structure of the current generation and that of its parents. He deduces that high socioeconomic status is significantly associated with fewer offspring and that the majority of Taiwanese families are nuclear. For researchers interested in Taiwan's family patterns, Wong's book serves as a good empirical source.

Chinese women, family and property in northern Taiwan.
See item no. 238.

Women and the family in rural Taiwan.
See item no. 239.

Variables for household division of labor as revealed by Chinese women in Taiwan.
See item no. 242.

Trends in fertility, family-size preferences, and family planning practice: Taiwan, 1961-85.
See item no. 244.

Statism and familism on Taiwan.
See item no. 361.

Marriage

209 **Affines and the rituals of kinship.**
Emily M. Ahern. In: *Religion and ritual in Chinese society*. Edited by Arthur P. Wolf. Stanford, California: Stanford University Press, 1974, p. 279-307.

Examines the relationship between affines (relatives by marriage) in the village of Chi-nan, about ten miles southwest of Taipei city. This study shows that marriage creates a ranking in which wife-givers are distinctly superior to wife-takers. From the time of betrothal the bride's family is defined as ritually superior to the groom's, irrespective of the previous economic and social positions of the two families.

210 **Deviant marriage patterns in Chinese society.**
James McGough. In: *Normal and abnormal behavior in Chinese culture.* Edited by Arthur Kleinman, Tsung-yi Lin. Boston, Massachusetts: D. Reidel, 1981, p. 171-201.

Describes deviant forms of marriage practised in traditional Chinese society, noting some cases from Taiwan. The author discusses the motivation for entering into such unions, and analyses why they are considered deviant.

211 **Affines, ambiguity, and meaning in Hokkien kin terms.**
Robert P. Weller. *Ethnology,* vol. 20, no. 1 (1981), p. 15-29.

Open-ended interviews conducted in three Taiwanese villages reveal a variation in terms for affines (relatives by marriage). Sociolinguistic analysis of the data shows that this variation reflects a fundamental ambiguity in the marriage tie – it is both the core of a new family and the evidence of a public alliance between two groups.

212 **Social contradiction and symbolic resolution: practical and idealized affines in Taiwan.**
Robert P. Weller. *Ethnology,* vol. 23, no. 4 (1984), p. 249-60.

Marriage in Taiwan creates problems for brides: in-laws are potential allies, yet they are also dangerous meddlers. How do these contradictory social relations affect symbolic expressions of kinship? This is the question addressed by Weller in this study.

213 **Marriage and adoption in northern Taiwan.**
Arthur P. Wolf. In: *Social organization and the applications of anthropology.* Edited by Robert J. Smith. Ithaca, New York: Cornell University Press, 1974, p. 128-60.

Describes the various forms of marriage and adoption recognized by customary law in northern Taiwan in the first two decades of the twentieth century. By customary law the author means the law acknowledged in the beliefs and practices of the farmers and shopkeepers who made up the great majority of the population of northern Taiwan at that time.

214 **Marriage and adoption in China, 1845-1945.**
Arthur P. Wolf, Chieh-shan Huang. Stanford, California: Stanford University Press, 1980. 426p. bibliog.

By utilizing Japanese colonial household registers in Taiwan, Wolf and Huang show that Chinese marriage and adoption practices were the complex reflections of a variety of forces – demographic, economic, and psychological – that interacted to shape family organization. The authors include a bibliographical listing of social science research in Hai-shan and its immediate vicinity. Hai-shan, an area in northern Taiwan, includes San-Hsia, Ying-ke, Shu-lin, and the southwest corner of Pan-chiao, all townships near Taipei. Demographers and sinologists will find this a stimulating study of the Chinese family.

Health, welfare, and the social services

215 **Chinese-style and Western-style doctors in northern Taiwan.**
Emily M. Ahern. In: *Medicine in Chinese culture.* Edited by Arthur Kleinman, et al. Washington, DC: Department of Health, Education, and Welfare Public Health Service, 1975, p. 209-18.

In San-hsia, a township on the southern edge of the Taipei basin, there are two distinct kinds of doctors: Chinese-style doctors (those who practice Chinese medicine), and Western-style doctors (those who are trained in Western medical science). This paper compares their methods of diagnosis and treatment, doctor-patient relations, patients' attitude toward both kinds of doctors, and other related topics. In this well-edited volume, the author also presents an essay entitled 'Sacred and secular medicine in a Taiwanese village: a study of cosmological disorders' (p. 91-113), which explores some of the basic concepts that play a part in Chinese villagers' understanding of bodily health and sickness.

216 **'Heating' and 'cooling' foods in Hong Kong and Taiwan.**
Eugene N. Anderson. *Social Science Information*, vol. 19, no. 2 (1980), p. 237-68.

The belief that certain foods are 'heating' and others 'cooling' is central to many traditional medical systems. The basic principles of such types of humoral medicine are outlined and the system as it works in Hong Kong and Taiwan is examined.

217 **Social statistics of Taiwan Province for forty years.**
Edited by Y. C. Chow. Nan-tou, Taiwan: Department of Social Affairs, Provincial Government of Taiwan, 1988. 326p.

Describes the achievements of the social services in Taiwan. The book covers welfare services, labour insurance, community development, social services organizations, and similar topics. In addition, ninety-four statistical tables are included.

218 **Conference on economic development and social welfare in Taiwan.**
Compiled by the Institute of Economics. Taipei: Institute of Economics, Academia Sinica, 1987. 2 vols.

Essays in this volume are based on a conference held in 1987 on economic development and social welfare in Taiwan. Thirteen articles, along with participants' comments, have been collected. Topics are varied, but include economic aspects of health insurance, the social security system, health care delivery, and related issues.

219 **Patients treated by physicians and folk healers; a comparative outcome study in Taiwan.**
Arthur Kleinman, James L. Gale. *Culture, Medicine and Psychiatry*, vol. 6, no. 4 (1982), p. 405-23.

The outcome for 118 patients treated by shamans (sacred folk healers) in Taipei is compared with that for 112 roughly matched patients treated by physicians. An impressive finding from follow-up evaluation was the fact that more than seventy-five percent of patients in both groups perceived that their health problems had improved.

220 **Why do indigenous practitioners successfully heal?**
Arthur Kleinman, L. H. Sung.   *Social Science and Medicine*, vol. 13B, no. 1 (1979), p. 7-26.

Findings from a follow-up study of patients treated by a shaman (*tang-ki*) are reported and related to early findings from a much larger study of indigenous healing in this Chinese cultural setting. Ninety per cent of patients treated by indigenous practitioners suffered from chronic, minor psychological disorders. In the follow-up study, ten out of twelve cases treated by the indigenous healer considered themselves to be cured.

221 **Forensic psychiatry in Taiwan.**
Sou-hong Kuo.   *International Journal of Law and Psychiatry*, vol. 6 (1983), p. 457-72.

Provides an introduction to forensic psychiatry in southern Taiwan based on the study of available case records. This report shows that the present attitude of Taiwan's legal system towards insanity remains inconclusive and inconsistent. The development of adequate legislation, including the amendment of the present law as well as the enactment of a mental health act, is a matter of necessity.

222 **Overview of mental disorders in Chinese cultures: review of epidemiological and clinical studies.**
Keh-ming Lin, Arthur Kleinman, Tsung-yi Lin.   In: *Normal and abnormal behavior in Chinese culture.* Edited by Arthur Kleinman, Tsung-yi Lin. Boston, Massachusetts: D. Reidel, 1981, p. 237-72.

The information derived from epidemiological studies of mental disorders not only provides a rational basis for planning mental health care services, but also helps us to understand better the causes and distribution of various mental illnesses. This essay reviews research on mental disorders, particularly studies undertaken in Taiwan, and suggests a future research agenda.

223 **Statistics relating to maternal and child health in Taiwan.**
Compiled by the Taiwan Provincial Maternal and Child Health Institute.   Taichung, Taiwan: Taiwan Provincial Maternal and Child Health Institute, 1986. 80p.

Summarizes statistics on population, live births, infant deaths, and maternal deaths in Taiwan. Data are presented alongside international statistics. This publication also gives information about maternal and child health services in Taiwan.

224 **Politics, ideology, and social welfare programs: critical evaluation of social welfare legislation in Taiwan.**
Wen-hui Tsai, Ly-yun Chang.   *National Taiwan University Journal of Sociology*, vol. 17 (1985), p. 233-62.

Analyses the effects of economic growth on social welfare legislation in Taiwan. At present, the four major welfare programmes provide for children, the aged, and the disabled, and offer general social assistance. The national government, however, has provided little financial support to make these laws effective.

225 **Traditional and modern psychiatric care in Taiwan.**
Wen-shing Tseng.   In: *Medicine in Chinese culture*. Edited by Arthur
Kleinman, et al. Washington, DC: Department of Health, Education,
and Welfare Public Health Service, 1975, p. 177-94.

Describes the various forms of traditional and modern psychiatric care that exist in
Taiwan. The authors compare styles of approach and problems treated, with the aim of
understanding the psychiatric care systems from professional, sociological, and cultural
points of view.

226 **Shen-k'uei syndrome: a culture-specific sexual neurosis in Taiwan.**
Jung-kwang Wen, Ching-lun Wang.   In: *Normal and abnormal
behavior in Chinese culture*. Edited by Arthur Kleinman, Tsung-yi Lin.
Boston, Massachusetts: D. Reidel, 1981, p. 357-69.

Shen-k'uei means 'vital or kidney deficiency' in classical Chinese medicine. Various
categories of sexual behaviour and diseases are described in contemporary Chinese
medicine texts where their pathogenesis is related to *shen-k'uei*. Therefore, *shen-k'uei*
syndrome is a culture-specific illness. This study evaluates eighty-seven cases and
discusses the underlying psychiatric diagnosis of *shen-k'uei* patients, with two cases of
shen-k'uei provided as detailed examples.

Induced abortion: reported and observed practice in Taiwan.
See item no. 260.

Women's Studies

227 **Sex, value, and change on Taiwan.**
Sheldon Appleton. In: *Value change in Chinese society*. Edited by
R. W. Wilson, A. A. Wilson, S. L. Greenblatt. New York: Praeger,
1979, p. 185-203.
In search of further insight into the changing values of men and women on Taiwan, this
paper analyses the relationship between sex and values among the island's residents.
The author reviews previously published data and in some cases reprocesses original
data. He finds the values expressed by men and women on Taiwan to be very similar,
with such concepts as 'family security', 'a world at peace', and 'inner harmony' near
the top of their value hierarchy.

228 **Economic and political control of women workers in multinational
electronics factories in Taiwan: martial law coercion and world market
uncertainty.**
Linda Gail Arrigo. *Contemporary Marxism*, vol. 11 (1985), p. 77-95.
Arrigo examines the multinational corporation's means of political control over
workers, basing her findings on a field study of women workers in Taiwan begun in
1977. The political conditions in Taiwan, including martial law, government control of
media, and security agencies, are discussed. It is argued that local martial law is
consciously employed by US management to coerce or control workers. Arrigo
explains that labour unions are extensions of the Nationalist Party.

229 **Women in Taiwan politics: overcoming barriers to women's
participation in a modernizing society.**
Bih-er Chou, Cal Clark, Janet Clark. Boulder, Colorado: Lynne
Rienner, 1990. 160p.
Basing their findings on extensive interviews with the women serving in the principal
assemblies of Taiwan, the authors explore how women overcome social and cultural
barriers to their political participation in a rapidly modernizing society. The traditional

male-dominated social norms have come under increasing pressure from the effects of rapid economic development and from the government's ideological commitment to the equality of the sexes. The findings indicate, however, that most women become active in politics only with the benefit of special social circumstances, and that direct or indirect discrimination against women demonstrates the practical difficulties involved in enacting institutional reforms to increase women's political participation.

230 **Women under Kuomintang rule: variations on the feminine mystique.**
Norma Diamond. *Modern China*, vol. 1, no. 1 (1975), p. 3-45.

Presents descriptive material on the life-style of the new urban middle class in Taiwan, concentrating particularly on how it relates to women, and examines family-related values and women's rôles in the society. This article supplements Diamond's earlier essay, 'The middle class family model in Taiwan: woman's place is in the home', *Asian Survey*, vol. 13, no. 9 (1973), p. 853-72. In the author's opinion, the low status of women in Taiwan is demonstrated by the fact that they are permitted only low paid and rather uninteresting jobs before marriage, and defined as a source of domestic labour after marriage, regardless of training, talents, or social class.

231 **Mothers-in-law and daughters-in-law: intergenerational relations within the Chinese family in Taiwan.**
Rita S. Gallin. *Journal of Cross-Cultural Gerontology*, vol. 1, no. 1 (1986), p. 31-49.

Examines the relations of mothers-in-law and daughters-in-law in a Taiwanese village that has changed over the past twenty-five years from an economic system based primarily on agriculture to one founded predominantly on off-farm employment. Data for this research were obtained from participant observation, in-depth interviews, township records, and from other official statistics accumulated during several field study periods in Taiwan dating from 1957 to 1982.

232 **Sexual stratification: the other side of 'growth with equity' in East Asia.**
Susan Greenhalgh. *Population and Development Review*, vol. 11, no. 2 (1985), p. 265-314.

Argues that Taiwan's economic growth may have been achieved at the cost of high or increasing inequality between the sexes. Using micro-level, longitudinal data from Taiwan, the author documents the growing inequality between sons and daughters with respect to four socioeconomic resources – education, occupation, income, and property – and three areas of personal autonomy – job selection, residence, and control over income.

233 **Family roles and female mortality differentials across cultures: an inquiry of cultural adaptation in industrialization.**
Yow-hwey Hu. *International Journal of Sociology of the Family*, vol. 18, no. 1 (1988), p. 57-78.

Compares the relationship between family support systems and female mortality patterns in the US and Taiwan. The author argues that, in Taiwan, older women seem to benefit more from family support than younger women, while the reverse seems valid in US society.

234   **The changing status of women in Taiwan: a conscious and collective struggle toward equality.**
Yen-lin Ku.   *Women's Studies International Forum*, vol. 11, no. 3 (1988), p. 179-86.

The contemporary women's movement in Taiwan started in the 1970s, earlier than certain other social movements such as those concerning consumers' rights and environmental protection. Ku asserts that equal partnership for women and men in all aspects of social life remains as a goal to be worked for, even though women's status in Taiwan has improved to some degree. The recent political liberalization offers a new opportunity for success for the women's movement.

235   **The feminist movement in Taiwan, 1972-87.**
Yen-lin Ku.   *Bulletin of Concerned Asian Scholars*, vol. 21, no. 1 (1989), p. 12-22.

Focuses on women's consciously organized collective attempts to change the *status quo* of gender relations in Taiwan. Ku describes the social context of the feminist movement, its stages of development, and its recent growth during the post-martial-law period of the late 1980s.

236   **Factory women in Taiwan.**
Lydia Kung.   Ann Arbor, Michigan: UMI Research, 1983. 231p.
bibliog.

Based on field-work undertaken in Taiwan in 1974, Kung's study indicates that factory work for young women merely provides a new channel for existing rôle expectations, and that the values on which rôle definitions are based have not changed. Kung examines the rôle of women in the family, the nature of women's work in traditional China, and the structure of industry and labour in Taiwan, in order to measure the level of women's status in contemporary Taiwanese society. Kung's work is a useful contribution to the field of women's studies.

237   **Sex differences in the perception of women's attributes for management positions: a cross-cultural comparison between American and Chinese business college students.**
Li-chen Ma, Sue Ann Ma, Kathryn White.   *National Taiwan University Journal of Sociology*, vol. 18, (1986), p. 191-205.

Examines a survey of 138 US and 173 Taiwanese business students to investigate whether or not the individual's sex determines his or her perception of women's ability to meet the demands of management positions. The result shows that female students in both societies perceive women more favourably than do the male students. The high educational or occupational status of the mother rather than the father improves students' perceptions of women's fitness for managerial jobs.

238   **Chinese women, family and property in northern Taiwan.**
Lung-sheng Sung.   *International Journal of Women's Studies*, vol. 6,
no. 1 (1983), p. 54-64.
Shows that Taiwanese women in the rural areas are not by any means powerless. Sung
demonstrates that women take an active part in family affairs and management and in
certain matters are always considered to be the decision makers. The field-work for
this paper was carried out in Shu-lin town, Taipei, during 1972 and 1981.

239   **Women and the family in rural Taiwan.**
Margery Wolf.   Stanford, California: Stanford University Press, 1972.
235p.
Wolf examines the socialization and life cycle of women in a Taiwanese village. She
begins by asking how a Chinese woman defines her own 'family'. She shows that the
Chinese woman feels closest to her uterine family – defined as a domestic unit centring
around her mother, including her brothers and sisters, but excluding her father. The
original uterine unit dissolves as the daughter marries and grows older. Yet the
daughter can create a new uterine family if she succeeds in bearing her own children.
Throughout the book, Wolf illustrates the conflict of interest between the uterine
family and the male-dominated domestic unit. Another aspect of Wolf's contribution is
the discussion of the 'women's community', which exists in all Chinese villages and is
composed of neighbours who wash clothes together, mind each other's children, and
exchange news. These neighbourhood groups exercise a considerable amount of social
control since gossip is usually a powerful weapon. Wolf has written an admirable and
very useful book for specialists as well as non-specialists.

240   **Contemporary period women in the Republic of China in Taiwan.**
Esther S. Lee Yao.   In: *Chinese women: past and present*. Esther S.
Lee Yao. Mesquite, Texas: Ide House, 1983, p. 199-241.
Yao describes women's status in Taiwan primarily after 1949, with sporadic reference
back to the period of Japanese colonization. She offers readers a quick glimpse into the
status of women in Taiwan, even though one may take issue with her argument that
the oppression of women is definitely a matter of historical record only.

241   **Successful professional Chinese women in Taiwan.**
Esther S. Lee Yao.   *Cornell Journal of Social Relations*, vol. 16, no. 1
(1981), p. 39-55.
Examines professional and personal experiences as revealed by thirty-five successful
professional Chinese women interviewed in Taiwan. The findings show that equal
rights are not enjoyed by all Chinese women since the majority of them are still
influenced or shaped by the traditional value systems of marriage and family.

242   **Variables for household division of labor as revealed by Chinese women
in Taiwan.**
Esther Lee Yao.   *International Journal of Sociology of the Family*,
vol. 17, no. 1 (1987), p. 67-86.
Assesses demographic characteristics, household divisions of labour, concepts of self,
and attitudes toward family life in a sample of Chinese women in Taiwan, drawing on
statistical analyses of questionnaires administered to 341 women in fourteen Taiwanese

villages. The study reveals that the household division of labour in contemporary Chinese families has become more egalitarian because of changes in women's education, employment, and rôle perceptions.

Do husbands and wives agree? fertility attitudes and later behavior.
See item no. 245.

Female employment and reproductive behavior in Taiwan, 1980.
See item no. 255.

Induced abortion: reported and observed practice in Taiwan.
See item no. 260.

Childhood association, sexual attraction, and fertility in Taiwan.
See item no. 261.

Modernity and fertility preference in Taiwan.
See item no. 262.

Women and industry in Taiwan.
See item no. 633.

The entry of Chinese women into the rural labour force: a case study from Taiwan.
See item no. 635.

Women, wages, and discrimination: some evidence from Taiwan.
See item no. 636.

Women in China: a selected and annotated bibliography.
See item no. 823.

Population

243 **Migration and fertility in Taiwan.**
Ming-cheng Chang. Taipei: Institute of Economics, Academia Sinica, 1982. 220p. (Institute of Economics Monograph Series, no. 22).
Urbanization has been associated with a decline in fertility levels, but relatively little is known about the determinants of fertility for people migrating from the country to urban centres. This study is concerned with the interrelationships between migration and fertility in Taiwan and is based on data, which were derived mainly from an island-wide survey undertaken in 1973. The results show that the fertility of the urban non-migrants is not any less than that of migrants to the city of rural origin who as a group are younger and less well educated.

244 **Trends in fertility, family-size preferences, and family planning practice: Taiwan, 1961-85.**
Ming-cheng Chang, Ronald Freedman, Te-hsiung Sun. *Studies in Family Planning*, vol. 18, no. 6 (1987), p. 320-37.
Traces major trends in the reproductive behaviour of Taiwan's population from 1961 until 1984-85, when the net reproduction rate was below 1.0. Taiwan's family planning programme has attained its demographic objective of moving from high to low birth rates. It has also made great improvements in the infant mortality rate on the island.

245 **Do husbands and wives agree? fertility attitudes and later behavior.**
Lolagene C. Coombs, Ming-cheng Chang. *Population and Environment*, vol. 4, no. 2 (1981), p. 109-27.
Analyses the extent to which husbands and wives agree in their attitudes toward a number of key issues that may affect fertility behaviour. Although aggregate views of men and women are remarkably similar, married couples are frequently in disagreement. The findings show that where there is disagreement, it is the wife's attitude that has more influence on fertility.

Population

246 **An old-age security incentive for children in the Philippines and Taiwan.**
Susan De Vos. *Economic Development and Cultural Change*, vol. 33,
no. 4 (1985), p. 793-814.
The old age security hypothesis states that the expectation of relying on children in
one's old age promotes the desire for large families in traditional societies. In this
report a comparable analysis of data from the Philippines and Taiwan is used to assess
the general validity of this old age hypothesis. Although the findings are generally
consistent with the hypothesis, the author feels that an examination of behaviour in
other countries is necessary in order to determine why this is so.

247 **Statistical sources on the population geography on Taiwan.**
Catherine Schurr Enderton. *China Geographer*, no. 2 (fall 1975),
p. 57-63.
Taiwan is unique among Third World countries as a resource for population
geographers because so much well-organized data exists. This is a brief review of the
sources for the study of the sociospatial demography of Taiwan.

248 **Household composition, extended kinship and reproduction in Taiwan,
1973-1980.**
Ronald Freedman, Ming-cheng Chang, Te-hsiung Sun. *Population
Studies*, vol. 36, no. 3 (1982), p. 395-412.
Taiwan today is an industrial-commercial society. Even its agricultural families obtain
most of their income from non-agricultural sources. This essay deals with the impact of
rapid economic and social development on the Chinese family structure, on
interpersonal relationships within the family, and on reproductive behaviour.

249 **Development with surplus population – the case of Taiwan.**
Yhi-min Ho. *Economic Development and Cultural Change*, vol. 20,
no. 2 (1972), p. 210-34.
Analyses Taiwan's development experience during the 1951-65 period. The author
finds little reason to doubt that Taiwan stands as an example of successful development
under severe pressure of overpopulation. Ho's results signify that the condition
governing labour supply may be less important as a factor in development than the
state of technology and the rate of change in technology directed at agriculture.

250 **The role of education in fertility transition in Taiwan.**
Paul K. C. Liu. *Economic Review*, no. 220 (1984), p. 1-28.
This report is based on a study of the trends and components of educational differences
as they relate to fertility in Taiwan for the period 1906-82. It shows that production
technology is one of the important factors determining the preference for number of
children and fertility level, and it is education that causes technological advances.
Improvement in education, therefore, will lead to a fertility transition from high to low
levels.

251 **Birth seasonality among peasant cultivators: the interrelationship of workload, diet, and fertility.**
Steven Westley Mosher. *Human Ecology*, vol. 7, no. 2 (1979), p. 151-81.

Examines human birth seasonality for a fishing village in Taiwan with 1,507 inhabitants in 1977. Data on monthly births entered in the town records are examined for the years 1926-76. Mosher demonstrates that such seasonality analysis can be extended to other cultures as well, as illustrated by examples from Germany and Mexico. This study indicates that seasonal changes in food intake are linked to the birth rate in Taiwan.

252 **The relation of income to fertility decisions in Taiwan.**
Eva Mueller, Richard Cohn. *Economic Development and Cultural Change*, vol. 25, no. 2 (1977), p. 325-47.

Explores the relation of income to fertility in Taiwan in 1969. The authors show that changes in tastes and economic attitudes are likely to be responsible in part for the decline in fertility which accompanies economic development.

253 **Fertility intentions and behavior: some findings from Taiwan.**
N. K. Nair, L. P. Chow. *Studies in Family Planning*, vol. 11, nos. 7-8 (1980), p. 255-63.

Shows that couples with a higher socioeconomic status appear less likely to desire additional children. Prior use of contraception seems to have a negative influence on desire for additional fertility. The authors report that the most important indicator of desire for additional fertility is the number of living children, closely followed by the number of living sons.

254 **Guests in the dragon: social demography of a Chinese district, 1895-1946.**
Burton Pasternak. New York: Columbia University Press, 1983. 224p.

In a volume packed with tables and statistical analyses, Pasternak focuses on three forms of Chinese marriage: the matching of young adults who then join the husband's family, the adoption of a female infant to be brought up in the home of her future husband as a 'child daughter-in-law', and the 'calling-in' of a son-in-law to live in the home of his parents-in-law. Readers will be amply rewarded by Pasternak's perception in explaining Chinese marriage patterns.

255 **Female employment and reproductive behavior in Taiwan, 1980.**
C. Shannon Stokes, Yeu-sheng Hsieh. *Demography*, vol. 20, no. 3 (1983), p. 313-31.

The impact of female employment on fertility preferences and behaviour is examined, using data from a 1980 national sample of Taiwanese women. Findings reveal that female employment in Taiwan is only slightly related to reproductive behaviour.

Population

256 **Household extension and reproductive behavior in Taiwan.**
C. Shannon Stokes, Felicia LeClere, Yeu-sheng Hsieh. *Journal of Biosocial Science*, vol. 19, no. 3 (1987), p. 273-82.
Using interview data drawn from a 1980 sample of Taiwanese married couples with wives aged fifteen to forty-nine, the authors examine the influence of household type on reproductive behaviour. They reveal that women in extended households have only slightly higher fertility preferences and current birth rate than women who have been married for the same length of time in nuclear families.

257 **Intergenerational relations and reproductive behavior in Taiwan.**
Arland Thornton, Ronald Freedman, Te-hsiung Sun, Ming-cheng Chang. *Demography*, vol. 23, no. 2 (1986), p. 185-97.
Examines the influence of intergenerational contact and authority relationships on reproductive behaviour in Taiwan. Possible influences from intergenerational relationships during young adulthood are outlined and tested using data drawn from an island-wide survey of Taiwanese wives.

258 **An econometric analysis of the effects of population change on economic growth: a study of Taiwan.**
S. L. Tung. *Applied Economics*, vol. 16, no. 4 (1984), p. 523-38.
Taiwan provides a good case for the study of the impact of rapid population growth on economic activities. Tung constructs an econometric model which presents a set of equations and takes into account major interrelationships between economic development and demographic change. His findings indicate that slow-growing populations produce substantially higher Gross Domestic Product (GDP) per capita than do fast-growing populations in the short run. Hence, it is beneficial for developing countries with higher birth rates to reduce fertility in order to achieve better economic performance in the short run.

259 **Taiwan, Republic of China.**
C. M. Wang, T. H. Sun. *Studies in Family Planning*, vol. 11 (Nov. 1980), p. 343-46.
The total population of Taiwan reached 17.5 million at the end of 1979, with a population density of 486 persons per square kilometer. This paper evaluates Taiwan's family planning system: its organizational structure, education and training programmes, overall achievements, and lingering problems.

260 **Induced abortion: reported and observed practice in Taiwan.**
Janet F. Wang. *Health Care for Women International*, vol. 6, nos. 5-6 (1985), p. 383-404.
In 1980 a survey was undertaken of a non-random sample of 500 Chinese women in Taiwan, where abortion was not legal at the time. Some 46.6 per cent (223) of the women admitted that they had obtained at least one induced abortion for birth control purposes in their lifetime. In this report, some questions are explored in relation to women's abortion experiences, attitudes toward sexual activity and marriage, guilt after abortion, and fear of complications.

261 **Childhood association, sexual attraction, and fertility in Taiwan.**
Arthur P. Wolf. In: *Demographic anthropology*. Edited by Ezra
B. W. Zubrow. Albuquerque, New Mexico: University of New Mexico
Press, 1975, p. 227-44.

During the first three decades of this century Chinese families living in the rural areas of northern Taiwan gave away the majority of their female children shortly after birth and raised in their places wives for their sons. The majority of these 'little daughters-in-law' were adopted before they were a year old and eventually married boys who were not more than three or four years old at the time the girls were adopted. This paper offers further evidence in support of the author's contention that the experience of intimate and prolonged childhood association lessened sexual attraction and thereby reduced the fertility of couples who were reared in the same family.

262 **Modernity and fertility preference in Taiwan.**
Keiko Yamanaka, H. C. Chang, Frederick O. Lorenz. *Sociological Quarterly*, vol. 23, no. 4 (1982), p. 539-51.

Changes that take place during societal modernization involve a transformation in individual attitudes toward family size. However, the complex processes by which institutional changes such as industrialization and urbanization are linked to reduction in family size are not clear. In this study, data drawn from interviews with 973 Taiwanese females, aged fifteen to forty-four, who had at least one child and who were currently living with their husbands, were used to demonstrate the direct relationship between modernity and desired family size.

Urban deconcentration in developing countries: an analysis of the processes of population dispersion in Taiwan and South Korea.
See item no. 169.

Indigenous Minority Peoples

263 **Taiwan aborigines: a genetic study of tribal variations.**
Chen Kang Chai. Cambridge, Massachusetts: Harvard University Press, 1967. 238p. bibliog.

The author applies concepts and methods in population genetics to the aboriginal population of Taiwan. Chai gives a detailed view of his operations in the field and a summary of demographic data on Taiwan's aborigines. He also presents an extensive bibliography on these people in addition to references cited in the text. All of these aspects make his book a welcome addition to the field. It is highly technical, however, and will be primarily of use to advanced students.

264 **Genetic markers of an aboriginal Taiwanese population.**
K. H. Chen, H. Cann, T. C. Chen, B. Van West, L. Cavalli-Sforza. *American Journal of Physical Anthropology*, vol. 66, no. 3 (1985), p. 327-38.

This project concentrates on a group of Taiwanese aborigines, the Toroko, as part of an ongoing programme aimed at a comprehensive study of Taiwan's aborigines and the results of this survey are compared with older findings from other tribes. The authors claim that the Toroko group of Taiwan aborigines show genetic affinities with people from the Philippines and Thailand, and, to a slightly lesser extent, with people from southern China and Vietnam.

265 **Studies on Taiwan plains aborigines: a classified bibliography.**
Edited by Ying-chang Chuang, Ying-hai Pan, Chia-in Weng, Su-chuang Jen. Taipei: Institute of Ethnology, Academia Sinica, 1988. 257p. (Taiwan History Field Research Office, Resource and Information Series, no. 1).

Contains articles and bibliographies on Taiwan plains aborigines. The bibliographies include both Chinese and foreign publications. Pan's discussion of study material written in Western languages will be most valuable for English readers.

266 **Aboriginal peoples of the southwestern Taiwan plain.**
Raleigh Ferrell. *Bulletin of the Institute of Ethnology, Academia Sinica*, no. 32, part 3 (1971), p. 217-35.
During the seventeenth century, there were many aboriginal groups living on the southwestern plain. In 1935 the Japanese estimated that approximately 23,000 descendants of these ethnic groups survived in Taiwan. Nonetheless, aboriginal languages are no longer used and the descendants have lost ties with their ancestry. This paper identifies and locates these groups and provides ethnographic data drawn from documents written by the Dutch in the early contact period.

267 **Ethnic groups of insular Southeast Asia. Volume 2: Philippines and Formosa.**
Edited by Frank M. LeBar. New Haven, Connecticut: Human Relations Area Files Press, 1975. 174p. bibliog.
This volume presents a survey of the peoples and cultures of the Philippines and Taiwan. It provides a series of descriptive ethnographic summaries, with accompanying bibliographies, ethnolinguistic maps and an index to ethnic names. The section on Taiwan is divided into four ethnic groups: Chinese, eastern lowland groups, western lowland groups, and central mountain groups. While the discussion on the Chinese is very brief, the other three groups are analysed quite extensively and are well documented in terms of settlement patterns and housing, economy, marriage and family, kin groups, sociopolitical organization, and religion. The volume also contains an excellent bibliographical survey.

268 **Plains aborigines and Chinese settlers on the Taiwan frontier in the seventeenth and eighteenth centuries.**
John R. Shepherd. PhD thesis, Stanford University, Stanford, California, 1981. 525p. (Available from University Microfilms, Ann Arbor, Michigan, order no. 8202038).
Studies the historical interaction of Chinese settlers and Malayo-Polynesian indigenous peoples on the Taiwan frontier. By documenting the relentless expansion of Chinese agricultural settlement, the author analyses the land tenure processes by which Han settlers obtained land from the aborigines. He demonstrates the impact of Chinese settlers on aboriginal societies and the mutual accommodation of Han settlers and plains aborigines.

269 **Sinicized Siraya worship of *A-li-tsu*.**
John R. Shepherd. *Bulletin of the Institute of Ethnology, Academia Sinica*, no. 58 (1984), p. 1-81.
The Siraya were the inhabitants of the southwestern Taiwan plain and constituted one of nearly twenty Malayo-Polynesian ethnolinguistic groups that inhabited Taiwan before Chinese settlement. Today, the most distinctive survival of Sirayan culture is the worship of the goddess known as A-li-tsu. This study discusses the worship of A-li-tsu in two Sinicized Siraya villages. The rituals combine a rich mixture of Chinese and Sirayan elements. They are shown to be part of a calendric series imposing taboos during the growing season and marking the passage between the separate seasons of agriculture and hunting. Some Chinese practices, such as the burning of incense and of spirit money, have been adopted by the Siraya.

Education

Educational system and problems

270 **The development of achievement and ability among Chinese children: a contribution to an old controversy.**
Laurence Chalip, James W. Stigler. *Journal of Educational Research*, vol. 79, no. 5 (1986), p. 302-07.
A study was conducted to investigate the relationship between ability and achievement among elementary school children in Taipei. The data collected are discussed in terms of both theoretical and policy implications.

271 **A study of cultural transmission in Taiwan.**
Kuang-ho Chen, L. L. Cavalli-Sforza, M. W. Feldman. *Human Ecology*, vol. 10, no. 3 (1982), p. 365-82.
This study of cultural transmission in Taiwan is based on a survey of 1,000 students, their families and friends. Areas investigated ranged from religion to customs and superstitious beliefs, as well as including entertainment and habits of hygiene. The findings show that the father's authority is more important than the mother's in cultural transmission in Taiwanese society. Girls appear to be influenced more than boys by elder siblings, and are perhaps themselves slightly more influential in the education of younger siblings.

272 **Some problems of economic development and education in Taiwan.**
Ching-han Chung. *Journal of Educational Sociology*, vol. 23, (1968), p. 124-43.
Describes the educational problems faced by Taiwan in a society undergoing rapid changes towards industrialization. Education is viewed as an end in itself, as a status symbol for both the students and their families, and as an entry into privileged occupations. Therefore, a sense of formalism exists and 'promotionism' still persists, which is responsible for teachers and students gearing course work towards the

requirements of the entrance examination to the next level of schooling, instead of the pursuit of knowledge. Most of the arguments employed here still reflect the current situation in Taiwan.

273 **Reformatory education in Chinese society.**
Irving I. Epstein. *International Journal of Offender Therapy and Comparative Criminology*, vol. 30, no. 2 (1986), p. 87-100.
Compares the approaches to institutional reform for juveniles in mainland China, Taiwan, and Hong Kong, focusing on issues of juvenile stigmatization, the development and maintenance of organizational rationality, and educational quality. Data are based on personal observations made during field trips, primary sources, and government publications.

274 **Research notes on modernization of education in the Republic of China since 1949.**
Ping-huang Huang. *Issues and Studies*, vol. 21, no. 9 (1985), p. 69-86.
Describes aspects of the development of Taiwan's educational system, such as the establishment of a compulsory schooling period of nine years for each pupil and the improvement of college entrance exams. The author suggests that further educational modernization would require active involvement of professional and public groups.

275 **An empirical analysis of China's brain drain into the United States.**
Charles H. C. Kao, Jae Won Lee. *Economic Development and Cultural Change*, vol. 21, no. 3 (1973), p. 500-13.
China, including Taiwan, has frequently been cited as the nation most susceptible to the brain-drain since 1945. This essay investigates economic, political, social, demographic, and professional factors which may account for Chinese scholars' decision to stay in the US.

276 **The recruitment of elites in the Republic of China: a case study in the social utility of education.**
Fred Chwan Hong Lee. PhD thesis, University of Oregon, Eugene, Oregon, 1983. 212p. (Available from University Microfilms, Ann Arbor, Michigan, order no. 8325281).
This study concentrates upon recruitment of personnel for the Ministry of Economic Affairs, the Ministry of Finance, the Nationalist Party, publicly-owned corporations, and two private corporations. The author argues that the educational system in Taiwan is well suited to the production of pragmatic bureaucrats, in its emphasis on achievement and obedience. Taiwan's government bureaucrats have consistently worked towards the goal of growth with equality.

277   **Classroom climate and science-related attitudes of junior-high school students in Taiwan.**
Bao-shan Lin, Frank E. Crawley, III.   *Teaching*, vol. 24, no. 6 (1987), p. 579-91.

This study examines classroom climate in the eighth grade of junior high school and its relationship to students' attitudes toward science. The authors draw on data collected from a survey on a sample of 1,269 students enrolled in forty science classes distributed equally among ten junior high schools, five metropolitan and five rural.

278   **The Republic of China (Taiwan).**
Ching-jiang Lin.   In: *Schooling in East Asia: forces of change.* Edited by R. Murray Thomas, T. Neville Postlethwaite. New York: Pergamon, 1983, p. 104-35.

Describes the educational progress and the evolving schooling structures in Taiwan. The author also analyses the relationship between socioeconomic planning and the educational system.

279   **The politics of national development and education in Taiwan.**
Christopher J. Lucas.   *Comparative Politics*, vol. 14, no. 2 (1982), p. 211-25.

Examines the extent to which schooling provides and equalizes opportunity for upward mobility in an expanding economy. This essay also considers problems of articulation between formal education and the nation's work-force development requirements, an important consideration for Taiwan.

280   **Middle school youth in modern Taiwan.**
Gerald A. McBeath.   *Asian Profile*, vol. 6, no. 2 (1978), p. 117-34.

Investigates the political learning process of young people in Taiwan. The findings show that students are more susceptible to influences from peers and youth associations, and are becoming less bound to the rigid structure of the Chinese family system.

281   **Moral education in Taiwan.**
Jeffrey F. Meyer.   *Comparative Education Review*, vol. 32, no. 1 (1988), p. 20-38.

Using data gathered in Taiwan in 1984, this study is based chiefly on eighty written responses to a series of ten questions completed by teachers in Taiwanese state schools. Meyer also examined textbooks, conducted interviews with teachers and administrators, and visited classrooms. His purpose was to study teachers' attitudes toward moral education in the face of social and political changes as a result of modernization on the island.

282 **Racial/ethnic identity of preschool children: comparing Taiwan, Hong Kong, and the United States.**
J. Kenneth Morland, Chien-hou Hwang. *Journal of Cross-Cultural Psychology*, vol. 12, no. 4 (1981), p. 409-24.
Pre-school children from four racial/ethnic groupings in three different sociocultural settings were given a picture interview in order to determine their sense of racial/ethnic identity. The chief finding was that a crucial factor in the type of identity young children develop has less to do with whether the society in which they grow up is homogeneous or multi-racial/ethnic in makeup, than whether it is stratified according to socioeconomic status.

283 **Lessons from afar: the Chinese high school in modern Taiwan and other essays.**
Douglas C. Smith. Taipei: Pacific Cultural Foundation, 1986. 224p. bibliog.
Analyses the Chinese high school in Taiwan today, establishing its historical-philosophical context and describing its current operational framework. The first section gives a historical description of Taiwan's educational system, while the second focuses on contemporary issues in the high school system. A list of persons interviewed for the study is appended.

284 **Sex difference in school adjustment in Taiwan.**
Wei-tsuen Soong, Ko-ping Soong. In: *Normal and abnormal behavior in Chinese culture*. Edited by Arthur Kleinman, Tsung-yi Lin. Boston, Massachusetts: D. Reidel, 1981, p. 157-65.
The authors demonstrate that in elementary schools in Taiwan boys have more adjustment problems than girls. They stress that school education in Taiwan should shift its focus from a rigid, test oriented, performance-dominated, teacher-centred approach to one which is flexible, growth-oriented, and child-centred.

285 **Consequences of skill: the case of abacus training in Taiwan.**
James W. Stigler, Laurence Chalip, Kevin F. Miller. *American Journal of Education*, vol. 94, no. 4 (1986), p. 447-79.
The abacus, a wood-framed tool composed of columns of movable beads, is used for arithmetic throughout Asia and is studied by children in Taiwan as part of the mathematics curriculum. The authors examine the consequences of abacus training on mathematical knowledge, the transfer of abacus skills to other tasks, and the context in which such skills develop.

286 **Curriculum and achievement in mathematics: a study of elementary school children in Japan, Taiwan, and the United States**
James W. Stigler, Shin-ying Lee, G. William Lucker, Harold Stevenson. *Journal of Educational Psychology*, vol. 74, no. 3 (1982), p. 315-22.
Describes a method for constructing a test of mathematical achievement for use in cross-national study. The mathematics curricula presented in elementary school textbooks from Japan, Taiwan, and the United States were analysed according to the

grade level at which various concepts and skills were introduced. Children from Japan and Taiwan consistently perform at a higher level than their American counterparts.

287 **Mathematics classrooms in Japan, Taiwan, and the United States.**
James W. Stigler, Shin-ying Lee, Harold W. Stevenson. *Child Development*, vol. 58, no. 5 (1987), p. 1272-85.

Presents observations which were made in Chinese, Japanese, and American classrooms during mathematics classes. The authors describe the large cross-cultural differences found in various aspects of classroom structure and management. These differences paralleled differences in achievement in mathematics among the three countries studied.

288 **Learning to be Chinese: the political socialization of children in Taiwan.**
Richard W. Wilson. Cambridge, Massachusetts: MIT Press, 1970. 203p.

This work is based on observations and data derived from a questionnaire undertaken in three elementary schools in or near Taipei. With frequent reference to the existing literature on the culture and personality of the Chinese, this volume reports on a study of political socialization of Chinese children in Taiwan. From this study Wilson attempts to make inferences about traditional Chinese political personality patterns. Supplementary discussions appear in his essays, 'A comparison of political attitudes of Taiwanese children and mainlander children in Taiwan', *Asian Survey*, vol. 8, no. 12 (1968), p. 988-1000; and 'The learning of political symbols in Chinese culture', *Journal of Asian and African Studies*, vol. 3, nos. 3-4 (1968), p. 241-56.

289 **Ethnicity as a determinant of political culture among Taiwan youth.**
Frank J. Young. *Asian Profile*, vol. 7, no. 6 (1979), p. 517-26.

Summarizes the author's findings drawn from surveys administered to 905 students at seven universities in Taiwan in 1975. This report analyses the content of student political culture in Taiwan while employing ethnicity as one of the variables presumed to influence student answers.

290 **Taiwan's international exchange program: a study in cultural diplomacy.**
Priscilla C. Yu. *Asian Affairs*, vol. 12, no. 2 (1985), p. 23-45.

Noting the significance of international exchange as a method of furthering a nation's interests, Yu seeks to examine the development and operation of one such scheme, the exchange programme of the Bureau of International Exchange of Publication of Taiwan's National Central Library. The author presents statistics and charts to indicate the growth and utilization of international exchange from 1920 to the present.

Colonial education in Korea and Taiwan.
See item no. 116.

Japanese colonial education in Taiwan, 1895-1945.
See item no. 117.

Social loafing in cross-cultural perspective: Chinese on Taiwan.
See item no. 161.

Youth change in Taiwan, 1975 to 1985.
See item no. 179.

Social classes and rural-urban patterning of socialization in Taiwan.
See item no. 192.

Changing family attitudes of Taiwanese youth.
See item no. 201.

The effect of family pathology on Taipei's juvenile delinquents.
See item no. 203.

The role of education in fertility transition in Taiwan.
See item no. 250.

Higher education

291 **The political socialization of college students on Taiwan.**
Sheldon Appleton. *Asian Survey*, vol. 10, no. 10 (1970), p. 910-23.
What are the thoughts, values, and orientations of Taiwan's college students, who will inherit the positions of leadership in Taiwan? How does the educational experience of these students affect their attitudes? Based on a survey questionnaire of some 800 high school and college students in Taiwan, Appleton attempts to find answers to these questions. This is just one of his excellent articles on student attitudes of the period 1960-70 in Taiwan. Readers looking for supplementary writings by Appleton on similar subjects may consult *Pacific Affairs*, vol. 143, no. 2 (1970), p. 227-39; and *China Quarterly*, no. 44 (1970), p. 38-65.

292 **The development of higher education in the Republic of China.**
Kenneth C. S. Gai. *Asian Thought and Society*, vol. 10, no. 30 (1985), p. 157-64.
Describes the growth of higher education in Taiwan since 1949 and the problems it has faced in the process. The author then discusses strategies to upgrade current higher education.

293 **The transformation of Junior Technological College education in Taiwan from 1945 to 1981.**
Chih-chen Lin. PhD thesis, New York University, New York, 1986. 304p. (Available from University Microfilms, Ann Arbor, Michigan, order no. 8625634).
Explores and identifies the factors influencing the development of Junior Technological College (JTC) education in Taiwan from 1945 to 1981. Official documents of the Republic of China in Taiwan were the chief source of material. This thesis contains recommendations for the future development of JTC education.

294 **Alienation of Chinese college students in Taiwan.**
Li-chen Ma. *Free Inquiry in Creative Sociology*, vol. 14, no. 2 (1986), p. 159-64.
Examines the extent of alienation among Taiwanese college students on the basis of questionnaire data obtained from 1,091 students. Alienation is seen as having four dimensions, powerlessness, social isolation, normlessness, and meaninglessness. Alienation appears to be very common in Taiwan, perhaps reflecting the stresses of a rapidly developing society.

295 **The Protestant ethic among college students in two Chinese societies.**
Li-chen Ma. *Sociological Spectrum*, vol. 7, no. 1 (1987), p. 45-59.
Investigates the Protestant ethic in Chinese culture by surveying Taiwanese and Hong Kong college students. The results indicate that, compared to Taiwanese students, Hong Kong college students are less likely to accept the Protestant ethic and beliefs in justice and fairness, and are less alienated and sexually permissive. However, Taiwanese students adhere less to authoritarianism than do their counterparts in Hong Kong.

296 **Social orientation and individual modernity among Chinese students in Taiwan.**
Kuo-shu Yang. *Journal of Social Psychology*, vol. 113, no. 2 (1981), p. 159-70.
Reviews a series of studies on the relationship between social orientation and individual modernity among Chinese students in Taiwan, and then reports on another piece of research in the series which surveyed ninety-two students at the National Taiwan University. The studies revealed a consistent negative correlation between social orientation and individual modernity.

297 **Colleges and universities in the ROC: a pictorial introduction.**
Edited by Yu-chao Yu. Taipei: Sinorama, 1987. 2 vols.
Describes colleges and universities in Taiwan in terms of their facilities, faculty quality, student activities, size, and specialities.

Sex roles and the subjective: a cross-cultural test.
See item no. 182.

Sex differences in the perception of women's attributes for management positions: a cross-cultural comparison between American and Chinese business college students.
See item no. 237.

Library education in the Republic of China.
See item no. 789.

Continuing education and staff development for librarians in the Republic of China.
See item no. 790.

Problems confronting library science education in the Republic of China.
See item no. 796.

Law and the Legal System

General

298 **Comparison of the Nationalist and Communist Chinese views of unequal treaties.**
Hungdah Chiu.   In: *China's practice of international law: some case studies*. Edited by Jerome Alan Cohen.   Cambridge, Massachusetts: Harvard University Press, 1972, p. 239-67.
Studies the problem of unequal treaties in the light of both the Nationalist government's and the Communist government's theory and practice. Both the Nationalist government and Communist China denounce the unequal treaties imposed by Western powers in the nineteenth and twentieth centuries. The Nationalist government argues, however, that China's unequal treaties should be revised or abrogated in accordance with the writings of Western international law. On the other hand, Communist China, which has been more vocal than the Nationalist government, tends to negate Western international law in its interpretation of treaties.

299 **The United States Status of Forces Agreement with the Republic of China: some criminal case studies.**
Hungdah Chiu.   *Boston College International and Comparative Law Review*, vol. 3, no. 1 (1979), p. 67-88.
The US sent military aid and an advisory group to Taiwan after the outbreak of the Korean War in 1950. By 1957, the number of the so-called Military Assistance Advisory Group (MAAG) had increased to 1,887. Although in 1965 the Agreement between the ROC and the US on the status of US armed forces in the ROC was concluded, MAAG personnel continued to be treated as diplomats and were immune to Chinese criminal jurisdiction. This article examines the 1965 Agreement through the discussion of several cases. It may serve to elucidate certain aspects of the US status of forces agreements with Japan and South Korea.

300 **Family partition as contractual procedure in Taiwan: a case study from south Taiwan.**
Myron L. Cohen. In: *Chinese family law and social change.* Edited by David C. Buxbaum. Seattle, Washington; London: University of Washington Press, 1978, p. 176-204.

The main objects of the study were residents of Yen-liao, located in Kaohsiung county in south Taiwan. Features of family partition and related matters are examined to identify the influence of technological modernization on traditional patterns, and in turn to ascertain the overall locus and direction of social change.

301 **Ending martial law in Taiwan: implications and prospects.**
John F. Copper. *Journal of Northeast Asian Studies*, vol. 7, no. 2 (1988), p. 3-19.

Assesses Taiwan's martial law in terms of its impact on politics while it was in force between 1949 and 1987. The author also discusses the prospects for a new and modern Taiwan without martial law or emergency decrees.

302 **A study tour of Taiwan's legal system.**
Ruth Bader Ginsberg. *American Bar Association Journal*, vol. 66 (Feb. 1980), p. 165-70.

Provides an overview of Taiwan's legal system and discusses the impact on it of the sudden termination of diplomatic ties with the US. The author also deals with the legal education programmes offered at several institutions in Taiwan.

303 **Martial law in Taiwan.**
Richard C. Kagan. *Bulletin of Concerned Asian Scholars*, vol. 14, no. 3 (1982), p. 48-54.

This essay was prepared for the subcommittee on Asian and Pacific Affairs, Committee on Foreign Affairs, US House of Representatives, in 1982. It describes the history and purpose of martial law in Taiwan, its application, and US policy toward martial law.

304 **A compilation of the laws of the Republic of China.**
Chi-chao Kang. Taipei: The Author, 1971. 3 vols.

Presents the Constitution of the Republic of China, the nation's Civil Code, Administrative Law, Criminal Code, Military Law, and laws governing customs duties and internal revenue. This compilation should be useful to those interested in the development of Taiwan's legal system and general aspects of business and civil law on the island.

305 **Guide to international trade and investment law in the Republic of China.**
Chin Kim. In: *Selected writing on Asian law.* Edited by Chin Kim. Littleton, Colorado: Fred B. Rothman, 1982, p. 425-37.

Provides American businesspeople and lawyers unfamiliar with Taiwan with the principal sources of information on trade and investment law in Taiwan. The author's approach is comparative and is addressed to those familiar with American laws.

306 **Forensic psychiatry in Taiwan: civil litigation.**
Sou-hong Kuo, Ching-piao Chien, Mark J. Mills. *International Journal of Law and Psychiatry*, vol. 10, no. 3 (1987), p. 297-309.
When forensic psychiatry was introduced in Taiwan two decades ago, the emphasis was on its rôle in criminal law proceedings. Noting that civil cases now constitute an important part of forensic practice in Taiwan, the authors discuss the process followed by the courts in obtaining psychiatric intervention in civil litigation. Those sections of the Taiwanese civil code that deal with mental disorder are discussed, and the problems of delivering psychiatric assessments within the present legal system are examined.

307 **The status and protection of aliens in Taiwan, Republic of China.**
Hsin-sun Liu. Taipei: Asia & World Forum, 1978. 169p. bibliog. (Asia and World Monograph Series, no. 9).
Taiwan has granted the right of entry to aliens on the principle of reciprocity. For the protection of the personal security of non-nationals in Taiwan, they are generally granted the same treatment as nationals. This study describes general regulations regarding aliens in Taiwan and exceptions to these regulations.

308 **Trade and investment in Taiwan: the legal and economic environment in the Republic of China.**
Edited by Herbert H. P. Ma. Taipei: Institute of American Culture, Academia Sinica, 1985. 2nd ed. 946p. bibliog.
Provides information on and analyses of Taiwan's legal system and a number of its laws. The volume meets a long-standing need for a readable and comprehensive view of Taiwan's legal system, the authors being well-known specialists in their own fields. The comprehensiveness of this book is evident from the contents of its chapters, which include: sales law; company law; contract law; the status of aliens and recognized foreign corporations; private international laws; the position of customary international law and treaties; general features of the law and legal system of the ROC; protection of intellectual property; export-import procedures and regulations applicable to foreign trade; US-ROC trade and investment relations; taxation regulations; monetary and banking system; joint ventures, chattel security interest; parent-subsidiary corporation; and technology transfer. Readers who are interested in Taiwan's legal system as well as its economic environment will find these essays valuable and stimulating. A bibliography of books and articles in English and Chinese primarily dealing with investment in the ROC and US-ROC trade relations is included.

309 **Law and social change in a Chinese community: a case study from rural Taiwan.**
Michael J. Moser. Dobbs Ferry, New York: Oceana, 1983. 200p.
Examines the influence of economic development and social change on legal institutions in rural Taiwan. Field-work in Taiwan was carried out during 1974-76. Sources include documents, interviews, and observations of disputes and their handling in the community and the courts. The author concludes that mediation works as long as only the disputants are involved, or the stakes are relatively small. Mediation gives way to litigation when external contacts or high stakes are involved. Readers will find in this book a wealth of suggestions for further research.

310 **The commercial laws of the Republic of China.**
Werner Y. F. Ning. In: *Digest of commercial laws of the world.*
Dobbs Ferry, New York: Oceana, 1988. 121p. looseleaf.

This listing includes laws concerning contracts, jurisdiction of the courts, arbitration, pledges and chattel mortgages, corporations, partnerships, trust receipts, and others.

311 **The joint venture and related contract laws of mainland China and Taiwan: a comparative analysis.**
Clyde D. Stoltenberg, David W. McClure. *Georgia Journal of International and Comparative Law*, vol. 17 (1987), p. 45-97.

Through a direct comparison of the joint venture laws as they relate to the selected issues of corporate control of the venture, capital contribution, profit repatriation, taxation, and relevant contract law principles in Taiwan and the PRC, the authors conclude that joint ventures in Taiwan enjoy considerable autonomy and can take advantage of a highly skilled labour force, while foreign investors in the PRC have faced numerous difficulties.

312 **There are no strikes in Taiwan: an analysis of labor law in the Republic of China on Taiwan.**
Jane Kaufman Winn. *Maryland Journal of International Law and Trade*, vol. 12, no. 1 (1987), p. 35-63.

Unlike South Korea, industrialization in Taiwan has not been accompanied by violent repression of labour movements or clashes between workers and authorities. Yet the government has adopted authoritarian, paternalistic industrial policies to exclude workers from the political process. As a result, while striving to maximize export-led growth in Taiwan, workers are denied the opportunity to form free trade unions. Winn provides a survey of the labour laws and regulations in Taiwan in order to examine the labour situation and workers' rights there.

China, seventy years after the 1911 Hsin-hai revolution.
See item no. 67.

Commercial contract law in late nineteenth-century Taiwan.
See item no. 71.

The US Constitution and the development of constitutionalism in China; proceedings of a conference held on December 10, 1987.
See item no. 324.

The international law of recognition and multi-system nations – with special reference to the Chinese (mainland-Taiwan) case.
See item no. 379.

Quasi-diplomatic relations of the Republic of China: their development and status in international law.
See item no. 418.

The Republic of China and the law of the sea.
See item no. 492.

Legal aspects of offshore banking in Taiwan.
See item no. 548.

Security interests under the law of the Republic of China on Taiwan: an introductory guide.
See item no. 555.

Chinese law past and present: a bibliography of enactments and commentaries in English text.
See item no. 814.

Copyright protection

313 **Protection from commercial counterfeiters in Taiwan for US firms.**
Edward Han. *Law and Policy in International Business*, vol. 16 (1984), p. 641-61.
Examines the efforts of US firms to protect their intellectual property from Taiwanese counterfeiters. The author discusses the inadequacy of US legislation and international agreements to control international counterfeiting. However, economic pressures have dictated that the government curtail piracy and strengthen the copyright law. Dramatic changes in Taiwan's laws on copyright, together with the granting of juristical status to US firms in Taiwan's courts, signal an impressive effort made by the government to stem the flow of counterfeit goods from Taiwan.

314 **Protecting intellectual property in Taiwan: non-recognized United States corporations and their treaty rights of access to courts.**
Michael M. Hickman. *Washington Law Review*, vol. 60, no. 1 (1984), p. 117-40.
Taiwan has an international reputation for commercial counterfeiting. US corporations with no presence in Taiwan are sometimes victims of infringement there. The author describes how American corporations can protect their intellectual property rights in Taiwan under the US-ROC Treaty of Friendship, Commerce, and Navigation, signed in 1946. A criminal case instituted by Apple Computers in Taiwan illustrates the issues involved. Hickman also provides a brief overview of Taiwan's civil law system.

315 **A comparative study of the copyright protection in the United States and the Republic of China.**
De-fen Ho. *Journal of Social Science* (Taipei), vol. 28 (1980), p. 303-412.
Discusses differences between the legal schemes for copyright protection in the US and in Taiwan. In comparison with the American legal framework for copyright protection, Taiwan's copyright law needs revision to meet the changing needs of society. It should enlarge the scope of works with copyright and increase the civil remedies and criminal punishments.

316 **Legal efforts of the United States and the Republic of China on Taiwan at controlling the transnational flow of commercial counterfeit goods.**
Mitchell A. Silk. *Maryland Journal of International Law and Trade*, vol. 10, no. 2 (fall 1986), p. 209-72.

By examining the effect of international agreements binding on the US and domestic US laws dealing with counterfeiting, the author focuses on how to take retaliatory measures against countries where counterfeiting occurs, examining, in particular, the case of Taiwan. Silk assesses Taiwan's efforts at controlling commercial counterfeiting, including legislative means, judicial action, administrative policy, and police action. This article also appears in the *Chinese Yearbook of International Law and Affairs*, vol. 5 (1985), p. 90-149.

317 **Protection of American copyrights in books on Taiwan.**
Joseph T. Simone, Jr. *Journal of the Copyright Society of the USA*, vol. 35, no. 2 (1988), p. 115-57.

Book piracy in Taiwan has been the result of an historical absence of legal protection of copyright in China, pressure for economic development, and the lack of foreign publishers enforcing their rights under existing law. The author concludes that Taiwan's recently strengthened copyright law, combined with growing market opportunities for books, should provide more protection for US copyrights. Yet the total elimination of book piracy will require special strategies and patience on the part of American publishers. Simone suggests that US publishers should encourage local distributors to pursue offenders and that publishers should also establish their own branches in Taiwan.

Politics and Government

General

318 **The State and Taiwan's economic development.**
Alice H. Amsden. In: *Bringing the state back in*. Edited by Peter
Evans, D. Rueschemeyer, Theda Skocpol. Cambridge, England:
Cambridge University Press, 1985, p. 78-106.
When the Nationalist government retreated to Taiwan, it was obsessed with the
objective of military build-up in order to recover mainland China from the
Communists. Amsden describes how economic development replaced military growth
as the first priority for the government. The change of policy priority furthered the
process of capital accumulation and encouraged export-led capitalist industrialization.

319 **Political development in Taiwan: the Sun Yat-sen model for national**
reconstruction.
David Wen-wei Chang. *Issues and Studies*, vol. 25, no. 5 (1989), p. 11-
32.
Discusses three models of political development: the capitalist-democratic model, the
Marxist-proletarian model, and the Third World militaristic-bureaucratic model. The
author argues that future political and ideological developments in Taiwan must
incorporate and integrate elements of three other traditions: the Confucian cultural
heritage, Dr. Sun Yat-sen's model for democracy, and the lessons of the failure of
Communism. In consequence, whatever model is adopted in Taiwan, future
development must come from its own situation and peaceful experimentation.

320 **Evolution of Taiwan's political leadership after Chiang Ching-kuo.**
Parris H. Chang. *AEI Foreign Policy and Defense Review*, vol. 6,
no. 3 (1986), p. 10-19.
Predicts that under Teng-hui Lee a collective leadership that is an extension of
Chiang's régime will emerge. Lee will share power with the premier and other top
leaders in the KMT and will largely continue the policies of Chiang's government.

321 **The reform movement among intellectuals in Taiwan since 1970.**
Guying Chen. *Bulletin of Concerned Asian Scholars*, vol. 14, no. 3
(1982), p. 32-47.
During the 1970s, intellectuals in Taiwan moved from discussion and contemplation of
social and political issues to active participation in them. Chen details the intellectuals'
efforts at effecting reform and radical changes in Taiwanese society, noting their active
participation in public opposition movements to end martial law and their attendance
at parliamentary elections to accelerate the process of democratization in Taiwan.

322 **Democratizing the quasi-Leninist regime in Taiwan.**
Tun-jen Cheng. *World Politics*, vol. 41, no. 4 (1989), p. 471-99.
That the movement toward democratization exists in Taiwan is beyond any doubt, but
the interpretation of this trend has been the subject of many debates, which have
attempted to determine its origin and the probable stability of such a democracy. The
author argues that the process of democratization in Taiwan can be attributed to the
capabilities of the political opposition in the setting of agendas, the shifting of
bargaining arenas, and the creation of incentives for the reformist leaders of the régime
to play the game. It seems that democratization will continue because the ruling party
has been able to maintain its dominant position in new political circumstances. This is
an excellent explanation of Taiwan's political development after the mid-1980s.

323 **Democratizing transition in Taiwan.**
Yangsun Chou, Andrew J. Nathan. *Asian Survey*, vol. 27, no. 3
(1987), p. 277-99.
In 1986, the Democratic Progressive Party (DPP) was established, signifying a change
in Taiwan's political development. The authors examine Taiwan's party system reform
process, the motives behind the new party formation, its potential impact within
Taiwan and worldwide, and its theoretical significance for Taiwan studies. They
conclude that the Taiwanese experience has confirmed the proposition that
democratizing reform can strengthen a political régime.

324 **The US Constitution and the development of constitutionalism in China;
proceedings of a conference held on December 10, 1987.**
Edited by Ray S. Cline, Hungdah Chiu. Washington, DC: United
States Global Strategy Council, 1988. 166p. bibliog.
Contains seven papers presented by Chinese and American scholars on the influence of
the US Constitution on China's political development. Several papers deal with topics
related to the ROC. John F. Copper discusses the development of constitutional
democracy in Taiwan. David C. Cheng analyses the attitudes of Chinese scholars in
Taiwan toward the US Constitution from the early 1950s to the present. His study is
based on objective data and a content analysis of relevant literature. Herbert H. P. Ma

demonstrates the influence of the US Constitution and constitutional law on the Constitution of the ROC.

325 **The evolution of political parties in Taiwan.**
John F. Copper. *Asian Affairs: an American Review*, vol. 16, no. 1 (1989), p. 3-21.
Argues that Taiwan is not only a model of economic development but also a model of political modernization. The author describes how a political party system has evolved in Taiwan in recent years that both embodies and promotes party competition. While party competition has been institutionalized, the Nationalist Party will remain dominant in Taiwan's political arena, at least for some time.

326 **A quiet revolution: political development in the Republic of China.**
John F. Copper. Washington, DC: Ethics and Public Policy Center, 1988. 76p.
The author points out that Taiwan's economic success has somewhat obscured its political progress. In fact, the Taiwanese government has handled internal and external challenges so well that it might serve as a model for other developing countries. Through various elections, Taiwan has demonstrated an emerging if not yet fully operational democratic process. Although the country will probably continue to be dominated by the Nationalist Party, it has made gradual policy changes conducive to social stability and economic growth.

327 **Taiwan: a nation in transition.**
John F. Copper. *Current History*, vol. 88, no. 537 (1989), p. 173-76, 198-99.
Taiwan's success has caused some observers to declare that Taiwan is a nation that thrives on adversity, while others say it is a model of development. The publicity surrounding its success has changed Taiwan's image abroad; it is no longer regarded as a pariah state. Copper discusses Taiwan's recent economy, political changes, defence and foreign policy. He concludes that China may be fearful of Taiwan's success, which may make the problem of unification with mainland China more difficult to achieve.

328 **Political differentiation in Taiwan: group formation within the ruling party and the opposition circles, 1979-1980.**
Jürgen Domes. *Asian Survey*, vol. 21, no. 10 (1981), p. 1011-28.
Argues that Taiwan is in the process of transition towards a pluralistic representative system, and a comparatively broad spectrum of political groups and circles has emerged. Group formation within the ruling party is of greater importance, however, than the political and organizational activities of a highly diversified opposition with no more than a minority base in society.

329 **The impact of the 1980 supplementary election on Nationalist China's Legislative Yuan.**
Richard L. Engstrom, Chi-hung Chu. *Asian Survey*, vol. 24, no. 4 (1984), p. 447-458.
The Legislative Yuan (governmental branch) has served as an important manifestation of the Nationalist government's claim that it is the only legitimate government for all of China. This article analyses the 1980 election for seats in the Legislative Yuan.

330 **Taiwan in 1988: the transition to a post-Chiang world.**
Thomas B. Gold. In: *China briefing, 1989*. Edited by Anthony J. Kane. Boulder, Colorado: Westview, 1989, p. 87-108.
The year of 1988 began with the death of President Chiang Ching-kuo, followed by the succession by Vice President Teng-hui Lee. Lee continued his predecessor's policies of liberalizing and democratizing Taiwan's ossified political system, of increasing openness towards mainland China, and of adopting a flexible foreign policy. This essay describes the development of domestic politics in Taiwan and its international interactions in 1988.

331 **Ideology and development: Sun Yat-sen and the economic history of Taiwan.**
A. James Gregor, Maria Hsia Chang, Andrew B. Zimmerman. Berkeley, California: University of California, Institute of East Asian Studies/Center for Chinese Studies, 1982. 107p.
By reviewing Dr. Sun Yat-sen's economic ideas and Taiwan's post-war economic history, the authors explore the issue of whether Taiwan's post-war economic policies and its successful economic development during the past decades can be traced to the teachings of Sun. Although the relationship is not satisfactorily established, this book is worth reading for anyone interested in Sun's viewpoints regarding economic development.

332 **Taiwan after Chiang Ching-kuo.**
Selig S. Harrison. *Foreign Affairs*, vol. 66, no. 4 (1988), p. 790-808.
Assesses Taiwan's political situation and foreign policies, and suggests that the United States should continue to resist playing an active rôle in Taiwan's politics. The US should neither endorse nor promote the 'one country, two systems' concept, an idea proposing a unified China with different coexistent political systems.

333 **The more things change, the more they stay the same: some external constraints on the ROC's bureaucracy.**
Szu-yin Ho. *Issues and Studies*, vol. 24, no. 5 (1988), p. 126-37.
Recent political reforms in Taiwan have changed the bureaucracy's sociopolitical environment and raised people's expectations of government administration. Ho discusses the consequences of political development on the bureaucracy.

334   Economic and political development in the Republic of China.
       John Fuh-sheng Hsieh, Chung-lih Wu. In: *China's global presence*.
       Edited by David M. Lampton, Catherine H. Keyser. Washington, DC:
       American Enterprise Institute for Public Policy Research, 1988, p. 35-
       66.

Discusses Taiwan's development since 1949 and considers what might lie ahead both
economically and politically. This essay stresses several non-statistical factors in
explaining Taiwan's growth record, for example, successful land reform, the
emergence of a strong middle class, and other social and cultural factors.

335   **Paradoxes in the politics of Taiwan: lessons for comparative politics.**
       J. Bruce Jacobs. *Politics*, vol. 13, no. 2 (1978). p. 239-47.

Examines Taiwan's politics by focusing on the Nationalist Party and Taiwan's interest
groups. This article encourages further research into the nation's politics because
Taiwan offers numerous important foci for cross-cultural comparisons.

336   **Political opposition and Taiwan's political future.**
       J. Bruce Jacobs. *Australian Journal of Chinese Affairs*, no. 6 (1981),
       p. 21-44.

True opposition to the Nationalist Party (KMT) on Taiwan has not come from the two
officially sanctioned minor parties, but from non-partisan groups and individuals,
including the Presbyterian Church. Non-partisan candidates won approximately twenty
per cent of the 1977 county executive and provincial assembly elections. However, an
unexpected riot known as the Kao-hsiung Incident in 1979 resulted in jail terms
ranging from twelve years to life for non-partisan leaders and temporarily ended the
trend toward democratization.

337   **A preliminary model of particularistic ties in Chinese political alliances:**
       Kan-ch'ing and Kuan-hsi in a rural Taiwanese township.
       J. Bruce Jacobs. *China Quarterly*, no. 78 (June 1979), p. 237-73.

The concept of *Kuan-hsi* (personal ties) means far more than the notion of social
contacts and actual acquaintance. One particular characteristic of *Kuan-hsi* is that its
existence or nonexistence affects the behaviour of not only those directly involved in
the personal relationship – it can potentially affect all who are to any degree associated
with any of the principal parties in this latent network of personal ties. The Chinese
have long suggested that personal ties play an important rôle in their politics. This
study looks into cultural influence on politics and seeks to develop an alternative
approach to Chinese politics. By examining the Matsu township in Taiwan, Jacobs
shows that the Chinese prefer persons sharing a *Kuan-hsi* base when seeking political
allies.

338   **Recent leadership and political trends in Taiwan.**
       J. Bruce Jacobs. *China Quarterly*, no. 45 (1971), p. 129-54.

Investigates political changes in Taiwan and analyses their importance. Taiwan's future
political and economic development depends on the result of the debate between the
younger technical experts and the older military security advisors. The author's
observations in some ways still reflect the 'macropolitical phenomenon' in Taiwan. This

phenomenon includes the political actions and policies of groups, institutions and classes, with the emphasis on collective political choices.

339 Taiwan's future?
Edited by Yung-hwan Jo. Tempe, Arizona: Center for Asian Studies, Arizona State University, 1974. 351p.

Based on an international conference on the future of Taiwan held in 1973, this volume contains fourteen papers analysing Taiwan's internal politics; its external relations with Japan, the US, the USSR, and mainland China; and other topics related to Taiwan's economy and society. The provocative issue of who owns Taiwan is also discussed.

340 The great transition: political change and the prospects for democracy in the Republic of China on Taiwan.
Tai-chun Kuo, Ramon H. Myers. *Asian Affairs*, vol. 15, no. 3 (fall 1988), p. 115-33.

Throughout the 1980s, the Philippines, South Korea, and Taiwan have all undergone political changes. The authors maintain that, of all these countries, Taiwan experienced the most successful transition from a powerful ruling party to a polity of new political opposition. They suggest that this smoothness of change depends upon social stability and tolerance of popular disagreement.

341 Existential imperatives and the future of the Kuomintang.
John Mingsien Lee. *Asian Affairs*, vol. 13, no. 2 (1986), p. 10-20.

The future of the Kuomintang (KMT), according to Lee, lies in its accomplishments in ensuring a peaceful coexistence between Mainlanders and Taiwanese, respecting human rights and dignity, promoting a public-spirited civic culture, promoting peaceful competition and the transition of power, and upgrading the quality of civic life.

342 National elite and local politician in Taiwan.
Arthur J. Lerman. *American Political Science Review*, vol. 71, no. 4 (1977), p. 1406-22.

Describes how the political culture of the national élite and that of the masses came to coexist in Taiwan and analyses trends in Taiwan's politics under the influence of their conflicting relationship. Lerman, however, is optimistic about the direction of Taiwan's politics because he believes that the national élite will move towards integration with the mass political culture.

343 Structural correlates of emerging political pluralism in Taiwan.
Wen Lang Li. *Journal of Asian and African Studies*, vol. 23, nos. 3-4 (1988), p. 305-17.

This study analyses the results of the Provincial Assembly elections among 360 Taiwanese townships to see whether Taiwanese society has achieved a two-party system. The percentage of votes for non-Nationalist Party candidates was calculated. It concludes that the most significant factor influencing a country's progress towards pluralist politics is its degree of industrialization. If a community experiences a dramatic increase in the percentage of its population working in the non-agricultural sector, that community is likely to become pluralistic in terms of local political competition, allowing non-nationalists to challenge the dominant Nationalist Party.

344 **Political development in the Republic of China on Taiwan.**
Ya-li Lu. *Issues and Studies*, vol.21, no. 9 (1985), p. 138-51.
While Taiwan's economic growth has been well explored, its political development has not received sufficient attention from scholars. Lu argues that Taiwan's achievement in increasing political participation, as well as modernizing the bureaucracy, could provide a useful example for other developing countries.

345 **The politics of Formosan nationalism.**
Douglas H. Mendel. Berkeley, California: University of California Press, 1970. 315p.
Supporters of an independent Taiwan, free from the KMT's rule, tend to describe themselves as Formosan, rather than Taiwanese, nationalists to emphasise their independence. This volume tackles three interrelated topics: the history of Taiwan with a selective analysis of post-1949 political and economic development; Taiwanese attitudes toward contemporary issues, especially economic development and military commitment; and foreign policy problems and the overseas Formosan movement. Certain data-gathering difficulties limit the possibility of in-depth discussion on some issues, such as the overseas Formosan movement. However, this pioneering book can serve as supplementary reading on the elusive problem of Formosan nationalism.

346 **Toward a normative theory of political development with special reference to the Republic of China in Taiwan.**
Thomas A. Metzger. *Republican China*, vol. 9, no. 3 (1984), p. 23-29.
Presents a list of questions for the discussion of Taiwan's political development. These questions are derived from debates between the author and liberal scholars in Taiwan who are highly critical of government policies. Metzger argues that scholars in Taiwan tend to evaluate governments by combining human rights theory with a modernization approach. This combination blurs the differences between descriptive and prescriptive questions. He hopes that as these questions are deliberated, normative discussions about Taiwan's political development will become more cerebral and less emotional.

347 **Dateline Taiwan: a dynasty ends.**
Thomas Omestad. *Foreign Policy*, no. 71 (1988), p. 176-98.
The reform programme in Taiwanese politics was engineered by the late Chiang Ching-kuo and continued until his death in 13 January 1988. This political liberalization represents the Nationalist Party's coming to terms with economic success. The author discusses Taiwan's post-Chiang vulnerability, manifested in worsening diplomatic isolation and dependence on exports. He also suggests some guidelines for the US government: the US should encourage Taiwan to continue relaxing its relations with mainland China; it should also urge Taiwan to foster democratization and respect for human rights.

348 **Formosa under Chinese Nationalist rule.**
Fred Warren Riggs. New York: Macmillan, 1952. 195p.
This concise study of Chinese Nationalist rule in Taiwan emphasizes early internal development. Although, in the early 1950s, tensions existed between the Taiwanese and the Mainlanders, and the Nationalist Army was not well enough equipped to undertake a significant defence of Taiwan, the island's productivity had already grown considerably since 1945 and the administration had become relatively efficient and

91

honest. Meanwhile, US aid was on its way to becoming a stabilizing factor in Taiwan's economic and social security.

349 **Taiwan in 1988.**
James D. Seymour. *Asian Survey*, vol. 29, no. 1 (1989), p. 54-63.

The year 1988 saw astonishing changes in Taiwan. It began with the death of President Chiang Ching-kuo and ended with Taiwan's Chinese Mainlanders struggling to fend off the increasingly restless Taiwanese. Seymour also discusses Taiwan's moves toward normalizing economic and cultural relations with mainland China.

350 **Taiwan in 1987: a year of political bombshells.**
James D. Seymour. *Asian Survey*, vol. 28, no. 1 (1988), p. 71-77.

In 1987 Taiwan experienced unprecedented development in politics as well as in its economy. Martial law was ended on the island and the economy was booming. Seymour argues that the year 1987 will be seen as a landmark year if the government carries through its promised political reforms.

351 **Building democracy in the Republic of China.**
Yu-ming Shaw. Taipei: The Asia and World Institute, 1984. 53p.
(Asia and World Monograph Series, no. 35).

This pamphlet contains three lectures delivered in Taipei by American scholars in 1983. In his preface, Shaw maintains that Taiwan is as much a democracy as any other country since no country in this world has fully realized democracy. Both Sidney Hook and Penn Kemble, without discussing Taiwan's situation, provide general lectures on democracy in developing countries. John Copper argues that the existence of local and national elections are a sign of Taiwan's progress in democratic reform.

352 **The Kuomintang: selected historical documents, 1894-1969.**
Milton J. T. Shieh. New York: St. John's University Press, 1970. 434p.

Designed to impart a preliminary understanding of the nationalist Kuomintang Party (KMT), this book provides a systematic study of selected documents. In addition to an introduction offering a general historical background, Shieh provides a chronology of the origin and development of the KMT, with reference to intraparty history and external relations. Fifty-four documents are discussed. A glossary of Chinese proper names is also provided.

353 **Taiwan's political economic development in the eighties: studies of structural transitions.**
Chih-yu Shih. *Asian Profile*, vol. 15, no. 4 (1987), p. 305-18.

Urges students of Taiwan to give more attention to the factional conflicts within the government and to emerging class conflicts. The dilemma becomes more vexing as these conflicts are added to previous tensions between Mainlanders and the Taiwanese and between the ruling party and non-party politicians.

354 **Taiwan: entering the 21st century.**
Robert G. Sutter. Lanham, Maryland; London: University Press of America, 1988. 82p.

Despite predictions of economic upheaval for the island of Taiwan, which is heavily dependent on foreign trade, and even fears of invasion from Communist China in 1979, when the US shifted its official recognition from the ROC to the PRC, Taiwan has survived and flourished. Sutter provides an in-depth analysis to explain why and how Taiwan has achieved its impressive economic success and political development.

355 **The great transition: political and social change in the Republic of China.**
Hung-mao Tien. Stanford, California: Hoover Institution Press, 1989. 324p. bibliog.

Concerns government and politics in Taiwan under the rule of the KMT. The author argues that the KMT was organized somewhat on the Leninist model of a disciplined single democratic-centralist, revolutionary party based on the élite, exercising leadership throughout the political system. In Taiwan a structural contradiction exists between a Leninist party-state and a capitalist socioeconomic system that promotes the values of liberal democracy in sociopolitical life, and this contradiction has caused the country to experience social strains and political conflicts. Tien also examines the KMT's internal transformation and gradual adaptation to change. Since 1986, reforms have made opposition parties legal and greatly liberalized political activities. For readers unfamiliar with the dynamics of the island's political process, this book offers a comprehensive treatment of Taiwan's politics as well as theoretical considerations of Taiwan's transition from authoritarianism to democracy.

356 **Taiwan's response to the Cultural Revolution.**
Stephen Uhalley, Jr. *Asian Survey*, vol. 7, no. 11 (1967), p. 824-29.

Presents a contemporary examination of Taiwan's response to the Cultural Revolution on mainland China. Uhalley demonstrates that Taiwan's response has been minimal and on the whole disappointing. The author argues that Taiwan has missed an opportunity for exploiting the unsettled mainland situation. However, he fails to explain in a concrete way how Taiwan could have exploited this golden opportunity.

357 **Economic development and democratization in Taiwan.**
Wou Wei. *Journal of Sunology* (Kaohsiung, Taiwan), vol. 4, no. 1 (1989), p. 184-203.

Argues that Taiwan's past economic development has created political stability and social prosperity, which in turn assure continued economic development. While most studies of Taiwan's economy address economic measures only, this essay shows the interactive process between economic growth and political development. The advancement of one aspect reinforces the positive change of the other.

358 **Elite political struggle, 1945-1985.**
Edwin A. Winckler. In: *Contending approaches to the political economy of Taiwan*. Edited by Edwin A. Winckler, Susan Greenhalgh. Armonk, New York: M. E. Sharpe, 1988, p. 151-71.

Discusses the principal conflicts in power within the Nationalist state on Taiwan since 1949 and the confrontations between economic élites within Taiwanese society since 1945. Winckler argues that for a time after 1945 the struggles within Taiwan were basically political conflicts between factions surviving from the Republican and civil war periods. Only gradually have these political confrontations become linked to economic conflicts within the bourgeoisie. However, economic élites remain more dependent on the Nationalist state than the reverse. Even in the 1980s, the Taiwanese élites have not gained autonomy in the arena of political competition and continue to rely on the increasingly sophisticated Nationalist Party mechanism.

359 **Institutionalization and participation on Taiwan: from hard to soft authoritarianism.**
Edwin A. Winckler. *China Quarterly*, no. 99 (1984), p. 481-99.

Points out that while Taiwan is in the process of moving from a mainland-based to a Taiwan-based leadership, it can best be described as a gerontocratic-authoritarian régime beginning a systemic transition from hard to soft authoritarianism. Hard authoritarianism means Mainlander-technocratic rule under a one-man dictatorship. Soft authoritarianism implies joint Mainlander-Taiwanese technocratic rule under a collective party leadership.

360 **Mass political incorporation, 1500-2000.**
Edwin A. Winckler. In: *Contending approaches to the political economy of Taiwan*. Edited by Edwin A. Winckler, Susan Greenhalgh. Armonk, New York: M. E. Sharpe, 1988, p. 41-66.

Describes Taiwan's external political status during the three major political eras in Taiwan's history: local administration by imperial China until 1895; colonial rule by imperialist Japan (1895-1945); and *de facto* independence under the Nationalist state since 1945. At the same time internal political conditions also went through a period of initial pacification under the Chinese Empire, the era of administrative modernization under the Japanese Empire, and political development under the Nationalist state and American influence. Winckler argues that during these three eras Taiwan has always remained half incorporated into regional and global politics and half independent as an internal political entity.

361 **Statism and familism on Taiwan.**
Edwin A. Winckler. In: *Ideology and national competitiveness*. Edited by George C. Lodge, Ezra F. Vogel. Boston, Massachusetts: Harvard Business School Press, 1987, p. 173-206.

Points out that Taiwan's business community is divided between two disparate ideologies: statism and familism. Statism asserts the independence of the state from domestic social forces. In this respect the economic development policies of Taiwan are the upshot of struggles among the various bureaux of the Nationalist state over how to minimize foreign dependence and maximize domestic autonomy. Familism argues that the economically corporate and spatially dispersed Taiwanese family pools resources and performs many of the functions of investment, production, and employment assumed by Western corporations. Postwar development in Taiwan reflects the ideological tension between statism and familism. Despite much convergence of interests since 1945, the state remains largely Mainlander-Nationalist, the families mostly islander-Taiwanese.

Taiwan in a time of transition.
See item no. 5.

Taiwan under Chiang Kai-shek's era: 1945-1976.
See item no. 65.

China, seventy years after the 1911 Hsin-hai revolution.
See item no. 67.

Taiwan in modern times.
See item no. 70.

Formosan political developments under Japanese colonial rule, 1914-1937.
See item no. 99.

Formosa: licensed revolution and the home rule movement, 1895-1945.
See item no. 106.

Japanese rule in Formosa.
See item no. 114

Jiang Jie-shi (1887-1975).
See item no. 122.

The anthropology of Taiwanese society.
See item no. 125.

City temples in Taipei under three regimes.
See item no. 127.

The politics of ritual disguise: repression and response in Taiwanese popular religion.
See item no. 149.

Sectarian religion and political action in China.
See item no. 150.

State and society in the Taiwan miracle.
See item no. 163.

Politics, ideology, and social welfare programs: critical evaluation of social welfare legislation in Taiwan.
See item no. 224.

Women in Taiwan politics: overcoming barriers to women's participation in a modernizing society.
See item no. 229.

Learning to be Chinese: the political socialization of children in Taiwan.
See item no. 288.

Ethnicity as a determinant of political culture among Taiwan youth.
See item no. 289.

The political socialization of college students on Taiwan.
See item no. 291.

Taiwan's politics: the provincial assemblyman's world.
See item no. 396.

Annual review of government administration, Republic of China.
See item no. 397.

Taiwan at the crossroads.
See item no. 400.

Economic development in Taiwan: a model of a political economy.
See item no. 506.

The Taiwan exception: implications for contending political economy paradigms.
See item no. 507.

The Taiwan ascent: system, state, and movement in the world economy.
See item no. 508.

Political institutions and economic performance: the government-business relationship in Japan, South Korea, and Taiwan.
See item no. 522.

Phoenix and the lame lion: modernization in Taiwan and mainland China, 1950-1980.
See item no. 533.

Taiwan to 1993: politics versus prosperity.
See item no. 534.

Taiwan politics.
See item no. 807.

Human rights

362 **Human rights in Taiwan, 1986-1987: an Asia Watch report, December 1987.**
Asia Watch Committee.   New York; Washington, DC: Asia Watch Committee, 1987. 269p.
This report is drawn from interviews and research into human rights conducted during the years 1986-87. It describes the judicial system of Taiwan, basic political rights, labour rights, academic freedom, and religious freedom of the people in Taiwan. In

addition, it discusses the electoral system employed in Taiwan. The report concludes on a note of cautious optimism about Taiwan's human rights record. It particularly commends Taiwan's decision to lift martial law in 1987 and to allow opposition parties to participate in political contests.

363 **Supporting democracy in the People's Republic of China and the Republic of China (Taiwan).**
Raymond D. Gastil, James D. Seymour. In: *Freedom in the world: political rights and civil liberties, 1983-1984.* Edited by Raymond D. Gastil. New York: Freedom House, 1984, p. 121-64.

Argues that both Chinese leaderships (PRC and ROC) merely give lip-service to the need for democracy. Taiwan's legitimacy is questioned because the Taiwanese people have little say in affairs of state. For the PRC, the Marxist/Maoist notion of ongoing class struggle obstructs the development of democracy. However, the authors' argument that neither the ROC nor the PRC are making much progress toward achieving democracy seems too pessimistic. The situation in Taiwan offers some hope, as evidenced by the political developments of the 1980s. The Taiwanese government has given more options and meaningful choices to people than has the PRC. A valuable and extensive discussion of this issue is included at the end of the article.

364 **The Republic of China and US policy: a study in human rights.**
A. James Gregor, Maria Hsia Chang. Washington, DC: Ethics and Public Policy Center, 1983. 145p.

In this survey of the circumstances affecting human rights in Taiwan, the authors argue that the continuing conflict with China justifies enforcement of martial law in order to restrict some aspects of civil and political rights. Moreover, they believe that the outlook for future protection of human rights is good since considerable progress has already been made.

365 **Democratization on Taiwan.**
Mab Huang. In: *Freedom in the world: political rights and civil liberties, 1983-1984.* Edited by Raymond D. Gastil. New York: Freedom House, 1984, p. 267-84.

While Taiwan has been given high marks for successfully managing its economic development, Huang argues that the political system has moved too slowly to accommodate the changing circumstances. Secret surveillance, intimidation, and selective persecution of political opponents have become an integral part of the political process. The author explains the discord between economic development and democratic rule, and explores the prospects for democratization in the near future. He urges the American government to convey to the Nationalist leaders on Taiwan its commitment to civilian rule and its concern for democratic reforms. In addition, private organizations should publicize and speak out against human rights violations on Taiwan. Comments and discussions of this article are also included.

366 **Intellectual ferment for political reforms in Taiwan, 1971-1973.**
Mab Huang. Ann Arbor, Michigan: Center for Chinese Studies, University of Michigan, 1976. 131p. (Michigan Monograph in Chinese Studies, no. 28).

This is a story of an intellectual attempt to revive political discourse in Taiwan. Although this attempt was proudly declared to be a parallel to the 1919 May Fourth Movement, it was unfortunately a failure. Huang's sad tale is an important document on Taiwan's political and social development.

367 **The court-martial of the Kaohsiung defendants.**
John Kaplan. Berkeley, California: Institute of Asian Studies, University of California, 1981. 79p. (Research Papers and Policy Studies, no. 2)

On 18 March 1980, a military court took up a trial which is politically significant in the modern history of Taiwan. A charge was filed by the government against a sizeable portion of the leadership of its electoral opposition. The accusation was that the eight defendants had plotted to overthrow the government with violence and had provoked a riot in the city of Kaohsiung. Kaplan discusses the whole Kaohsiung incident and the legal issues relevant to the trial.

368 **Human rights in Taiwan: convergence of two political cultures?**
Hung-chao Tai. In: *Human rights in East Asia.* Edited by James C. Hsiung. New York: Paragon House, 1985, p. 77-108.

The author examines the Western concept of human rights, contrasting it with the Chinese concept in traditional Chinese political culture, and goes on to discuss present and future developments affecting human rights in Taiwan.

Ending martial law in Taiwan: implications and prospects.
See item no. 301.

Martial law in Taiwan.
See item no. 303.

Taiwan Independence Movement

369 **The future of Taiwan.**
Trong R. Chai. *Asian Survey*, vol. 26, no. 12 (1986), p. 1309-23.

Discusses the nature of the Taiwan question and examines various approaches to its solution. Chai concludes that the United States should urge the Nationalist party to hold a plebiscite and then declare Taiwan a new nation if that is the wish of the Taiwanese people.

370 **Formosa, China, and the United Nations: Formosa in the world community.**
Lung-chu Chen, Harold D. Lasswell. New York: St. Martin's, 1967. 428p.

The authors believe in the importance of the rôle played by the United Nations in determining the future status of Taiwan. They argue that a UN decision to admit the PRC as the only China, with a native-ruled Republic of Formosa eligible for a separate membership, would either force the Nationalists to hand over power to the Taiwanese peacefully or inspire a revolt by natives and dissident Mainlanders on the island. In their view, it would be better to have a UN-supervised plebiscite so that the people in Taiwan could declare independence through peaceful means. In essence, their solution is a 'one China, one Taiwan' proposal.

371 **Self-determination for the people of Taiwan.**
Kent L. Christiansen. *California Western International Law Journal*, vol. 14, no. 3 (1984), p. 471-500.

After discussing the historical background of the island, the author reviews the principle of self-determination in international law in the case of Taiwan. He argues that the Taiwan Relations Act of 1979, which was passed by the US Congress to regulate US-Taiwan relations, has offered a positive means for the people of Taiwan to establish an independent state through the principle of self-determination.

372 **One China or two: facing up to the Taiwan question.**
Marc J. Cohen. *World Policy Journal*, vol. 4, no. 4 (1987), p. 621-49.

Although self-determination would not immediately solve all of Taiwan's problems, the author argues that it offers the best hope for an outcome that is just, encourages stability, and promotes American objectives in the Pacific Basin. He notes that in the meantime, American arms sales must be based on the defensive needs of the people on the island, and that continued economic and security relations must be linked to accelerated democratization and respect for human rights.

373 **The Taiwan Independence Movement: the failure of political persuasion.**
A. James Gregor, Maria Hsia Chang. *Political Communication and Persuasion*, vol. 2, no. 4 (1985), p. 363-91.

Argues that the failure of the Taiwan Independence Movement (TIM) to achieve independence from KMT rule has led its leadership to take recourse to terrorist tactics. The change is understood to be the consequence of the failure of political persuasion and the inability of the revolutionary leadership to win support in an environment of expanding economic opportunity and a surprisingly equitable distribution of welfare benefits.

374 **Toward Taiwan's independence.**
Lillian Craig Harris. *Pacific Review*, vol. 1, no. 1 (1988), p. 24-37.

Most discussions about Taiwan's future begin from the basic Chinese premise that Taiwan is an integral part of China. Harris, however, refutes this position, and asserts that we should adopt the Taiwanese point of view. She asks the questions 'where has history led Taiwan?' and 'where do the Taiwanese themselves wish to go from here?'

Politics and Government. The unification issue (mainland China-Taiwan)

Through a discussion of Taiwan's future, the author examines the arguments in support of, and against, the establishment of an independent state in Taiwan.

375 **Formosa betrayed.**
George H. Kerr. Boston, Massachusetts: Houghton Mifflin, 1965. 514p.

This is a polemical study dealing with how the Chen Yi régime ruled Taiwan between 1945 and 1947. As a teacher and US State Department official living in Taiwan both before and after the Second World War, Kerr reports that the Nationalists engaged in the systematic slaughter of Taiwanese leaders, including the murders of potential leaders among the youth in the infamous rebellion of 28 February 1947. The author's personal observation and interpretation of the Chen Yi régime might be correct; however, readers should be cautious of his remarks concerning the 1960s because, drawing on his past experiences, he sometimes makes sweeping generalizations about that decade.

376 **Terrorism and the Taiwan Independence Movement.**
Joseph Martin. Taipei: Institute on Contemporary China, 1985. 69p.

This is a preliminary study of terrorism associated with the Taiwan Independence Movement (TIM). In the past TIM radicals have adopted terrorist tactics in order to effect a drastic change of the political, economic, and social *status quo* in Taiwan. The author pieces together documented sources on the movement's evolution and its terrorist aspects so as to assess the TIM in terms of a terrorism-oriented political movement, emphasizing its historical origin. The author's six years of extensive research in the US, Japan, and Taiwan, including interviews with former TIM leaders, have made this volume a useful introduction to the Movement.

Christians and the Taiwanese Independence Movement: a commentary.
See item no. 158.

The unification issue (mainland China-Taiwan)

377 **The process of assimilation of Hong Kong (1997) and the implication for Taiwan.**
John P. Burns. *AEI Foreign Policy and Defense Review*, vol. 6, no. 3 (1986), p. 19-26.

The author points out that Hong Kong's transition to Chinese rule has several implications for Taiwan. Taiwan must accept Chinese rule in Hong Kong if it wishes to preserve important economic links with the island. Should the Hong Kong experiment prove successful, some elements in Taiwan may be tempted to advocate negotiating a similar agreement with China. If mainland China seeks future reunification with Taiwan by peaceful means, the Chinese authorities must treat Hong Kong carefully.

Politics and Government. The unification issue (mainland China-Taiwan)

378 **China and the Taiwan issue.**
Edited by Hungdah Chiu. New York: Praeger, 1979. 285p.
In this volume, three chapters describe the relationship between Taiwan and mainland China. They attempt to explore the historical ties between these two countries, the legal and political status of Taiwan, and mainland China's strategy for achieving the goal of unification. Two other chapters deal separately with Taiwan's political advances and economic development. In addition to the scholarly contribution of the essays, this volume is noteworthy for the valuable official documents which it contains and its well-prepared bibliography of published works on Taiwan.

379 **The international law of recognition and multi-system nations – with special reference to the Chinese (mainland-Taiwan) case.**
Hungdah Chiu. In: *Multi-system nations and international law*. Edited by Hungdah Chiu, Robert Downen. Baltimore, Maryland: School of Law, University of Maryland, 1981, p. 41-57. (Occasional Papers/Reprint Series in Contemporary Asian Studies, no. 8).
Argues that it would be in the interest of the PRC to stabilize the Taiwanese situation within the context of the ultimate goal of unification. To achieve this goal, the PRC must tolerate Taiwan's acquisition of appropriate international legal status in the global community. This status is essential to prevent Taiwan from moving toward a 'two-China' policy. Readers interested in a more theoretical discussion of multi-system nations may consult Yung Wei's essay in the same volume, entitled 'The unification and division of multi-system nations' (p. 59-74).

380 **An American view of 'one country, two systems.'**
J. Terry Emerson. *Issues and Studies*, vol. 24, no. 9 (1988), p. 36-49.
Mainland China has proposed the concept of 'one country, two systems' as a model for the unification of China, which will contain two different socioeconomic structures. The author examines the feasibility of this proposal.

381 **The status quo is not static: mainland-Taiwan relations.**
Thomas B. Gold. *Asian Survey*, vol. 27, no. 3 (1987), p. 300-15.
According to the author, the essence of the Taiwan issue is the relationship between the political authorities and civil societies of China and of Taiwan, and how and when such a relationship should be established. Gold argues that the only possible measure suitable for the Taiwan issue is the Taoist option of 'doing nothing so that nothing will not be done' (*Wu-wei* in Chinese). Yet, *status quo* does not mean stagnation. A gradual change of policies on both sides will facilitate a resolution, whereas a sudden change before the requisite forces have sufficiently matured will bring tragic consequences.

Politics and Government. The unification issue (mainland China-Taiwan)

382 **The Hong Kong Accord as a model for dealing with other disputed territories.**
Kevin M. Harris, with remarks by Herbert J. Hansell, Robert E. Lutz, James V. Feinerman, Hurst Hannum, Hungdah Chiu, Chun Li.
American Society of International Law Proceedings, vol. 80 (1986), p. 348-68.

Great Britain seized Hong Kong island in 1841 to punish the Chinese for confiscating large amounts of opium that the British were importing into China. As a result of three specific treaties, Hong Kong became a British colony. A set of documents, called the Hong Kong Accord, was formulated to return Hong Kong to Chinese sovereignty. In this panel discussion, scholars attempt to evaluate the possibility of using the Hong Kong Accord as a model for the return of other disputed territories, focusing especially on Taiwan.

383 **The Hong Kong settlement: effects on Taiwan and prospects for Peking's reunification bid.**
James C. Hsiung. *Asian Affairs*, vol. 12, no. 2 (1985), p. 47-58.

By examining the Hong Kong issue, Hsiung argues that the peaceful unification route is still the most desirable for mainland China in its bid to reunite with Taiwan.

384 **An analysis of attitudes of Taiwan residents returning from visits to mainland China.**
Chang Hu. *Issues and Studies*, vol. 25, no. 6 (1989), p. 95-112.

On 2 November 1987, Taiwan lifted its ban on residents visiting mainland China; since then, numerous Taiwanese residents have made trips to the mainland. This paper examines the Taiwanese government's policy regarding the mainland, as well as the attitudes of returning visitors as reflected in public opinion surveys and interviews conducted by the author.

385 **Taiwan: a view from Beijing.**
Guo-cang Huan. *Foreign Affairs*, vol. 63, no. 5 (1985), p. 1064-80.

Three related factors determine the texture of the relationship between Taiwan and mainland China: the policies evolving in mainland China, internal developments on Taiwan, and the international environment. The author evaluates each of these factors and discusses Taipei's policy options. These options include a policy of independence, a conservative approach to maintaining the *status quo*, a realistic choice to accept the PRC's proposal of unification, and a cautious policy to reduce tensions and to expand informal contacts.

386 **Policy in evolution: the US role in China's reunification.**
Martin L. Lasater. Boulder, Colorado: Westview, 1988. 206p.

As mainland China has claimed, the reunification of Taiwan with China is one of the most important policy issues for the US as well as a central component of Sino-US relations. Lasater evaluates the Reagan administration's policy towards the reunification issue and suggests various policy options for the US following an assessment of current political trends in Taiwan and China.

387 The contest between two Chinese states.
Ramon H. Myers. *Asian Survey*, vol. 23, no. 4 (1983) p. 536-52.
Argues that Communist China can neither achieve economic modernization nor convince the Nationalists to unite with them without radically altering the current relationship between state and society. Therefore, the contest between these two Chinese states will be resolved either by war or by a fundamental restructuring of relationships between state and society in one of the two states.

388 The future association of Taiwan with the People's Republic of China.
Dan C. Sanford. Berkeley, California: Institute of East Asian Studies, University of California, 1981. 93p. bibliog.
Assesses the possibility of unification between Taiwan and mainland China and examines the political impact of the increasing trade relations between these political entities. Sanford concludes that China's peculiar arrangement with Hong Kong indicates the probable course it will pursue with Taiwan.

389 Taiwan: a view from Taipei.
Yu-ming Shaw. *Foreign Affairs*, vol. 63, no. 5 (1985), p. 1050-63.
Shaw states that officials in Taiwan feel that the island has become a modern, international force without losing its traditional Chinese values, which are essential in the prevention of a communist system of government. Through the media, people in mainland China are well aware of the island's achievements, and understand that Taiwan has become a democratic, viable alternative for the rest of China.

390 Taiwan and the reunification of China.
Lee Lai To. *Pacific Review*, vol. 2, no. 2 (1989), p. 132-40.
Examines the reunification proposals of the post-Mao leaders in mainland China, and the reasons for Taipei's responses. The author also analyses the Nationalist Party's strategy on reunification in the light of Taiwan's domestic developments and international realities.

391 Can the Hong Kong settlement serve as a model for Taiwan?
An-chia Wu. In: *The future of Hong Kong*. Edited by Hungdah Chiu, Y. C. Jao, Yuan-li Wu. New York: London: Quorum, 1987, p. 155-77.
The PRC has suggested the concept of 'one country, two systems' as a strategy for the settlement of issues involving Taiwan and Hong Kong. It proposes that after China is unified, the PRC will maintain its socialist system, while Hong Kong and Taiwan will continue their capitalist way of life. The Hong Kong issue has been settled between Britain and the PRC, but the Taiwan matter is still unresolved. This paper examines the feasibility of using the Hong Kong model for Taiwan. It concludes that ideological confusion is bound to occur under the so-called 'one country, two systems' scheme. Because of the differences in economic and social development between the PRC and the ROC, the possibility of peaceful unification for these two political entities remains remote.

392 **Unification in China and Korea: implications for regional security.**
      Herbert S. Yee. *International Journal*, vol. 38, no. 2 (spring 1983),
      p. 269-86.
Argues that whether North and South Korea, or the PRC and ROC, remain separated,
or are reunited, rests on the choice of the people. The use of military force could only
result in a prolonged war or civil strife with unacceptable costs to the eventual victor.
All major powers should maintain a 'hands-off' policy to encourage the pursuit of non-
military solutions.

Reaching across the water.
See item no. 576.

Administration and
Local Government

393 **Taiwan's 1985 elections.**
John F. Copper. *Asian Affairs*, vol. 13, no. 1 (1986), p. 27-45.
In 1985, voters in Taiwan went through a series of local elections which the author considers to be important to Taiwan's political process. These competitive local elections indicate that Taiwan continues to experience significant democratic political development.

394 **Information management in the public administration of the Republic of China.**
Koong-lian Kao. In: *Proceedings of IMC's 1985 Asia-Pacific regional information and micrographic management congress.* Taipei, 11-13 July 1985, p. 51-93.
Policy makers in Taiwan have long recognized the effectiveness of computer systems in processing data for policy design and implementation. This study details the development of an information management system in Taiwan's public administration and explores ways of upgrading the utilization level of the system in order to increase the productivity of civil services.

395 **Taiwan's provincial and local political decision-makers: Taiwanization.**
Kuo-wei Lee. *Asian Profile*, vol. 15, no. 2 (1987), p. 179-96.
Surveys the social backgrounds and the recruitment process of political decision makers in Taiwan's provincial and local governments from 1950 to the present. The author shows that the majority of political decision makers at the provincial and local levels are recruited from those Taiwanese who enjoy relatively high social status. The Nationalist Party is too powerful as a political recruitment machine to be challenged by the other parties and nonpartisans.

396 **Taiwan's politics: the provincial assemblyman's world.**
Arthur J. Lerman. Washington, DC: University Press of America,
1978. 298p. bibliog.

Rather than discussing Taiwan's overall political system, Lerman investigates the provincial assemblyman's network of political interaction. His study shows that the assemblyman's political behaviour is shaped by three political factors: political groupings based on support or lack of support for the Nationalist governing élite; groups derived from local electoral factions, lineage, clans, territorial groups, and others resulting from competition for local political resources; and the assemblyman's relations with the growing number of economic enterprises. Lerman's analysis of the local exchange network and patron-client relationship is fascinating and stimulating.

397 **Annual review of government administration, Republic of China.**
Research, Development and Evaluation Commission. Taipei: The
Commission, Executive Yuan. annual.

Systematically illustrates the annual policies and performance of the Chinese government in Taiwan. Readers can get an overview of the functioning of the national and local governments, national defence, the economy, the education system, the social security system, and the international relations of Taiwan. This volume also provides statistical and graphic information supplemented by concise explanations and analyses.

The more things change, the more they stay the same: some external constraints on the ROC's bureaucracy.
See item no. 333.

Economics, economic bureaucracy, and Taiwan's economic development.
See item no. 521.

Foreign Relations

General

398 **Japan and Taiwan: community of economic interest held together by paradiplomacy.**
Walter Arnold.   In: *Japan's foreign relations*. Edited by Robert S. Ozaki, Walter Arnold. Boulder, Colorado: Westview, 1985, p. 187-99.
Explains why and how Japan and Taiwan have been able to maintain and expand effective and viable economic ties over the last decade without formal diplomatic relations. The author provides a description of the institutional arrangements and the general environment of Japanese-Taiwanese economic ties.

399 **The 'two-Chinas' problem and the Olympic formula.**
Gerald Chan.   *Pacific Affairs*, vol. 58, no. 3 (1985), p. 473-90.
By tracing the history of China's relations with the International Olympic Committee (IOU), Chan illustrates how the so-called IOU formula has been devised to solve the 'two Chinas' problem, when both mainland China and Taiwan claim to be the sole legitimate representative of China in the Olympic Games.

400 **Taiwan at the crossroads.**
Marc J. Cohen.   Washington, DC: Asia Resource Center, 1988. 431p.
This book is the product of the author's 'Taiwan-watching'. Drawing on hundreds of interviews conducted during two trips to Taiwan, he seeks to explain how Taiwan has undergone dramatic political reforms, changing from a once largely quiescent society to a place of remarkable grass roots activism. Despite the opening up of political space, serious obstacles to democracy remain: conservatives are still dominant in the Nationalist Party and the danger of renewed authoritarian rule from within and the threat of Communist Chinese takeover from without have put Taiwan at a virtual crossroads. Cohen also discusses Taiwan's international status with emphasis on the concept of self-determination and the island's ties with the US. The author claims that

self-determination best serves the interests of all parties concerned. His association with *Taiwan Communiqué* (q.v.), a periodical focusing on human rights in Taiwan, leads him to examine issues from a rather critical perspective. Photographs of several important figures in Taiwan's political development are provided. There is, however, no bibliography, though chapter notes may prove helpful.

401 **European and Soviet perspectives on future responses in Taiwan to international and regional developments.**
Reinhard Drifte. *Asian Survey*, vol. 25, no. 11 (1985), p. 1115-22.
Argues that Taiwan exists in European thinking only as an object of trade and tourism. There is no discernible concern in Europe about Taiwan making any destabilizing moves in East Asia. Although the title of his article mentions the Soviet Union, the author includes no extensive discussion about the Soviet perspective on Taiwan.

402 **Taiwan's Russian option: image and reality.**
John W. Garver. *Asian Survey*, vol. 18, no. 7 (1978), p. 751-66.
Discusses the possibility of a Taiwan-Soviet rapprochement. Such an alliance would obviously involve ideological problems on both sides, yet the history of international relations is full of cases of such ideologically improbable alignments.

403 **Strategy for survival: the foreign policy and external relations of the Republic of China on Taiwan, 1949-79.**
Chiao Chiao Hsieh. London: Sherwood, 1985. 371p. bibliog.
Traces the evolution of Taiwan's foreign policy. An initial obsession with the military recovery of mainland China was replaced by a revised strategy, emphasizing a political as well as military counterattack, which evolved as the hope of direct US assistance in an invasion of the mainland began to fade. Hsieh also discusses Taiwan's foreign aid to Third World countries, undertaken to enlist their support for Taiwan's seat in the United Nations. This policy later shifted to emphasize informal diplomatic links by expanding commercial relations with as many countries as possible.

404 **Slighting Taiwan is behind the times.**
Hidenori Ijiri. *Japan Quarterly*, vol. 36, no. 1 (1989), p. 69-74.
Argues that Taiwan has made real progress toward representative democracy and might act as a guide to China in accomplishing economic, social, and political change. For these very reasons, the author suggests, it is vital that Japan should deepen its relations with Taiwan.

405 **The future of Taiwan: a difference of opinion.**
Edited by Victor H. Li. White Plains, New York: M. E. Sharpe, 1980. 187p.
This volume explores the nature and complexity of the international and domestic issues involved in the so-called 'Taiwan problem' and is a useful introduction for lay people and public officials. Fifteen Chinese-American scholars present conflicting views, sometimes without supporting evidence or careful documentation. It is best read as a collection of opinions, speculations, and value judgements made by concerned scholars. The whole volume is reprinted in a special issue of the *International Journal of Politics*, vol. 9, no. 4 (1980).

406 Informal 'diplomatic relations': the case of Japan and the Republic of China, 1972-1974.
David Nelson Rowe. Hamden, Connecticut: Shoe String, 1975. 82p.
Beginning in 1972 Japan established diplomatic relations with the Chinese communist régime and simultaneously severed its official ties with the ROC on Taiwan. The author discusses this change in Japan's policy towards China and Taiwan's responses to it. After terminating formal diplomatic relations with Taiwan, the Japanese set up the Inter-Change Association (ICA), naming Taiwan's unit, the East Asia Relations Association. Although said to be unofficial, the ICA in fact functions as an official diplomatic agency, handling Taiwanese/Japanese commercial, cultural, and other official business. These organizations and the substantive relations between Japan and Taiwan following the rupture of their official relations are the topics addressed here.

407 The Taiwan issue in Peking's foreign relations in the 1970s: a systematic review.
Lyushun Shen. Chinese Yearbook of International Law and Affairs, vol. 1 (1981), p. 74-96.
Argues that Peking's approach to the Taiwan issue in its foreign relations during the 1970s can be summarized in a single phrase: a pragmatic effort to legitimize the PRC's claim over Taiwan in the international arena so as to ensure a free hand in the future.

408 Foreign policy behavior of the Republic of China in the 1970s: a cross-sectional analysis.
Chung-chien Teng. Journal of National Chengchi University, vol. 49 (1984), p. 105-31.
Examines the ways in which the ROC government has adjusted its foreign behaviour to deal with its changing place in global society and the determinants influencing its policy change. Using statistical analysis, this study shows that there is a simple relationship between the ROC's attributes and its foreign behaviour.

409 Peking versus Taipei in Africa, 1960-1978.
Liang-tsai Wei. Taipei: The Asia and World Institute, 1982. 457p. bibliog. (Asia and World Monograph Series, no. 25).
Deals with the competition between Peking and Taiwan in Africa, noting the tactics that were used by both governments, the response of the African nations to the competition and the short-range and long-range goals of the two Chinese governments. Wei investigates these questions in detail and reviews the African states' perspective on the Chinese membership problem in the United Nations.

410 Third party response in foreign policy: Taiwan's response to Canadian and Japanese China policies.
Herbert S. Yee. Asia Quarterly, no. 4 (1979), p. 309-25.
Canada and Japan established diplomatic relations with mainland China in 1970 and 1972 respectively. The author shows how Taipei has made effective use of nondiplomatic channels to maintain economic, cultural, and other relations with countries which do not extend diplomatic relations to Taiwan.

411 **The development of relations between the Republic of China and Japan since 1972.**
Tzong-shian Yu. *Asian Survey*, vol. 21, no. 6 (1981), p. 632-44.

Deals with the evolution of relations between Taiwan and Japan since 1972, when Japan severed diplomatic ties with Taiwan. Yu argues that Japan's policy towards China is one of 'keeping two feet on two different boats' – a balanced development in relations with both Taiwan and mainland China. This expression still reflects to some degree Japan's current policy towards Taiwan and China.

Taiwan in a time of transition.
See item no. 5.

Contemporary Republic of China: the Taiwan experience 1950-1980.
See item no. 170.

Comparison of the Nationalist and Communist Chinese views of unequal treaties.
See item no. 298.

Taiwan's future?
See item no. 339.

Taiwan: entering the 21st century.
See item no. 354.

Taiwan at the crossroads.
See item no. 400.

Taiwan's international status

412 **The case for Taipei's membership in international economic organizations.**
Andrew B. Brick. *Backgrounder* (Heritage Foundation), no. 82 (Oct. 1988), p. 1-9.

While Taiwan is labelled as an economic mini-superpower, many major international economic organizations maintain that the ROC officially does not exist. The author argues that Taiwan is an overwhelming presence in the world trade picture. Hence economic reality requires that the international economic organizations address or bypass contentious politics and adopt policies of inclusion for Taiwan.

413   **China and international organizations: participation in non-governmental organizations since 1971.**
Gerald Chan.   New York: Oxford University Press, 1989. 225p. bibliog.

This book is a revised version of the author's doctoral dissertation, investigating the figures, issues, and policy changes involved in Chinese participation in international non-governmental organizations. The so-called 'two-China' problem is singled out as the primary issue for detailed examination because it remains one of the important elements affecting China's decisions on whether to participate in specific organizations and how this can be done. The 'two-China' problem refers to the political complications arising out of the competing claims of the PRC and the ROC to be the sole legitimate government of all China, including Taiwan. International non-governmental organizations included in this study are the International Olympic Committee, International Red Cross, International Council of Scientific Unions, International PEN, the Asia-Pacific Broadcasting Union, and the Universal Esperanto Association. Information about the membership of China and Taiwan in selective non-governmental organizations is appended.

414   **China and the question of Taiwan: documents and analysis.**
Edited by Hungdah Chiu.   New York: Praeger, 1973. 395p.

This is a collection of analytical essays and documents on the Chinese viewpoint of the legal status of Taiwan. The essays, written by specialists from various backgrounds, deal with the economic development, history, political development, and foreign relations of Taiwan. The 118 documents range from the Koxinga-Dutch treaty of 1662 to the Nixon-Chou communiqué of 1972, and are divided into official and unofficial documents. For readers who intend to carry out further research in the field, this book constitutes an invaluable source of information on Taiwan.

415   **The international status of the Republic of China.**
David S. Chou.   *Issues and Studies*, vol. 20, no. 5 (1984), p. 11-21.

Argues that both international law and the United Nations Charter recognize the ROC as a fully sovereign state, as demonstrated by Taiwan's history and its official and semi-official relations with numerous other states.

416   **Taiwan's international status.**
Ralph N. Clough.   In: *Multi-system nations and international law*.
Edited by Hungdah Chiu, Robert Downen. Baltimore, Maryland:
School of Law, University of Maryland, 1981, p. 141-59. (Occasional
Papers/Reprint Series in Contemporary Asian Studies, no. 8).

Despite the loss of diplomatic links with most nations and its exclusion from international organizations, Taiwan has prospered and has developed unorthodox ways of dealing with the rest of the world. The author discusses Taiwan's techniques for survival and the attitudes of Taipei and Peking toward each other. An essay written by the author on the same topic also appears in *Chinese Yearbook of International Law and Affairs*, vol. 1 (1981), p. 17-34.

417   **The legal status of Taiwan in the normalization of Sino-American relations.**
Gene T. Hsiao.   *Rutgers Law Journal*, vol. 14 (1983), p. 839-913.

Discusses the origins of American involvement in Taiwan and the status of Taiwan under the Taiwan Relations Act after the US recognition of the People's Republic of China. Hsiao argues that the Taiwan issue should be settled by the Chinese themselves, a solution consistent with the traditional non-intervention policy of the US and with international law.

418   **Quasi-diplomatic relations of the Republic of China: their development and status in international law.**
Thomas B. Lee.   *Issues and Studies*, vol. 24, no. 7 (1988), p. 104-17.

As Taiwan's substantive relations with other nations develop and expand, it is clear that the absence of diplomatic relations does not totally prevent Taiwan from dealing with other states. Lee examines several cases to show that Taiwan, recognized or unrecognized, is a legal person in international law.

419   **China and the United Nations.**
Evan Luard.   *International Affairs*, vol. 47, no. 4 (1971), p. 729-44.

The question of Chinese membership of the United Nations is not a question of 'admission'; China has been a member of the UN since its foundation. It is a question of 'representation'. The author presents an historical background of the China issue in the UN and suggests possible procedures to solve the representation problem.

420   **The status of Formosa and the Chinese recognition problem.**
D. P. O'Connell.   *American Journal of International Law*, vol. 50, no. 2 (1956), p. 405-16.

Connell acknowledges that the status of Formosa has long been a problem in international law: some have suggested that the island be internationalized, neutralized, or made independent under United Nations auspices and guarantee, while others have advocated handing Formosa over to mainland China. He considers the various views of the legal status of Taiwan current in the mid 1950s and examines whether or not the question of recognition of Communist China and the question of Formosa's disposition should be separated into different issues.

421   **The China question: essays on current relations between mainland China and Taiwan.**
Edited by Yu-san Wang.   New York: Praeger, 1985. 164p.

Most essays in this volume are drawn from conference papers presented in 1983-84 or articles from professional journals. They compare economic development in Taiwan and mainland China, explore the conditions of unification, and explain the Taiwan Relations Act of 1979, which has served as a framework for the status of the ROC. Although this volume can be criticized for its pro-Taiwan stance, it is a valuable guide to the China-Taiwan question.

422   **Taiwan's international status today.**
      Byron S. J. Weng.   *China Quarterly*, no. 99 (Sept. 1984), p. 462-80.
While gaining in the realm of economic development in the past decades, Taiwan has waned in terms of international status. Weng analyses how Taiwan's choices, mainland China's strategies, and Washington's policy changes have affected Taiwan's international status over the years.

US-Taiwan relations

423   **Commitment, policy legacy, and policy options: the US-ROC relations after Reagan.**
      David C. L. Auw.   *Issues and Studies*, vol. 18, no. 3 (1982), p. 8-26.
Indicates that US policy towards Taiwan should not be restricted to the Taiwan Relations Act or to the United States' interest in playing the 'China card'. Auw argues that the US must regard Taiwan as a valuable ally within the strategic and economic contexts.

424   **The Committee of One Million: 'China lobby' politics, 1953-1971.**
      Stanley D. Bachrack.   New York: Columbia University Press, 1976. 371p.
Making excellent use of available sources, among them the papers of Marvin Liebman, who served as secretary of the Committee of One Million for sixteen years, Bachrack presents a well-researched study of the major interest group seeking to influence American policy towards China. He describes the origins of the Committee and their efforts to influence American administrations from Eisenhower to Nixon. The study includes accounts of intra-Committee debates, fund-raising activities, and contacts between the Committee and Chinese Nationalist diplomats.

425   **Autonomy and diversity in the American state on Taiwan.**
      Richard E. Barrett.   In: *Contending approaches to the political economy of Taiwan.* Edited by Edwin A. Winckler, Susan Greenhalgh. Armonk, New York: M. E. Sharpe, 1988, p. 121-37.
Relying upon existing historical studies and recently released documents, Barrett examines American policy towards Taiwan in the late 1940s. He argues that because American businesses had no strong interests in Taiwan, bureaucrats in the US were able to decide the nation's policy without domestic economic pressure. The author's examination of the diversity of views about what to do with Taiwan demonstrates this relative autonomy.

426 **The President's unilateral termination of the Taiwan treaty.**
Raoul Berger. *Northwestern University Law Review*, vol. 75, no. 4
(1980), p. 577-634.
US rapprochement with mainland China required a political sacrifice – the termination
of the Mutual Defense Treaty between Taiwan and the US by President Carter. He did
so without consulting the Senate or Congress, reflecting the executive's unremitting
drive for a monopoly on foreign affairs. This touched off an examination of the treaty
termination power in the constitutional history of the US. Berger deals with the legal
aspect of this controversial issue.

427 **The United States and the long-term disposition of Taiwan in the making
of peace with Japan, 1950-1952.**
Su-ya Chang. *Asian Profile*, vol. 16, no. 5 (1988), p. 459-70.
Argues that through skilful manipulation in the negotiating and signing of the peace
treaty between Japan and Taiwan, the US largely achieved the anti-Communist policy
goal. The treaty prevented Peking from gaining international recognition in the world
community, while at the same time restricting the Nationalists' authority to Taiwan
only. This study reveals the emergence of a two-China policy on the part of the US in
the early 1950s.

428 **China policy and national security.**
Edited by Frederick Tse-shyang Chen.   New York: Transnational,
1984. 253p.
Presents the proceedings of a workshop sponsored by the Standing Committee on Law
and National Security and the International Law Section of the American Bar
Association, in cooperation with the University of Bridgeport, School of Law. The
focus of discussion is the national security consideration involved when relations with
mainland China were normalized in 1979. Eight sections touch upon different
dimensions of US-China relations, including cultural exchange, military relations,
diplomatic interaction, economic policy, human rights issues, legal impact, historical
overview, and a framework of inquiry. All the principal papers as well as subsequent
commentaries are written by well-known experts and presented in a clear and
accessible form.

429 **The future of US-Taiwan relations.**
Hungdah Chiu.   *Asian Affairs*, vol. 9, no. 1 (1981), p. 20-30.
Beginning with a discussion of the Taiwan Relations Act of 1979, Chiu tackles issues
related to the future of US-Taiwan relations, including Reagan's policy towards
Taiwan and US arms sales to Taiwan.

430 **Recent legal issues between the US and the People's Republic of China.**
Hungdah Chiu.   *Maryland Journal of International Law and Trade*,
vol. 12, no. 1 (1987), p. 1-33.
While readers should have no difficulty in finding studies on recent political relations
between the US and China, most of these studies do not adequately address the legal
aspects of such dealings. This article fills a gap by discussing several major legal issues
in Sino-US relations, such as human rights issues, how to protect US nationals in
mainland China, and trade law disputes. In particular, Chiu discusses the controversy

generated by the US alliance with Taiwan because mainland China had pressured the US to agree to the principle of gradually phasing out arms sales to Taiwan.

431 Taiwan's identity crisis.
Charles T. Cross. *Foreign Policy*, no. 51 (summer 1983), p. 47-63.

Taiwan has been a persistently contentious issue in Sino-American relations. However, since the normalization of relations, the US perceptions of the strategic threat in the western Pacific has changed markedly. Cross discusses US policy towards Taiwan in terms of arms sales as well as East Asian security considerations.

432 Arms sales, the Taiwan question, and Sino-US relations.
John W. Garver. *Orbis*, vol. 26, no. 4 (1983), p. 999-1035.

Since 1950 the 'Taiwan Question' has been one of the prickliest issues in Sino-US relations. Garver analyses the fundamental issues underlying the confrontation with China over US arms sales to Taiwan. He also puts the Taiwan issue in the context of a broader pattern of world politics and speculates on the strategic orientation underlying China's firm approach to the issue of US arms sales to Taiwan in 1981-82.

433 The isolation of island China.
Stephen P. Gibert. In: *Security in Northeast Asia*. Edited by Stephen P. Gibert. Boulder, Colorado: Westview, 1988, p. 117-36.

Briefly describes the confused and uncertain policy regarding China which the Reagan government inherited in 1981. The author then addresses the current state of US-Taiwan relations and the problems that remain between the two governments. The author feels that while Taiwan needs to continue its process of democratization and the cautious expansion of contacts between mainland China and itself, the US should continue to support Taiwan.

434 Foreign relations of the United States, 1955-1957; volume II, III: China.
Edited by John P. Glennon, Harriet D. Schwar, Louis J. Smith. Washington, DC: US Government Printing Office, 1986. 2 vols.

Volume two documents US policy in the Taiwan Strait crisis and the diplomatic efforts to end the crisis. Materials on the ambassadorial talks in Geneva between representatives of the US and of mainland China, as well as on US relations with Taiwan during the period, are included in volume three. Additional documentation concerning the ambassadorial talks in Geneva is available as a microfiche supplement published in 1987. The supplement reproduces all the reports on the talks sent to the US government by the US representative, Ambassador U. Alexis Johnson, along with his comments, the government's instructions, and other related materials. Some earlier volumes in this series, *Foreign Relations of the United States*, cover the period 1949-54 and contain records of the US policy of assistance with regard to Nationalist forces, Taiwan's commitment to consulting the US prior to any major offensive operations against the Chinese mainland, negotiation of a mutual security treaty, and the 1949 State Department's report on American policy towards China. Readers interested in US-ROC relations or US policy towards China will find these newly-released documents a mine of information for a better understanding of a turbulent period.

435 **The iron triangle: a US security policy for Northeast Asia.**
A. James Gregor, Maria Hsia Chang. Stanford, California: Hoover
Institution Press, 1984. 160p.

This document warns that it would be unwise for the US to proceed too far in creating
a close military association with China. It also recommends a gradual enhancement of
the military capabilities of such traditional allies of the US as Japan, South Korea, and
Taiwan, to ensure that any future Sino-Soviet rapprochement will not affect US
security interests in northeast Asia. The authors conclude that the US should provide
Taiwan with the military assets needed for its defence.

436 **Unilateral presidential treaty termination power by default: an analysis
of *Goldwater* v. *Carter*.**
Cynthia J. Hill. *Texas International Law Journal*, vol. 15 (spring
1980), p. 317-78.

Because of the normalization of relations with the PRC, President Carter decided to
terminate the Mutual Defense Treaty with Taiwan. This decision met with swift and, in
some instances, violent opposition from the Taipei government and the US Congress.
Senator Goldwater, with other colleagues on Capitol Hill, filed a suit against the
President, seeking declaratory and injunctive relief from the President's act of
termination without prior consultation with the Congress. The author describes the
case of *Goldwater v. Carter*, and, having disposed of the jurisdictional and procedural
questions involved in this litigation concerning the President's treaty termination
power, examines the political impact of this case on American foreign policy, as well
as the relationship between the executive branch and the legislative branch of the US
government.

437 **US aid to Taiwan: a study of foreign aid, self-help, and development.**
Neil H. Jacoby. New York: Praeger, 1966. 364p.

Examines the effects of US aid on Taiwan's economic development. Throughout the
book, Jacoby makes candid observations on a number of controversial issues and
summarizes the flaws and errors in the Taiwan aid programme. This volume is further
strengthened by the author's attempts to develop methods for aid evaluation. His
skilful interpretations of data sources make this a stimulating book and help the reader
to understand the relationships between aid and socioeconomic development.

438 **A matter of two Chinas: the China-Taiwan issue in US foreign policy.**
William R. Kintner, John F. Copper. Philadelphia: Foreign Policy
Research Institute, 1979. 127p.

The authors argue that Sino-American relations should not include the sacrifice of
Taiwan. They criticize the Carter administration for incorrectly assessing China as a
superpower, overestimating commercial benefits to be gained, and jeopardizing the
balance of power in East Asia.

439 **China and the United States: from 'special' to 'normal' relations.**
Paul H. Kreisberg. In: *China Briefing, 1989*. Edited by Anthony J.
Kane. Boulder, Colorado: Westview, 1989, p. 109-25.

During 1988, the US and the PRC continued to share important policy interests in
Cambodia, Afghanistan, and the Persian Gulf. Differences remain, however, on a
broad range of issues particularly sensitive for China, such as US policy toward Taiwan

and US human rights concerns. The author discusses how the Taiwan problem affects the Sino-US relationship in terms of its development in 1988 and its potential impact.

440 **The Taiwan issue in Sino-American strategic relations.**
Martin L. Lasater. Boulder, Colorado: Westview, 1984. 283p.
Lasater argues that US security policy in Asia should rest more on American strength and on the support of its traditional regional allies than on an optimistic projection of China as an ally against the Soviet Union. However, he suggests that the current dual-track China policy should be maintained by the US.

441 **A perspective on Taiwan.**
Victor H. Li. *International Lawyer*, vol. 14 (winter 1980), p. 73-77.
Even though the normalization of Sino-US relations has been completed, there are still many problems to be resolved. Li briefly examines the process by which normalization has been achieved, and then focuses on some of the issues that may arise in the future, such as the American response should Taiwan move toward independence, and the future direction of Taiwan's domestic politics.

442 **Taipei-Washington relations: moving toward institutionalization.**
Bih-jaw Lin. *Issues and Studies*, vol. 24, no. 11 (1988), p. 42-55.
Argues that the leaders of Taiwan and the US have carefully managed their mutual interests, although no official diplomatic relationship exists. Taipei-Washington relations have moved from the initial stage of uncertainty to an era of growing institutionalization.

443 **The fungibility of foreign assistance and resource allocation in the recipient country.**
Shenn-yi Lo. PhD thesis, University of Maryland, College Park, Maryland, 1984. 171p. (Available from University Microfilms, Ann Arbor, Michigan, order no. 8510261).
Focuses on post-war Nationalist Taiwan where large amounts of US assistance were received from the early 1950s to the 1970s. Lo shows that economic assistance tends to be more fungible or interchangeable than military aid since the former has more alternative uses. While the impact of US military assistance was to reduce Taiwan's defence burden by lowering the cost of military spending, economic aid provided the government with fungible revenue which was largely used to stimulate private sector income growth in Taiwan through tax reduction.

444 **Chinese perspectives on Sino-American relations.**
Minako K. Maykovich. *Bulletin of the Institute of Ethnology, Academia Sinica*, no. 50 (1980), p. 171-88.
In an occupationally stratified survey, interviews were conducted with 1,560 individuals – civil servants, students, professors, workers, and farmers – in order to assess Taiwanese attitudes towards Sino-American relations after the US Derecognition of Taiwan in 1979. Farmers and industrial workers show significant deviation from the rest of the sample in that they tended to view Americans negatively, considering them to be non-diligent, hypocritical, and warlike. On the other hand, they were more supportive of the Taiwanese government.

117

445 **Clandestine Chinese nationalist efforts to punish their American detractors.**
Robert P. Newman. *Diplomatic History*, vol. 7, no. 3 (1983), p. 205-22.

Drawing on Federal Bureau of Investigation (FBI) files and other primary sources, the author argues that in order to secure American support the Taiwanese government manufactured documents to impeach the credibility of American officials unfavorably disposed toward the Nationalist government. The documents suggest that the officials were pro-Communist.

446 **The status of agreements between the American Institute in Taiwan and the Coordination Council for North American Affairs.**
R. Sean Randolph. *International Lawyer*, vol. 15, no. 2 (1981), p. 249-62.

As 1979 dawned, the US broke diplomatic relations with the ROC in Taiwan in favour of an association with the PRC. The US established the American Institute in Taiwan (AIT) to carry on all future relations of a governmental nature between the US and the ROC. Its Taiwanese counterpart was the Coordination Council for North American Affairs (CCNAA). Lack of experience with these new species of organizations posed significant legal and political problems for the US. The author examines the relations between AIT and CCNAA, and argues that the agreements between these two organizations must be accorded recognition as valid international agreements of equivalent status.

447 **International bargaining and domestic politics: US-China relations since 1972.**
Robert S. Ross. *World Politics*, vol. 38, no. 2 (1986), p. 255-87.

The interplay between domestic and international politics and the international behaviour of states has provided subjects for research in international politics and foreign policy studies. Ross explains the ups and downs in Sino-US relations since 1972 as being primarily a function of the shifting bargaining position of each country. Changes in this bargaining relationship affected China's strategies for unification of Taiwan with the mainland.

448 **Note: presidential power to terminate treaties without congressional action.**
David I. Salem, Howard Jack Price, Jr. *International Trade Law Journal*, vol. 5 (1979), p. 68-72.

In 1978 President Carter gave a unilateral notice of termination of the 1954 Mutual Defense Treaty. Some Congressional members, including Senator Barry Goldwater, challenged the decision through legal channels, contending that Carter's decision violated the legislative right of Congress to be consulted and to vote on the Treaty's termination, thus impairing the effectiveness of their original votes approving the treaty. This essay is a summary of the litigation history of *Goldwater v. Carter* (100 S. Ct. 533, 1979).

449 **The United States and Taiwan after derecognition: consequences and legal remedies.**
Ahmed Sheikh. *Washington and Lee Law Review*, vol. 37 (spring 1980), p. 323-41.

As far as international law and its current practices are concerned, US derecognition of Taiwan's government does not spell the end of the world for Taiwan. Taiwan still has a legal personality, enjoys certain rights, and retains significant responsibilities in the global community. Meanwhile, the US has attempted to continue economic and other non-political activities with Taiwan. The author discusses Taiwan's legal status and considers how the US has maintained commercial relations with Taiwan.

450 **The US and free China: how the US sold out its ally.**
James C. H. Shen. Washington, DC: Acropolis, 1983. 310p.

As the ambassador of the ROC to the US in the years 1971-78, Shen was privy to details of the denouncement of Washington-Taipei relations. His purpose in this account is to leave behind a record of what happened so that people would know what went wrong and avoid the same mistakes again. His conclusion is that over a period of ten years the US sold Taiwan, its loyal friend and long-term ally, down the river, a bit at a time, but down the river just the same.

451 **US-China relations in 1980.**
John Bryan Starr. In: *China Briefing, 1981*. Edited by Robert B. Oxnam, Richard C. Bush. Boulder, Colorado: Westview, 1981, p. 79-91.

Discusses the Reagan administration's position on Taiwan in 1980. The authors focus on two issues: the status of US representation in Taiwan and the scope of US arms sales to Taiwan. Both issues are analysed within the broader US-PRC relations.

452 **Mainland China, Taiwan, and US policy.**
Edited by Hung-mao Tien. Cambridge, Massachusetts: Oelgeschlager, Gunn & Hain, 1983. 270p.

Consists primarily of reports and summaries of a conference held at the Wingspread Conference Center of the Johnson Foundation, Wisconsin, 28-30 August 1981. Twenty experts of Chinese origin joined together to discuss the China-Taiwan issue and US policy towards the two nations. Inevitably papers in such a collection vary in scope and quality, however, they represent a broad spectrum of divergent views which constitute a good introduction for readers to explore feasible solutions. Fu-mei C. Chen, for example, argues that the US should at least play the rôle of mediator to ensure the continuation of peaceful competition between both sides. Victor Li notes that the future solution of the Taiwan issue depends on domestic developments in mainland China and Taiwan, not on US-USSR relations and other international matters. James C. Hsiung evaluates the Reagan administration's foreign policy towards mainland China and Taiwan. The sixteen documents included in this book will prove useful for further research.

453 **Derecognition worked.**
Leonard Unger. *Foreign Policy*, no. 36 (1979), p. 105-21.
In the late 1970s many Americans feared that the US policy of normalizing relations with mainland China would endanger the security and prosperity of Taiwan. Unger evaluates Taiwan's situation one year after the announcement of the severance of diplomatic ties with Taiwan and concludes that Taiwan continues to prosper.

454 **The Taiwan issue.**
Richard Walker, comments by Yuan-li Wu. *International Trade Law Journal*, vol. 5 (1979), p. 19-26.
Walker points out that despite the policy of normalization towards the PRC, which seemed to break American links with Taiwan, the island remains a US responsibility. The most important part of the continuing responsibility which the United States has for the future of Taiwan lies in the commercial dealings and social interactions between the two nations. Therefore the US should ensure that the island remain secure and unimpaired.

455 **Relations between Peking, Washington, Taipei.**
Peter Kien-hong Yu. In: *Changes and continuities in Chinese communism, volume I: ideology, politics, and foreign policy.* Edited by Yu-ming Shaw. Boulder, Colorado: Westview, 1988, p. 337-57.
Studies Peking's perspective on the triangular relationship between itself, the US and the ROC, dwelling on Taipei's strategy toward Peking and Washington in the future.

The United States status of forces agreement with the Republic of China: some criminal case studies.
See item no. 299.

Protection from commercial counterfeiters in Taiwan for US firms.
See item no. 313.

Protecting intellectual property in Taiwan: non-recognized United States corporations and their treaty rights of access to courts.
See item no. 314.

The Republic of China and US policy: a study in human rights.
See item no. 364.

Policy in evolution: the US role in China's reunification.
See item no. 386.

The legal status of Taiwan in the normalization of Sino-American relations.
See item no. 417.

US arms sales to Taiwan: institutional ambiguity.
See item no. 472.

The Washington-Peking controversy over United States arms sales to Taiwan: diplomacy of ambiguity and escalation.
See item no. 477.

US arms sales to Taiwan: implications for American interests.
See item no. 479.

The Taiwan Relations Act of 1979

456 **Some legal problems in Sino-US relations.**
Tiqiang Chen. *Columbia Journal of Transnational Law*, vol. 22, no. 1
(1983), p. 41-60.
The Taiwan question is the major issue around which all other problems of Sino-American relations revolve. The author deals with the 1979 Taiwan Relations Act and the US arms sales to Taiwan. Chen is a prominent scholar of international law and a senior advisor to the PRC Foreign Ministry, his views, while stated in his private capacity as a scholar, coincide with the official position of the PRC on the issue of the legal status of Taiwan. Readers will find his article valuable reading, even though they may not agree with all his opinions.

457 **ROC-US political relations as seen from the implementation of the Taiwan Relations Act.**
David S. Chou. *Issues and Studies*, vol. 24, no. 11 (1988), p. 13-41.
Reviews the implementation of the Taiwan Relations Act of 1979, which has served as a framework for US-Taiwan relations. The author concludes with an identification of factors which may influence relations in the post-Reagan era.

458 **The role of the US Congress in supervising the implementation of the Taiwan Relations Act.**
Chi-hung Chu. In: *The prospects for ROC-US relations under the Reagan administration.* Edited by Yu-ming Shaw. Taipei: The Asia and World Institute, 1983, p. 42-54.
The 1979 Taiwan Relations Act was enacted to preserve and promote close commercial and cultural ties and other relationships between the US and Taiwan. It also stipulated that Congressional Committees on Foreign Affairs should monitor the implementation of the provisions of the Act. The author discusses whether Congress has been successful in its supervisory function as specified in the Act. The findings show that Congress has done little to make certain that the policies mandated in the Act have been implemented faithfully and effectively.

459 **The Taiwan pawn in the China game: Congress to the rescue.**
Robert Downen. Washington, DC: Center for Strategic and International Studies, Georgetown University, 1979. 80p.
When President Carter announced his decision to terminate diplomatic ties with the Republic of China, the US Congress was shocked by his sudden move. His action was extremely controversial and highly emotionally charged. This monograph argues that the President's decision put Taiwan, a small but intrinsically American ally, in jeopardy on the international geopolitical chessboard. Therefore, Congress had to

adopt adequate legislative guarantees of security to protect Taiwan, the pawn that had been so carelessly exposed. Appendices include a summary of conditions for PRC-US normalization, the Taiwan Relations Act, and other related documents.

460   **The Taiwan Relations Act: legislative recognition of the Republic of China.**
      J. Terry Emerson.   *Issues and Studies*, vol. 24, no. 11 (1988), p. 56-69.
Describes how US-Taiwan relations have survived and flourished without interruption under the 1979 Taiwan Relations Act. The Act represents an example of the US Congress exercising its independent rôle in deciding American foreign policy.

461   **The Taiwan Relations Act: successful foreign policy making by Congress.**
      J. Terry Emerson.   *The American Asian Review*, vol. 6, no. 3 (1988), p. 1-22.
Argues that US-ROC relations rest on a stable legal foundation and the proven record of years of successful practice under the Taiwan Relations Act of 1979. The author discusses the processes whereby the Act was created and the impact it has had on American foreign policy towards Taiwan.

462   **What determines US relations with China: the Taiwan Relations Act or the August 17 Communique with Beijing?**
      J. Terry Emerson.   *Backgrounder* (Heritage Foundation), no. 72 (Nov. 1987). p. 1-12.
In 1979 the US Congress enacted the Taiwan Relations Act, considering it essential for preserving the military security and economic, political and social stability of Taiwan. On 17 August 1982, the US and the PRC issued a joint communiqué to set qualitative and quantitative limits on future US arms sales to Taiwan. Questions have arisen over the potential conflict between the 1979 act and the 1982 communiqué. The author argues that under the laws of the US the act would have precedence in any contest between the communiqué and the act.

463   **Taiwan's security and United States policy: executive and congressional strategies in 1978-1979.**
      Michael S. Frost.   Baltimore, Maryland: School of Law, University of Maryland, 1982. 39p. (Occasional Papers/Reprints Series in Contemporary Asian Studies, no. 4).
Shows how the Carter administration downgraded Taiwan's security rôle in the Pacific Basin in order to pave the way for the US normalization of diplomacy with the PRC. Although Congress passed the Taiwan Relations Act (TRA) to provide some security protection for the ROC, Frost argues that the TRA does not legally obligate the US to do anything for Taiwan if the PRC invades the island. He suggests that the establishment of relations between the PRC and the US should not be at the expense of Taiwan's security.

464 **Congress and foreign relations: the Taiwan Relations Act.**
Jacob K. Javits. *Foreign Affairs*, vol. 60, no. 1 (1981), p. 54-62.
The rôle of Congress in American foreign policy is unique among the legislative bodies of the world. As one who participated in the congressional deliberations that led to the Taiwan Relations Act of 1979, Javits provides a short review of the rôle of Congress in making this Act and evaluates the significance of Congress in deciding foreign policy.

465 **US-ROC economic relations since the Taiwan Relations Act: an American view.**
Jan S. Prybyla. *Issues and Studies*, vol. 24, no. 11 (1988), p. 70-82.
Discusses the achievements as well as the problems in the US-ROC economic relationship. Given the strength and dynamism of the two economies and of the market system to which they both belong, there is every reason to be optimistic about the future of the US-ROC relationship.

466 **United States-China relations: has President Reagan's communique revised international obligations towards Taiwan?**
John E. Wolfinger. *California Western International Law Journal*, vol. 14 (spring 1984), p. 326-50.
The US Constitution requires that international agreements be made by a treaty with Senate approval. Presidents throughout US history, however, have circumvented this requirement by entering into executive agreements with foreign states without Senate approval. In August 1982 President Reagan issued a joint communiqué with the PRC that appeared to contradict and amend congressional legislation, the Taiwan Relations Act of 1979. The 1982 communiqué indicated that the US intended to reduce arms sales to Taiwan, and that the quantity and quality of arms would not exceed the nature and number of arms sold to Taiwan in the previous years. Wolfinger compares Reagan's communiqué with the Taiwan Relations Act and focuses on the executive branch's response to a congressional inquiry into the propriety of Reagan's action. The conclusion suggests a need for a judicial review of the communiqué.

467 **The main legal problems in the bilateral relations between China and the United States.**
Lihai Zhao. *New York University Journal of International Law and Politics*, vol. 16 (spring 1984), p. 543-79.
Discusses the many problems which remain in Sino-US relations. Zhao comments on, for example, the passing of the Taiwan Relations Act of 1979, by US Congress which granted diplomatic privileges and immunities to Taiwan's unofficial organization in the US, and the continuing arms sales to Taiwan. The author is a legal scholar from the PRC and analyses these issues from the perspective of public international law.

The Taiwan Relations Act and the defence of the Republic of China.
See item no. 478.

Military Affairs

National security and defence forces

468 US arms sales: the China-Taiwan tangle.
A. Doak Barnett. Washington, DC: Brookings Institution, 1982. 70p.
Argues that Sino-American political relations will remain uncertain and fragile until there is further compromise and progress on the Taiwan issue. In developing its China policy, the author feels that the US must give priority to strengthening sound, sustainable political and economic ties with China, and not to making arms sales or developing military links. Barnett calls for great restraint in US military relations (including arms sales) with both China and Taiwan.

469 Defence burden and economic growth: unraveling the Taiwanese enigma.
Steve Chan. *American Political Science Review*, vol. 82, no. 3 (1988), p. 913-20.
Historically, Taiwan has combined a comparatively heavy defence burden with rapid economic growth, but the Taiwanese case appears to be exceptional because it is generally supposed that high military spending has a negative impact on economic performance. The author analyses different models of the effects of defence spending on economic growth and concludes that the models capture only part of the empirical reality. In order to unravel the Taiwanese puzzle, Chan suggests that one should probe deeply into the historical context of Taiwan's political economy.

470 **Party-military relations: a comparative study of two Chinese armies.**
Hsiao-shih Cheng. Boulder, Colorado: Westview, 1989. 224p.
Examines how Leninist party-states have been able to maintain stable civil-military
relations. By presenting detailed case studies of the political commissar systems in the
armies of China and Taiwan, Cheng argues that military participation in politics,
instead of the party control of the military, is the key stabilizing factor. His observation
is valuable for our study of civil-military relations and raises questions about the impact
of professionalism, the political neutrality of the military, and civilian supremacy.

471 **Maintaining the dragon's teeth: balanced sales of advanced weapons and
high technology to the two Chinas.**
Christian C. Day. *Syracuse Journal of International Law and
Commerce*, vol. 13, no. 1 (1986), p. 29-82.
Argues that American foreign policy will be enhanced by the balanced sales of arms to
the PRC and Taiwan. Taiwan is critically important to the defence of the Northeastern
Pacific Basin. With the recognition of the PRC by the US, the ROC has become
increasingly isolated from the West. In consequence, Taiwan may not be able to resist
the PRC's overtures for reunification. The US should pursue a policy of selective sales
of weapons and military materials to the ROC in order to allow Taiwan to defend itself
against communist military invasions.

472 **US arms sales to Taiwan: institutional ambiguity.**
Dennis Van Vranken Hickey. *Asian Survey*, vol. 26, no. 12 (1986),
p. 1324-36.
Outlines present US policy on arms transfers to Taiwan, examines other policy options
that the US might consider, and suggests that the current policy may be in the best
interests of the US.

473 **Taiwan as a strategic asset.**
Tun Hwa Ko. *Global Affairs*, vol. 4, no. 2 (1989), p. 65-83.
Claims that Taiwan possesses the attributes that make it important for US security,
especially its geostrategic position. If the US is forced to give up its military bases in
the Philippines, Taiwan should be considered as a possible alternative.

474 **Beijing's blockade threat to Taiwan.**
Edited by Martin L. Lasater. Washington, DC: Heritage Foundation,
1986. 31p. (Heritage Lectures, no. 80).
Based on a seminar discussion held in 1985, this volume evaluates the military
capability of the PRC to enforce a blockade of Taiwan. The author considers how such
a blockade might be put into force and the impact that it would have on US interests in
the northeast Asian region.

475 **Military industry in Taiwan and South Korea.**
Janne E. Nolan. London: Macmillan, 1986. 205p.
Drawing primarily on American sources, the author analyses the means by which
Taiwan and South Korea acquired the capability to manufacture more sophisticated
types of weapons in the 1970s, often through agreements with the US weapons industry.

Nolan focuses on the international factors which prompted the development of military industry in these two countries.

476 **The military balance in the Taiwan Strait and the implications of China's military modernization.**
Jonathan D. Pollack. *AEI Foreign Policy and Defence Review*, vol. 6, no. 3 (1986), p. 35-42.

Among the consequences of the Sino-American normalization process, the reduction of military tension in the Taiwan Strait constitutes an important accomplishment. Mainland China has reduced the armed forces it deploys against Taiwan, yet Taiwan insists that Communist China's threat remains unchanged. Pollack analyses both sides' concerns and the regional strategic situation in East Asia.

477 **The Washington-Peking controversy over United States arms sales to Taiwan: diplomacy of ambiguity and escalation.**
Lyu-shun Shen. *Chinese Yearbook of International Law and Affairs*, vol. 2 (1982), p. 98-120.

A major source of friction between the US and the People's Republic of China in 1982 was the arms sales to Taiwan. The author scrutinizes each side's interpretation of the documents relevant to Sino-US relations, in particular those concerning the arms sales issue. The factors that have influenced Peking's attitudes towards the issue both before and after normalization are also analysed.

478 **The Taiwan Relations Act and the defence of the Republic of China.**
Edwin K. Snyder, A. James Gregor, Maria Hsia Chang. Berkeley, California: Institute of International Studies, University of California, 1980. 132p. bibliog. (Policy Papers in International Affairs, no. 12).

Evaluates the military balance in the Taiwan Strait region and gives some pragmatic insights into the serious consequences of altering that balance. Should the defence capabilities of Taiwan be enhanced to the level where a military solution to the Taiwan question appears increasingly unattractive to mainland China, a period of stability in the Taiwan Strait region of the western Pacific can be expected. Appendices include the joint communiqué of the establishment of Sino-US diplomatic relations and the text of Taiwan Relations Act of 1979.

479 **US arms sales to Taiwan: implications for American interests.**
Robert Sutter. *Journal of Northeast Asian Studies*, vol. 1, no. 3 (1982), p. 27-40.

Evaluates arguments for and against US sales of arms to Taiwan, the changing policies of the Reagan administration, and implications for future US-Taiwan relations.

480 **Military preparedness and security needs: perceptions from the Republic of China on Taiwan.**
Chi-wu Wang. *Asian Survey*, vol. 21, no. 6 (1981), p. 651-63.
Refutes the argument that Taiwan's security risks are diminishing because mainland China has placed more emphasis on modernization projects, instead of posing a military threat to Taiwan. The author also evaluates Taiwan's military preparedness for defence and strategic plans for stopping a communist invasion.

481 **United States export control policies and the modernization of China's armed forces.**
Larry M. Wortzel.   In: *China's military modernization: international implications*. Edited by Larry M. Wortzel. New York: Greenwood, 1988, p. 159-92.
Discusses the growing Sino-American defence relationship in terms of US strategic arms exports to mainland China. Wortzel describes the fears of Taiwan and of China's other regional neighbours about US arms sales to the PRC as a number of scientific and technical agreements between these two countries will benefit China's military modernization efforts.

Arms sales, the Taiwan question, and Sino-US relations.
See item no. 432.

The iron triangle: a US security policy for Northeast Asia.
See item no. 435.

US aid to Taiwan: a study of foreign aid, self-help, and development.
See item no. 437.

Taiwan's security and United States policy: executive and congressional strategies in 1978-1979.
See item no. 463.

Taiwan Straits Crisis

482 **The odd day.**
DeWitt Copp, Marshall Peck.   New York: William Morrow, 1962.
212p.
In the late summer and early autumn of 1958, mainland China ceaselessly shelled the offshore islands of Quemoy for forty-four days. Failing in their attempt to occupy the islands, the Chinese Communists decided to continue their shelling on every odd-numbered day. The authors describe the situation on the offshore islands and on Taiwan. Names of people interviewed appear in the appendix.

483 **United States opposition to use of force in the Taiwan Strait, 1954-62.**
Leonard H. Gordon. *Journal of American History*, vol. 72, no. 3 (1985),
p. 637-60.

This examination of US policy in the Taiwan Strait, during the 1950s, is based on
documentation recently declassified by the US Department of State and reveals the
Eisenhower-John Foster Dulles view of Chiang Kai-shek and the Nationalist
government on Taiwan. Although the US remained sympathetic to the cause and
ultimate objectives of the Nationalist policy of returning to the mainland, Taiwan
received considerably less assistance than it requested as US policy was designed only
to give Taiwan sufficient military aid for self-defence, not for a successful
counterattack. The author feels that both Eisenhower and Dulles exhibited moderation,
vision, and unwavering commitment to settling the Taiwan question without the use of
force and presents a detailed account of an important aspect of US-China policy in the
1950s.

484 **The Taiwan Strait crisis revisited: politics and foreign policy in Chinese**
motives.
Melvin Gurtov. *Modern China*, vol. 2, no. 1 (1976), p. 49-103.

The PRC suffered a major setback in the 1958 Taiwan Strait crisis. The conventional
explanation of this crisis is that it was initiated by the leaders of the PRC. Gurtov
argues that had it not been for American actions, in Taiwan, elsewhere in Asia, and in
the Middle East, Mao would have had no reason to order the bombardment of the
offshore islands on 23 August 1958.

485 **The 1958 Quemoy crisis.**
Morton H. Halperin, Tang Tsou. In: *Sino-Soviet relations and arms*
control. Edited by Morton H. Halperin. Cambridge, Massachusetts:
MIT Press, 1967, p. 265-303.

Explores Sino-Soviet relations during the 1958 Taiwan Strait crisis and concludes from
the available evidence that there may not have been any major Sino-Soviet
disagreement about strategy during the crisis. Another article by the authors on the
same subject appeared in *Public Policy*, vol. 15 (1966), p. 119-38.

486 **The abortive liberation of Taiwan.**
Jon W. Huebner. *China Quarterly*, no. 110 (1987), p. 256-75.

Considers China's attempts to 'liberate' Taiwan from capitalist exploitation during the
early 1950s and examines why these attempts ended in failure. Huebner concludes that
several important constraints, for example, poorly trained and ill equipped Chinese
invasion forces and the possibility of American intervention, diminished the likelihood
of a Chinese invasion at this time.

487 **Public opinion and American foreign policy: the Quemoy crisis of 1958.**
Marian D. Irish. *Political Quarterly*, vol. 31, no. 2 (1960), p. 151-62.

Discusses the impact of public opinion in the US on American policy toward the
Quemoy crisis. The author concludes that even though public opinion in September
and October of 1958 was extremely intense and voluble, it apparently did not affect the
substance of American foreign policy.

488   **China, Taiwan, and the offshore islands.**
Thomas E. Stolper.   Armonk, New York: M. E. Sharpe, 1985. 170p.
bibliog.

The author investigates Mao Tse-tung's decisions during the Taiwan Strait crises of
1954-55 and 1958. He argues that Mao's overriding objective during both crises was to
prevent the United States from engineering the international acceptance of Taiwan as a
political entity separate from China. In neither crisis did Mao intend to seize the
Taiwanese-administered islands of Matsu and Quemoy. Rather each served Mao's
purpose to keep America entangled in China's unfinished civil war, thus making it
clear to the US that it could not avoid conflict with China if it supported Taiwan.

489   **The limits of alliance: the Quemoy crisis of 1958.**
John R. Thomas.   In: *Sino-Soviet military relations*. Edited by
Raymond L. Garthoff. New York: Frederick A. Praeger, 1966, p. 114-
49.

The Quemoy crisis of 1958 stands as a very significant case in which Sino-Soviet unity
was tested under fire. The author examines the workings of the Sino-Soviet alliance in
a crisis affecting the vital interests of China and the Soviet Union.

490   **Mao's limited war in the Taiwan Strait.**
Tang Tsou.   *Orbis*, vol. 3, no. 3 (1959), p. 332-50.

Discusses Mao's basic principles of limited war and how these principles have guided
Mao in his political-military strategy against the United States and Taiwan. Tsou uses
the Taiwan Strait crisis of 1958 to examine the application of Mao's principles.

491   **The Quemoy imbroglio: Chiang Kai-shek and the United States.**
Tang Tsou.   *Western Political Quarterly*, vol. 12, no. 4 (1959), p. 1075-
91.

The 1958 crisis over Quemoy and Matsu, two islands off the shore of mainland China,
revealed a fascinating relationship between Taiwan and the US. The author analyses
the intentions and tactics of Chiang Kai-shek in making it difficult for the US to force
him to withdraw his troops from the offshore islands. His strategy included pushing the
US toward the brink of war with Communist China.

Ocean Policy

492 **The Republic of China and the law of the sea.**
Kuo-tsai Chao. In: *The law of the sea: problems from the East Asian perspective*. Edited by Choon-ho Park, Jae Kyu Park. Honolulu, Hawaii: Law of the Sea Institute, University of Hawaii, 1987, p. 336-52.
After a discussion of Chinese experiences at the First and Second United Nations Conferences on the Law of the Sea, Chao analyses Taiwan's attitude toward the Third United Nations Convention on the Law of the Sea, as well as its current practices in ocean politics.

493 **The law of the sea and the delimitation of maritime boundaries in the East China Sea.**
Hungdah Chiu. In: *Energy, security and economic development in East Asia*. Edited by Ronald C. Keith. New York: St. Martin's, 1986, p. 222-48.
Begins with a survey of the maritime claims made by four East Asian political entities: Japan, South Korea, Taiwan, and mainland China. Chiu examines closely the legal issues which have emerged with the new Law of the Sea, especially with reference to the resolution of conflicting maritime jurisdictions in the East China Sea.

494 **Some problems concerning the delimitation of the maritime boundary between the Republic of China (Taiwan) and the Philippines.**
Hungdah Chiu. *Ocean Development and International Law*, vol. 14, no. 1 (1984), p. 79-105.
The delimitation of the maritime boundary between Taiwan and the Philippines in the Bashi Channel and the South China Sea involves several complicated issues of international law, namely, the legality the Philippines' claim to the entire sea area, the use of the archipelagic state principle and other delimitation principles provided in the 1982 United Nations Convention on the Law of the Sea, and the territorial claims of Taiwan and the Philippines to certain islands in the South China Sea. Chiu evaluates

these issues and suggests that the maritime boundaries of certain disputed islands in the South China Sea be declared neutral zones open to nationals of both countries. This article also appeared in the *Chinese Yearbook of International Law and Affairs*, vol. 3 (1983), p. 1-21.

495 **South China Sea islands: implications for delimiting the seabed and future shipping routes.**
Hungdah Chiu. *China Quarterly*, no. 72 (1977), p. 743-65.
Studies the possible implications of the rôle of the South China Sea islands in delimiting the seabed and considers future shipping routes in the light of the recent developments in international law concerning archipelago problems and the claims made by the coastal states of the South China Sea. Taiwan's position is discussed at length in this essay.

496 **A proposed fishery conservation and management act for the Republic of China.**
Joseph W. Dellapenna, Ar-young Wang. *Fordham International Law Journal*, vol. 5 (winter 1981-82), p. 35-89.
Drawing on the US Fishery Conservation and Management Act of 1976, the authors drafted a fishery conservation and management law for the ROC. Their proposed text is presented here with a brief section-by-section analysis. Because of the changes in the political climate in East Asia, however, the proposed draft has not been enacted. The authors' purpose here is to illustrate the thinking which is now going on in Third World countries as they attempt to modernize their fishery conservation and management practices. In this sense, the draft sheds light on what is happening in Taiwan today and serves as a model for other nations on issues pertaining to fishery.

497 **The Republic of China's claims relating to the territorial sea, continental shelf, and exclusive economic zones: legal and economic aspects.**
Joseph W. Dellapenna, Ar-young Wang. *Boston College International and Comparative Law Review*, vol. 3, no. 2 (1980), p. 353-76.
Argues that the emerging new consensus on the Law of the Sea presents an opportunity for Taiwan to extend the protection of its vital interests and thus enhance its economic development, without producing any serious difficulties for its relations with other nations. The authors suggest that Taiwan should enlarge the breadth of its ocean territories from three to twelve nautical miles, claim effective control of that portion of the Asian continental shelf adjacent to the territory presently controlled by Taiwan, and declare an exclusive economic zone of 200 miles breadth.

498 **Foreign investment in the troubled waters of the East China Sea.**
Ying-jeou Ma. *Chinese Yearbook of International Law and Affairs*, vol. 1 (1981), p. 35-73.
Six American oil companies have invested in the offshore oil development programmes of the ROC. This study concentrates on the impact of jurisdictional risks in the East China Sea on contractual terms and performance.

Ocean Policy

499 Legal problems of seabed boundary delimitation in the East China Sea.
Ying-jeou Ma, foreword by Louis B. Sohn. Baltimore, Maryland:
School of Law, University of Maryland, 1984. 308p. bibliog.
Following a description of the geophysical, political, and economic backgrounds of the
East China Sea oil controversy, the author reviews the conflicting claims and
overlapping concessions of the coastal states. In particular, Ma examines the relevance
of the Tiao-yu-tai territorial dispute (in which Japan and Taiwan both claim
sovereignty over the islands) to the seabed boundary issue. This decade-old boundary
problem is analysed in the light of recent developments during and after the Third
United Nations Convention on the Law of the Sea. Ma also examines the Peking-
Taipei rivalry over the seabed dispute in detail. This is an excellent study in which the
author shows his ability to master complex problems by offering well-documented and
clearly organized arguments. The appendix includes tables and maps.

500 Contest for the South China Sea.
Marwyn S. Samuels. New York: Methuen, 1982. 203p. bibliog. maps.
Provides an account of the origins, dimensions, and implications of the dispute among
mainland China, Taiwan, Vietnam and the Philippines over the Paracel and Spratly
Islands in the South China Sea. As the author indicates, the resources of the seabed
surrounding the islands and their waters, the strategic significance for shipping and air
transit throughout the basin, and the legal advantages of ownership are the major
incentives for the various claims to this area. Samuels should be commended for his
use of a variety of relevant scholarly literature, as well as for refraining from
interpreting issues or events that lie outside his special field of geography. The book's
value is further enhanced by a guide to place names.

501 The Spratly islands: dangerous ground in the South China Sea.
Mark J. Valencia. *Pacific Review*, vol. 1, no. 4 (1988), p. 438-43.
The Spratly Islands in the South China Sea have long borne the seeds of international
conflict. The author analyses why these islands are so important to China, Vietnam,
the Philippines, Taiwan, and Malaysia, and discusses each country's policy and claim to
these islands.

East China Sea: boundary problems relating to the Tiao-yu-tai Islands.
See item no. 23.

**The East Asian seabed controversy revisited: relevance (or irrelevance) of the
Tiao-yu-tai (Senkaku) Islands territorial dispute.**
See item no. 31.

**Protecting the Republic of China from oil pollution in the sea: accounting for
damages from oil spills.**
See item no. 646.

Economic
Development

502 **Taiwan's economic history: a case of etatisme and a challenge to dependency theory.**
Alice H. Amsden. *Modern China,* vol. 5, no. 3 (1979), p. 341-79.
Dependency theory argues that Third World countries will stay underdeveloped as long as they are integrated in the world capitalist system. Amsden counters that dependency theory is unable to come to grips with the Taiwanese case. Only when internally productive systems and social relations are taken into consideration can we understand both successful cases of economic development (like Taiwan) and unsuccessful instances as well.

503 **Dependency theory and Taiwan: analysis of a deviant case.**
Richard E. Barrett, Martin King Whyte. *American Journal of Sociology,* vol. 87, no. 5 (1982), p. 1064-89.
Dependency theory posits that the greater the degree of reliance on foreign investment and foreign aid in a country, the slower the rate of economic growth and the greater the inequality of incomes there. This study shows that Taiwan has become a deviant case. None of these results has occurred as the dependency theorists predict.

504 **Economic growth and income disparity in Taiwan.**
Han-yu Chang. In: *Asian socioeconomic development: a national accounts approach.* Edited by Kazushi Ohkawa, Bernard Key.
Honolulu, Hawaii: University Press of Hawaii, 1980, p. 215-32.
Attempts to examine Taiwan's income distribution and to identify the overall pattern of change during its post-war period of rapid economic growth. The author also offers a brief comparison of income distribution between Taiwan and other countries.

133

505 **Economic development in Taiwan and mainland China: a comparison of strategies and performance.**
Chu-yuan Cheng. *Asian Affairs*, vol. 10, no. 1 (1983), p. 60-86.
Cheng compares the economic performances of Taiwan and of mainland China, analyses the essence of each development, and draws some general implications from this comparison.

506 **Economic development in Taiwan: a model of a political economy.**
Cal Clark. *Journal of Asian and African Studies*, vol. 22, nos. 1-2 (1987), p. 1-16.
After summarizing Taiwan's impressive aggregate economic record, Clark attempts to develop an overall model for the political economy of the ROC based on the relationships between social structure and inequality, and economic structure and performance. He also incorporates the rôle of the state, the nature of domestic élites, and foreign economic and political relations.

507 **The Taiwan exception: implications for contending political economy paradigms.**
Cal Clark. *International Studies Quarterly*, vol. 31, no. 3 (1987), p. 327-56.
Points out that the Taiwanese experience since 1945 presents major challenges to several paradigms for studying international political economy. While Taiwan demonstrates that growth with equity is possible in an externally oriented market-based economy, its case also suggests that the eradication of colonial institutions, effective land reform, government-directed regulation of foreign multinational corporations, and a fairly egalitarian distribution of wealth all play major rôles in stimulating development. References at the end of the article are very useful for further research.

508 **The Taiwanese ascent: system, state, and movement in the world economy.**
George T. Crane. In: *Ascent and decline in the world system*. Edited by Edward Friedman. Beverly Hills, California: Sage, 1982, p. 93-113.
Argues that Taiwan's economic success can be explained by placing it within the context of the capitalist world economy. Taiwan's ascent in the capitalist world system did not occur overnight. The foundation of its rise was established during the era of Japanese colonial rule, while its dynamic and rapid period of growth took place later, around 1950-70.

509 **The origins and development of the Northeast Asian political economy: industrial sectors, product cycles, and political consequences.**
Bruce Cumings. *International Organization*, vol. 38 (winter 1984), p. 1-40.
The author applies several theories of international relations, for example, the product cycle, hegemony, and the world system, to analyse the creation and development of the northeast Asian political economy in this century. Taiwan, Japan, and South Korea have each developed in a particular relationship to each other; the three combined

together form a hierarchical, constantly interacting political-economic unit. After 1945, elements of the pre-war model survived in Taiwan and South Korea, two former Japanese colonies. Today, both Taiwan and South Korea are receptacles for Japan's declining industries. The most recent export-led competition has seen Taiwan succeed where South Korea has been burdened with rapidly increasing external debt. This article is a must for anyone interested in the East Asian political economy.

510 **Economic development of Taiwan, 1950-80.**
John C. H. Fei. In: *Development and cultural change: cross-cultural perspectives*. Edited by Ilpyong J. Kim. New York: Paragon House, 1986, p. 71-94.
Assesses the transition process of Taiwan's economy from pre-Second World War agrarian colonialism to the epoch of modern economic growth based on science and technology. Fei divides Taiwan's economic development into three phases: import substitution (1953-63); external orientation (1963-80); and technology-sensitive external orientation (1980-).

511 **Economic development in historical perspective: Japan, Korea, and Taiwan.**
John C. H. Fei, Kazushi Ohkawa, Gustav Ranis. In: *Japan and the developing countries*. Edited by Kazushi Ohkawa, Gustav Ranis, Larry Meissner. New York: Basil Blackwell, 1985. p. 35-64.
Presents an overview of the phases of economic development that Japan, Korea and Taiwan have passed through. These three countries began economic development with a large labour surplus, limited natural resources, and fairly equally distributed land areas. The authors examine substantial similarities as well as some differences in the early phases of economic development in the three countries. Topics covered include wage rates, capital/labour ratios, and income distribution.

512 **Taiwan: a resource analysis of an oriental economy.**
Norton S. Ginsburg. *Economic Development and Cultural Change*, vol. 1 (1952-53), p. 37-56, 110-131.
Discusses the character and problems of Taiwan's economic development in the early 1950s. Ginsburg describes the agricultural resources and development of the island, its industrial potential, and its course of economic development under the Japanese (1895-1945). This essay allows readers to compare previous scholarly opinions with current academic views on Taiwan's development experience.

513 **Colonial origins of Taiwanese capitalism.**
Thomas B. Gold. In: *Contending approaches to the political economy of Taiwan*. Edited by Edwin A. Winckler, Susan Greenhalgh. Armonk, New York: M. E. Sharpe, 1988, p. 101-17.
Taiwan's colonial interlude poses an anomaly for theories of imperialist occupation. By examining key aspects of Taiwan's experience of colonialism and decolonization that differed from those in other Third World countries, Gold evaluates their consequences for later economic development. While the Japanese demonstrated to the Taiwanese how to accomplish economic growth, it was the Taiwanese who began achieving it during the post-Japanese period. In other words, the Japanese developed Taiwan's

productive forces but restricted access to the major benefits. The Nationalist Chinese removed the remaining barriers, providing the incentive for the release of those forces.

514 **Entrepreneurs, multinationals, and the State.**
     Thomas B. Gold. In: *Contending approaches to the political economy of Taiwan*. Edited by Edwin A. Winckler, Susan Greenhalgh. Armonk, New York: M. E. Sharpe, 1988, p. 175-205.
Provides a chronological examinination of interactions among key members of Taiwan's economic élite: private capital, multinational corporations, and the State. Because the State played a much larger rôle than in Latin America, Taiwan has avoided much of the social, economic, and political disarticulation and exclusion prevalent in Latin America and has begun a transition toward a pluralist democratic system.

515 **Taiwanese economic development: an alternative interpretation.**
     Richard Grabowski. *Development and Change*, vol. 19, no. 1 (1988), p. 53-67.
Analyses economic development in Taiwan during both the Japanese colonial period and the Nationalist rule of the 1950s. It is argued that Taiwan does not represent a model of development that can be easily reproduced in many of today's less-developed nations.

516 **Supranational processes of income distribution.**
     Susan Greenhalgh. In: *Contending approaches to the political economy of Taiwan*. Edited by Edwin A. Winckler, Susan Greenhalgh. Armonk, New York: M. E. Sharpe, 1988, p. 67-100.
Evaluates the rôle of external links in explaining Taiwan's relatively egalitarian income distribution. The author reviews the available data about economic distribution in Taiwan from the mid-1800s to the present. She then examines various theoretical approaches to Taiwan's economic success. Given the limitation of these approaches, a new synthesis is offered, asserting the strong influence of supranational economic and political factors – in particular, conditions in the global economy – on Taiwan's income distribution, land reforms, and export expansion policies.

517 **Capitalist industrialization in East Asia's four little tigers.**
     Clive Hamilton. *Journal of Contemporary Asia*, vol. 13, no. 1 (1983), p. 35-73.
Describes the conjunctive forces which combined to sponsor the development of industry of a certain type in four newly industrialized East Asian countries: Taiwan, South Korea, Singapore and Hong Kong. Their social and historical backgrounds were favourable to the accumulation of capital through industrial development. The political régimes allied with the capitalist classes to sponsor the process of industrialization. Hamilton uses various theories of political economy to test their applicability in explaining East Asian economic success.

518 **Comment on dependency theory and Taiwan: analysis of a deviant case.**
Heather-jo Hammer. *American Journal of Sociology*, vol. 89, no. 4 (1984), p. 932-40.
This is a comment on Barrett and Whyte's analysis of Taiwan (*American Journal of Sociology*, vol. 87 (1982), p. 1064-89, (q.v.), which argues that Taiwan is a deviant case, dependent but not underdeveloped or peripheral in the capitalist world system. Hammer's primary argument is that Barrett and Whyte have interpreted dependency too broadly. She suggests that dependency refers to direct private foreign capital investment, while colonialism and reliance on foreign aid are actually 'external reliance' and not dependency. Barrett and Whyte's reply follows Hammer's comment.

519 **Road to prosperity: a macro-view on the magical growth in Taiwan.**
Fei-pang Ho, Sarah Ho. Taipei: Excellence, 1987. 237p.
Divides Taiwan's economic development into five chapters: 'Reminiscence among gunfire' (before 1952); 'The process of growing out of underdevelopment' (1952-60); 'A glorious economic miracle' (1973-80), and 'A turning point in the 1980s'. Numerous photos are used to depict the process of Taiwan's economic development.

520 **Economic development in Taiwan, 1860-1970.**
Samuel P. S. Ho. New Haven, Connecticut: Yale University Press, 1978. 461p.
Ho argues that Taiwan's economic development has depended on three primary factors: a cheap and elastic labour supply, heavy doses of foreign capital at critical times, and government willingness to promote capitalism by moving away from its 1940s and 1950s pattern of state control of the economy. Thus an export-oriented economic policy serves as an advantage for resource-poor Taiwan.

521 **Economics, economic bureaucracy, and Taiwan's economic development.**
Samuel P. S. Ho. *Pacific Affairs*, vol. 60, no. 2 (1987), p. 226-47.
Using Taiwan as a case study, Ho discusses the rôle of economic bureaucracy in the formulation, debate, and implementation of two major economic policies, namely the 1949-53 land reform and the 1958-60 adoption of an export-oriented strategy of industrialization.

522 **Political institutions and economic performance: the government-business relationship in Japan, South Korea, and Taiwan.**
Chalmers Johnson. In: *The political economy of the new Asian industrialism*. Edited by Frederic C. Deyo. Ithaca, New York: Cornell University Press, 1987, p. 136-64.
Through a comparison of state led development in Japan, South Korea, and Taiwan, Johnson argues that state intervention in East Asian capitalist countries has relied on organizational and institutional links between politically-insulated state development agencies and major private firms. The public agencies have been able to manipulate economic incentives in accordance with changing strategic goals by maintaining controls over access to credit, export licences, and the like. At the same time, state-linked, private-sector conglomerates, banks and trading organizations have dominated strategic economic sectors to amplify the efficacy of intervention.

523 **The interplay of state, social class, and world system in East Asian development: the case of South Korea and Taiwan.**
Hagen Koo. In: *The political economy of the new Asian industrialism.*
Edited by Frederic C. Deyo. Ithaca, New York: Cornell University
Press, 1987, p. 165-81.

Koo argues that, in most developing societies, the landlord and similar social classes tend to penetrate state structures and influence the decision making process in economic developments for their own self-interests. However, in Taiwan and South Korea, the strength of the landlord class was undermined by long-term Japanese colonial rule which also reorganized the economic structure of these two societies. The result for South Korea and Taiwan was the relative autonomy of the State in economic planning with an emerging industrial bourgeoisie and a growing industrial proletariat.

524 **The Taiwan economy in transition.**
Shirley W. Y. Kuo. Boulder, Colorado: Westview, 1983. 362p.

Although Taiwan experienced decelerated growth in its economic development after the 1973 oil crisis, it has maintained growth rates far beyond those of the advanced nations, steering clear of economic obstacles imposed by the global economy. The author undertakes a quantitative analysis to identify the factors responsible for the successful transition of Taiwan's economy, whilst facing those external challenges. Kuo offers a wealth of information on an extensive range of topics: labour absorption and income distribution; trade, prices, and external shocks; technical change and economic policies. Kuo argues that continuous progress towards greater equality in income distribution can be attributed to two factors: rapid labour absorption and an even geographical distribution of industries contributing to growing non-agricultural incomes in farm households. She also shows that the successful transition from import substitution to export promotion in Taiwan's manufacturing sector rested on the appropriateness of the government's economic policies and the private sector's promotion of specialization in labour-intensive industries.

525 **The Taiwan success story: rapid growth with improved distribution in the Republic of China, 1952-1979.**
Shirley W. Y. Kuo, Gustav Ranis, John C. H. Fei. Boulder,
Colorado: Westview, 1981. 161p.

The Taiwan experience in the post-war decades shows that economic growth need not preclude equity. The early land reform, government policies emphasizing industrialization and relatively free markets, an energetic and trainable labour force, flexible import substitution and export promotion policies, and foreign aid all contributed to the success of Taiwan's economy. The author concludes that it is possible for economic growth to be compatible with an improved distribution of income during every phase of the transition from colonialism to a modern developed economy. This book is well written and documented with abundant sources.

526 **An East Asian model of economic development: Japan, Taiwan, and South Korea.**
Paul W. Kuznets. *Economic Development and Cultural Change*,
vol. 36, no. 3 (1988), p. S11-S43.

The East Asian model of development stresses five shared economic characteristics that seem significant in the contemporary economic development of Japan, Taiwan, and South Korea. They include high investment ratios, small public sectors, competitive labour markets, export expansion, and government intervention in the economy. Kuznets discusses each of these characteristics in detail.

527 **Guerrilla capitalism: export oriented firms and the economic miracle in Taiwan (1973-87).**
Danny Kin-kong Lam. *Journal of Sunology* (Kaohsiung, Taiwan), vol. 4, no. 1 (1989), p. 167-83.

Argues that Taiwan's economic development is represented by the so-called 'guerrilla capitalism' model. One feature of this system of capitalism is its ability to carry out the structural adjustment of a national economy. In Taiwan a network of multinational market links was created by the overseas Taiwanese community, which brought technology and market knowledge from the developed nations into Taiwan. Multinational corporations also unintentionally transferred their technology to local managers. These factors were mixed with the successful exploitation of market opportunities for manufactured goods in the developed countries by small to medium firms in Taiwan, and the result was termed guerrilla capitalism. According to this study, the period 1973-87 witnessed the existence of this model in Taiwan.

528 **Models of development: a comparative study of economic growth in South Korea and Taiwan.**
Edited by Lawrence J. Lau. San Francisco, California: Institute for Contemporary Studies, 1986. 217p.

This volume offers an explanation of the successful economic development of South Korea and Taiwan. Following an individual description of the economy of each country, one section is reserved for a comparative analysis of development policies. Lau concludes that both countries have succeeded because of efficient economic management and the availability and quality of human resources.

529 **Development strategies in Taiwan.**
T. H. Lee, Kuo-shu Liang. In: *Development strategies in semi-industrial economies.* Edited by Bela Balassa, et al. Baltimore, Maryland: Johns Hopkins University Press, 1982, p. 310-50.

Provides a brief history of Taiwan's successful transition from its initial import-substitution strategy to a scheme oriented towards the expansion of exports. The author then discusses possible policy changes for future development.

530 **The evolution of policy behind Taiwan's development success.**
K. T. Li. New Haven, Connecticut: Yale University Press, 1988. 208p.

The author was one of the main architects of the organizational and policy changes in Taiwan over the past forty years. His account of Taiwan's economic development provides insight into the institutional underpinnings of a successful development experience. A lesson to be learnt from the Taiwanese experiences, Li argues, is the necessity of controlling inflation by adopting high interest rates to absorb savings, promoting automation and technology, and establishing adequate infrastructure. Two lengthy introductory essays by Gustav Ranis and John C. H. Fei are included to put Taiwan's experience in perspective. This volume is aimed at those interested in an overview of development in Taiwan and in the relationship between government policy and development.

531 **Experiences and lessons of economic development in Taiwan.**
Edited by Kwoh-ting Li, Tzong-shian Yu. Taipei: Institute of Economics, Academia Sinica, 1982. 536p.

This collection of papers presented at a 1981 conference held by the Institute of Economics, Academia Sinica, Taipei, covers almost every aspect of Taiwan's economic development. For example, John C. H. Fei explains the ideology of economic development in Taiwan; Simon Kuznets discusses modern economic growth and the less-developed countries; and Shirley W. Y. Kuo presents an excellent study of Taiwan's industrial development, 1952-79. The papers and records of follow-up discussions should prove worthwhile reading for students of Taiwan's economic development.

532 **What China can learn from Taiwan.**
Shaomin Li. *Orbis*, vol. 33, no. 3 (1989), p. 327-40.

Having reviewed the paths taken by both China and Taiwan, grappled with the problem of Chinese communism, and observed the close historic and cultural links between these two Chinese societies, the author argues that Taiwan may well serve as China's foremost model in the area of political and economic development.

533 **Phoenix and the lame lion: modernization in Taiwan and mainland China, 1950-1980.**
Alan P. L. Liu. Stanford: Hoover Institution Press, 1987. 182p.

One school of thought assumes that Taiwan has achieved economic success simply because it had many material advantages – small size, an established infrastructure, and substantial US aid. Through a comparison of the two Chinese societies – mainland China and Taiwan – Liu challenges this view by arguing that Taiwan's undoubted advantages still would not have enabled the country to modernize its economy without wise political and economic leadership, a sound government strategy of development, and the educated participation and goodwill of the people. He compares Mao Tse-tung and Chiang Kai-shek in terms of personality and leadership, and comments on the differences in the social backgrounds and political careers of the top economic planners, local officials, and business leaders of both societies. This is a solid comparative study substantiated with well-researched facts and sources.

534 **Taiwan to 1993: politics versus prosperity.**
Simon Long. London: Economist Intelligence Unit, 1989. 112p. (Special Report, no. 1159).

Identifies the policies which moved Taiwan's economy from the export of products with a low profit margin such as textiles in the 1960s through successive stages of technological upgrading until it stood at the edge of developed status in the late 1980s. Some structural weaknesses in Taiwan's buoyant economy are also explored. The report maintains that political change and economic reform are likely to continue, and Taiwan will achieve moderate growth of 4.3 per cent a year. Although the domestic political context and foreign relations are addressed, the author deals mostly with Taiwan's future economic trends.

535 **The economic transformation of the Republic of China on Taiwan.**
Ramon H. Myers. *China Quarterly*, no. 99 (1984), p. 500-28.

The transformation of Taiwan's economy has been neither easy nor smooth. After discussing Taiwan's achievements in economic growth, income distribution and industrial productivity. Myers analyses Taiwan's future challenge of restructuring its economy for continued development.

536 **Contending forces in Taiwan's economic policy making: the case of Hua Tung Heavy Trucks.**
Gregory W. Noble. *Asian Survey*, vol. 27, no. 6 (1987), p. 683-704.

A joint venture with US General Machinery Manufacturing Corporation was set up in Taiwan to build trucks, buses and diesel engines. The negotiations were intermittently tough and rancorous, and the final agreement was highly disadvantageous to Taiwan. Drawing on the Hua Tung affair, Noble investigates the organizations, people, and concepts determining economic policy in Taiwan. He indicates the salience of national security concerns and the prominent rôle played by the military in heavy industry and high technology.

537 **The economies of island and mainland China: Taiwan as a systemic model.**
Jan S. Prybyla. *Issues and Studies*, vol. 24, no. 12 (1988), p. 12-28.

Following a comparison of the economies of Taiwan and mainland China, Prybyla argues for the transfer of the Taiwanese model to the mainland.

538 **The new China: comparative economic development in mainland China, Taiwan, and Hong Kong.**
Alvin Rabushka.   Boulder, Colorado: Westview; San Francisco,
California: Pacific Research Institute for Public Policy, 1987. 254p.

Compares the development experiences of mainland China, Taiwan, and Hong Kong, three societies with similar cultures but very different political and economic institutions. Various factors behind economic growth – population, resources, politics, and economic systems – are analysed. The author looks at the way in which incentives and institutions of the market economy have combined with the Confucian traditions of thrift, hard work, and education to create prosperity for Hong Kong and Taiwan. On the other hand, the Chinese Communists have followed the model of central economic planning with disappointing results. China's economic development has improved since 1978, however, because of greater reliance on market forces and pragmatic policies. This book is useful for the scholar as well as the layperson.

539 **Social space and the periodization of economic history: a case from Taiwan.**
P. Steven Sangren. *Comparative Studies in Society and History*,
vol. 27, no. 3 (1985), p. 531-61.

Examines the economic history of the north Taiwanese town of Ta-chi. The author demonstrates that shifts in the structure of Ta-chi's ties to higher-level economic regions were among the most important factors underlying development within the town's own marketing community. For example, the shift from traditional frontier expansion to the export-oriented exploitation of camphor and tea that began in the 1850s resulted from the incorporation of Taiwan into the world economic system.

540 **The modernization of four Chinese societies: China, Taiwan, Hong Kong, and Singapore.**
Wen-hui Tsai. *National Taiwan University Journal of Sociology*, vol. 18 (1986), p. 163-90.

Compares the modernization processes of four countries: Taiwan, mainland China, Singapore, and Hong Kong. This study reveals that industrialization leads to economic growth, which then leads to social modernization. Interesting contrasts are drawn between Taiwan's mixture of planning and private enterprise, mainland China's socialism, Singapore's mix of socialism and capitalism, and Hong Kong's wholehearted capitalism.

541 **Taiwan's economic miracle: lessons in economic development.**
S. C. Tsiang. In: *World economic growth*. Edited by Arnold C. Harberger. San Francisco, California: Institute for Contemporary Studies, 1984, p. 301-31.

According to Tsiang, Taiwan's consistent success contains important lessons for other countries. In the light of this he examines closely how a market-based strategy helped to produce Taiwan's economic miracle. This essay is followed by a commentary by Lawrence J. Lau, another well-known expert on Taiwan's economic development.

542 **State intervention in 'outward-looking' development: neoclassical theory and Taiwanese practice.**
Robert Wade. In: *Developmental states in East Asia*. Edited by Gordon White. New York: St. Martin's, 1988, p. 30-67.

The theme of minimal government runs as a leitmotif through most of the literature on Taiwan's development. Wade argues, however, that existing accounts exaggerate the importance of markets and give little attention to how much the State has done in guiding Taiwan's economic development.

543 **Republic of China's experiences with economic development.**
Yi-ting Wong. In: *Confucianism and economic development*. Edited by Hung-chao Tai. Washington, DC: Washington Institute for Values in Public Policy, 1989, p. 115-27.

Discusses Taiwan's changing economic structure and economic development. The author suggests that other developing countries could acquire the prerequisites of industrialization – capital, technology, and markets – with relative ease, but maintains that the development of the social ethic needed to sustain industrialization is a difficult process, because the ethic has to be inherent in the social and cultural traditions of the countries concerned.

544   Asia's 'miracle' economies.
      Jon Woronoff.   Armonk, New York: M. E. Sharpe, 1986. 404p.
      bibliog.
Examines the economic success of the five Asian 'miracle' economies of Japan, South
Korea, Taiwan, Hong Kong, and Singapore. In a comprehensive survey of the history,
processes, and prospects of these economies, the author explains how they turned
themselves around and launched into accelerated growth, and how they overcame a
poor endowment and lack of experience to create a varied and resilient industry.
Woronoff suggests that other nations may adopt similar policies and strategies to give
their own economies a new impetus.

545   Becoming an industrialized nation: ROC's development on Taiwan.
      Yuan-li Wu.   New York: Praeger, 1985. 138p.
Examines the evolution of Taiwan's national economic policy since 1980, concentrating
on: the promotion of knowledge-intensive industries by government; institutional
development and the mobilization of capital; specialized manpower development; and
trade performance. By focusing on Taiwan's strategy for economic achievement, Wu
draws lessons for developing countries. He particularly stresses the importance of
behavioural characteristics in Taiwan's economic advance, including a willingness to
adopt new ideas and an alert response to change. This book is an important addition to
the growing literature on Taiwan studies, especially because it is not so strictly
mathematically and statistically oriented as some of the recent monographs on
Taiwan's economy.

546   Taiwan in the regional economy of the Pacific Basin.
      Yuan-li Wu.   *Journal of Sunology* (Kaohsiung, Taiwan), vol. 4, no. 1
      (1989), p. 139-66.
Describes the course of Taiwan's economic development and its underlying strategy
since 1950. The author also emphasizes that Taiwan's economy has a rôle to play in the
Pacific Basin region within the foreseeable future.

547   Economic performance in five East Asian countries: a comparative
      analysis.
      Yuan-li Wu, Hung-chao Tai.   In: *Confucianism and economic
      development*. Edited by Hung-chao Tai. Washington, DC: The
      Washington Institute for Values in Public Policy, 1989, p. 38-54.
The economic development of Japan, Taiwan, South Korea, Singapore and Hong
Kong following the Second World War has been one of the most striking events in the
economic history of these nations. The author compares the economic record of these
five countries with that of the rest of the world and assesses the significance of their
performance to the international community.

Taiwan: an economic and social geography.
See item no. 26.

China, seventy years after the 1911 Hsin-hai revolution.
See item no. 67.

Capital formation in Taiwan and Korea.
See item no. 115.

State and society in the Taiwan miracle.
See item no. 163.

Entrepreneurial role and societal development in Taiwan.
See item no. 174.

Economic growth and quality of life: a comparative indicator analysis between China (Taiwan), USA and other developed countries.
See item no. 176.

Families and networks in Taiwan's economic development.
See item no. 198.

Conference on economic development and social welfare in Taiwan.
See item no. 218.

An econometric analysis of the effects of population change on economic growth: a study of Taiwan.
See item no. 258.

Some problems of economic development and education in Taiwan.
See item no. 272.

Trade and investment in Taiwan: the legal and economic environment in the Republic of China.
See item no. 308.

The joint venture and related contract laws of mainland China and Taiwan: a comparative analysis.
See item no. 311.

The State and Taiwan's economic development.
See item no. 318.

Ideology and development: Sun Yat-sen and the economic history of Taiwan.
See item no. 331.

Economic and political development in the Republic of China.
See item no. 334.

Economic development and democratization in Taiwan.
See item no. 357.

Defence burden and economic growth: unraveling the Taiwanese enigma.
See item no. 469.

Networks of Taiwanese big business: a preliminary analysis.
See item no. 594.

Land reform in Taiwan.
See item no. 602.

Intersectoral capital flows in the economic development of Taiwan, 1895-1960.
See item no. 611.

Economic growth and the rise of civil society: agriculture in Taiwan and South Korea.
See item no. 615.

Agricultural development on Taiwan since World War II.
See item no. 619.

Technology transfer and national autonomy.
See item no. 652.

Economic development in Taiwan: a selected bibliography.
See item no. 803.

Finance and Banking

548 Legal aspects of offshore banking in Taiwan.
Ya-huei Chen. *Maryland Journal of International Law and Trade*,
vol. 8, no. 2 (1984), p. 237-76.

Progress has been made towards enhancing Taiwan's economic position by making the country an international financial centre. Reforms include the plan to have branches of many of Taiwan's banks in foreign states and the creation of an offshore banking centre in Taiwan. The author considers the legal framework underlying the establishment of the offshore banking centre and the impact of Taiwan's domestic environment on the centre.

549 Evolving open market operations in a developing economy: the Taiwan experience.
Deena R. Khatkhate. *Journal of Development Studies*, vol. 13, no. 2 (1977), p. 92-101.

Sketches the institutional background of the development of the government bond market during the late 1950s and the early 1960s. Historically, the discount rate and open market operations have evolved together as techniques of the central banking policy. The author discusses why the operation of an open market as a technique of monetary control was denied any chance to succeed by the pursuit of a high interest rate policy which, though primarily designed to promote a rapid rate of economic growth, a high savings ratio and a good export performance, also contributed to the development of a market for government bonds.

550 Financial institutions and markets in Taiwan.
Ching-ing Hou Liang, Michael T. Skully. In: *Financial institutions and markets in the Far East*. Edited by Michael T. Skully. New York: St. Martin's, 1982, p. 170-203.

Provides an overview of the financial sector by reviewing banking institutions, non-banking financial institutions, and financial markets. The authors conclude that US derecognition of the ROC after 1979 did not affect Taiwan's financial sector. Taiwan is expected to continue this trend in its development.

551 Fiscal and monetary policies.

Erik Lundberg. In: *Economic growth and structural change in Taiwan*. Edited by Walter Galenson. Ithaca, New York: Cornell University Press, 1979, p. 263-307.

Compares Taiwan's achievements and failures with those of other less developec countries. Lundberg gives an account of some relevant features of Taiwan's financial system and considers the rôle of monetary policy and interest rates in Taiwan's economic development.

552 Voluntary rural savings capacities in Taiwan, 1960-70.

Marcia L. Ong, Dale W. Adams, I. J. Singh. *American Journal of Agricultural Economics*, vol. 58, no. 3 (1976), p. 578-82.

Provides information on rural household savings and on some of the determining factors for savings in Taiwan during the 1960s. Taiwan's savings performance is due to appropriate policies rather than frugal cultural characteristics. These policies have aggressively promoted mobilization of savings in rural areas.

553 Government finance of the Republic of China.

Edited by Taxation and Tariff Commission. Taipei: Ministry of Finance, Republic of China, 1987. 59p.

After describing the organization and functions of the Ministry of Finance, this report then characterizes the structure of the national treasury, Taiwanese tax structure, management of financial institutions and securities, and fiscal measures to facilitate economic development. Readers with no knowledge of Taiwan's financial system are encouraged to consult this concise volume. Charts, tables, and figures are generously presented along with brief explanations.

554 East Asian financial systems as a challenge to economics: lessons from Taiwan.

Robert Wade. *California Management Review*, vol. 27, no. 4 (1985), p. 106-27.

Western economic theory tends to argue that financial controls are bad because bureaucratic or political factors interrupt the market process. Yet the financial systems of East Asian countries, particularly Taiwan, demonstrate that liberal use of controls plays a positive rôle in their industrialization. Financial controls have not led to the disasters that mainstream economics had predicted. The reason is that the public sector in general is more effective in these East Asian countries than in many other developing countries, that is, more effective in promoting a competitive will to produce.

555 **Security interests under the laws of the Republic of China on Taiwan: an introductory guide.**
Jane Kaufman Winn. *Texas International Law Journal*, vol. 23 (1988), p. 395-416.
In the late 1970s and early 1980s, the banking market in Taiwan became highly competitive. Many foreign banks made the decision to move down-market and lend to medium-sized businesses. The author discusses the financial transactions entered into most often by foreign banks or businesses operating in Taiwan and points out some of the problems experienced by such creditors in recent years.

556 **An empirical study of Taiwan's debt policy: 1950s-1984.**
Tsong-min Wu. *Economic Essays* (National Taiwan University, Taipei), vol. 15, no. 1 (1986), p. 19-44.
Studies the public debt structure of Taiwan from the mid-1950s to 1984. The author's main concern is the relationship between the dynamic pattern of government debt and the paths of government spending and national output.

Trade and investment in Taiwan: the legal and economic environment in the Republic of China.
See item no. 308.

Trade

557 **Taiwan.**
Alice H. Amsden. *World Development*, vol. 12, no. 516 (1984),
p. 491-503.
Shows that Taiwan's technology exports do not reflect accurately the level of Taiwan's
overall technological development. There are numerous industrial branches in Taiwan
whose technology seems to be fairly well developed but whose technological exports
are minuscule or nonexistent. Amsden also examines the so-called plant exports in
Taiwan.

558 **The hopes and fears of foreign direct investment: a comparative
evaluation of FDI regulation in the People's Republic of China and
Taiwan.**
Jeffrey K. D. Au. *Journal of Chinese Law*, vol. 2, no. 2 (1988), p. 359-
403.
Examines government regulation of foreign direct investment (FDI) in both mainland
China and Taiwan. The author compares the two governments' relative openness with
regard to four apparent policy objectives: the promotion of domestic capital
accumulation; the regulation of foreign exchange; the promotion of advanced
technology; and the maintenance of domestic control over FDI activities.

559 **Marketing in Taiwan.**
Frank E. Bair. In: *International marketing handbook*. Edited by
Frank E. Bair. Detroit, Michigan: Gale Research, 1988, vol. 2, p. 2510-
46.
Provides the reader with concise information about Taiwan's economy, foreign trade,
distribution and sales channels, transportation and utilities, advertising, credit,
guidance for business travellers, and sources of economic and commercial information.
The Information included is revised periodically.

560 **The US-Republic of China trade relationship: time for a new strategy.**
Edited by Roger A. Brooks. Washington, DC: Heritage Foundation,
1988. 90p.

Contains valuable observations and analyses of the current state of the US-ROC trade
relationship and suggests ways to improve that relationship through the establishment
of a free trade area between the two countries. These views are presented by
government officials, legislators, scholars, and public policy experts who participated in
a conference on US-ROC trade relations in 1988 sponsored by the Heritage
Foundation of the US and the Institute of International Relations in Taipei.

561 **A 'super 301' trade ruling: too early for Seoul and Taipei.**
Roger A. Brooks, Andrew B. Brick. *Backgrounder*, no. 91 (May
1989), p. 1-12.

In an attempt to correct the trade imbalance, the US Congress passed the Omnibus
Trade and Competitiveness Act. The most renowned provision is Section 301 – or
'Super 301' – whereby retaliatory measures may be taken against countries practising
unfair trade toward the US. The authors argue that more must be done by Seoul and
Taipei to maintain a balance of trade with the US, but the 'Super 301' process is not
the appropriate way to achieve this.

562 **The mouse that roared: Taiwan's management of trade relations with
the United States.**
Steve Chan. *Comparative Political Studies*, vol. 20 (Oct. 1987), p. 251-
92.

The author begins by outlining some general problems that often arise when a small,
less powerful country enters into trade negotiations with a larger one, using Taiwan-US
relations as a case study. After discussing the historical relationship between Taiwan
and the US, Chan elaborates on policy decisions in the two countries that have affected
their relations. Finally, he outlines Taiwan's method of coping with the trade problems
it faces in dealing with the US.

563 **The economic impact of American investment in Taiwan, Republic of
China.**
Chung-shyong Chang. *Issues and Studies*, vol. 24, no. 11 (1988),
p. 101-16.

Acting as one of the pioneer investors, an American firm first came to Taiwan in 1953.
Among the foreign investors in Taiwan, the US has been ahead of the others in terms
of the amount of capital invested. Chang discusses the impact of American investment
on Taiwan's economy.

564 **The production characteristics of multinational firms and the effects of
tax incentives: the case of Taiwan's electronics industry.**
Tain-jy Chen, De-piao Tang. *Journal of Development Economics*,
vol. 24, no. 1 (1986), p. 119-29.

Investigates the production characteristics of multinational firms in Taiwan, focusing
on the electronics industry, which provides a good sample for this study, since some
firms are export oriented, while others are oriented towards the local market. The

findings show that tax incentives which reduce capital cost for multinational firms have different effects on labour, depending on the firm's orientation.

565 **United States-Taiwan economic relations: trade and investment.**
Chu-yuan Cheng. *Columbia Journal of World Business*, vol. 21, no. 1 (1986), p. 87-95.
US-Taiwan economic relations have undergone radical changes during the past thirty-two years. In 1984 Taiwan became the sixth largest exporter to the US with two-way trade reaching the twenty billion dollar level. Cheng predicts an annual growth rate of eight to ten per cent for US-Taiwan trade in the ten years ahead.

566 **Concentration, profitability and trade in a simultaneous equation analysis: the case of Taiwan.**
Tein-chen Chou. *Journal of Industrial Economics*, vol. 34, no. 4 (1986), p. 429-43.
Studies the rôle of foreign trade in the analysis of market structure and performance in Taiwan. The author also indicates the significant influence of public enterprise on market structure and performance.

567 **Taiwan's trade surplus, US responses, and adjustment policies.**
Yunpeng Chu. *Issues and Studies*, vol. 24, no. 11 (1988), p. 83-100.
Taiwan's trade surplus has become a serious problem in the 1980s because the US is not happy about either its growing trade imbalance with Taiwan or the foreign exchange reserves Taiwan has accumulated. The author examines the trade relations between Taiwan and the US and predicts likely developments in the future.

568 **Legal aspects of European investment in the Republic of China.**
Peter Fischer. *Issues and Studies*, vol. 25, no. 4 (1989), p. 12-35.
This paper is divided into four sections covering: a brief history of foreign investment in China, the legal methods of regulating foreign investment in general; a discussion of the ROC's legal principles governing European investment in Taiwan; and, finally, the ROC's economic results. The author concludes that international confidence in the functioning of the ROC's legal and political system, its stability and the reduction of foreign exchange controls make the country very attractive for European investors.

569 **Export processing zones in Taiwan and the People's Republic of China.**
George Fitting. *Asian Survey*, vol. 22, no. 8 (1982), p. 732-44.
Export processing zones in Taiwan are used to encourage investment in the production of goods for export by offering a variety of benefits to investors. In a similar way, the Special Economic Zones (SEZs) are allowed a great deal of leeway in experimenting with new economic policies. Fitting analyses the impact of the export processing zones on economic, social, and political developments in Taiwan and draws some tentative conclusions about the impact of the Special Economic Zones in the PRC.

570 **Pathways from the periphery: the newly industrializing countries in the international system.**
Stephen Mark Haggard. PhD thesis, University of California, Berkeley, California, 1983. (Available from University Microfilms, Ann Arbor, Michigan, order no. 8328900).
Addresses two sets of theoretical and substantive questions. The first concerns the domestic political foundations of the relative success enjoyed by the newly industrializing countries (NICs). The author comments on the strategies they have pursued, and examines their adjustments to the external constraints associated with their growth strategies. The second set of questions relates to the effect of the NICs on the international system. Haggard states that they have altered the structure of North-South relations, contributing to greater changes in the distribution of international capabilities, patterns of trade and capital flows. The thesis concludes that the NICs represent the growing involvement of the State in determining the pattern of international economic relations. Detailed case studies of Korea, Taiwan and Mexico are presented, with a comparative analysis of Brazil and Hong Kong.

571 **Marketing in Taiwan.**
Jeffrey Hardee, Beth Johns, with contributions by the American Institute in Taiwan. Washington, DC: Department of Commerce, Sep. 1988. 68p. (International Marketing Information Series, OBR 88-10).
Provides an overview of Taiwan's foreign trade, economy, major marketing channels, advertising industry, trade regulation, foreign investment, and financial credit situation. In addition to sources of economic and commercial information, this report is a useful guide for business travellers.

572 **The entrepôt trade of Hong Kong with special reference to Taiwan and the Chinese mainland.**
Ronald Hsia. Taipei, Taiwan: Chung-hua Institution for Economic Research, 1984. 86p.
Deals with the pattern of Hong Kong's entrepôt trade; Hong Kong's rôle as an entrepôt for mainland China; and Hong Kong's part in trade between mainland China and Taiwan. This book is concisely written, provides a useful and handy reference work for quick access to data and remains within easy comprehension of the general reader.

573 **Causes and roles of export expansion in the Republic of China.**
Shirley W. Y. Kuo, John C. H. Fei. In: *Foreign trade and investment*. Edited by Walter Galenson. Madison, Wisconsin: University of Wisconsin Press, 1985, p. 45-84.
The first section of this article investigates the causes of trade expansion and structural change for the period 1952-70. The second section elaborates on trading partners, commodity contents, and comparative advantages during 1952-81. The remainder of the article provides a quantitative appraisal of the contribution of export expansion to economic growth and employment, and highlights growth, inflation and trade balance after the oil crisis in the 1970s.

574   **US-Republic of China economic issues: problems and prospects.**
Edited by Martin L. Lasater.   Washington, DC: Heritage Foundation,
1988. 61p. (Heritage Lectures, no. 150)
Drawing on conferences held separately in 1986 and 1987, the author evaluates the
longstanding economic relationship between the US and Taiwan and suggests how it
may be strengthened through a Free Trade Area.

575   **Direct foreign investment in Taiwan's development.**
Gustav Ranis, Chi Schive.   In: *Foreign trade and investment.* Edited by
Walter Galenson. Madison, Wisconsin: University of Wisconsin Press,
1985, p. 85-137.
The rôle of direct foreign investment played a significant part in the process of growth
in Taiwan, as the country moved from a pre-war colony to its present status as one of
the world's most successful cases of contemporary economic development. The author
aims to provide an objective assessment of the rôle direct foreign investment played in
Taiwan's growth, in association with many other factors determining the economy's
performance.

576   **Reaching across the water.**
Mitchell A. Silk.   *China Business Review*, vol. 15, no. 6 (1988), p. 10-
15.
Taiwan's previous 'Three No's' policy toward the mainland régime – no negotiation, no
compromise, no contact – is undergoing a dramatic change into 'no avoidance, no
restriction, no interference'. Aided by incentives from Peking and indirect sanction
from Taipei, Taiwan-mainland trade has increased continuously.

577   **Subsidies under United States countervailing duty law: the case of
Taiwan.**
Clyde D. Stoltenberg.   *Northwestern Journal of International Law and
Business*, vol. 9 (1988), p. 138-90.
According to US law, countervailing duties can be imposed when the US government
determines that a country is providing a subsidy with respect to goods imported into
the US, and that an industry in the US is materially threatened or injured by reason of
that subsidized merchandise. After describing the evolution of Taiwan's laws and
regulations affecting production of exports, the author discusses recent countervailing
duty proceedings involving Taiwanese products, and concludes that the Taiwanese
government subsidizes its exports only minimally. Indirectly, this finding refutes the
recurring argument that Taiwanese export subsidies have contributed to the US-
Taiwan trade deficit.

578   **Foreign trade and investment as boosters for take-off: the experiences of
the four Asian newly industrializing countries.**
S. C. Tsiang, Rong-i Wu.   In: *Foreign trade and investment.* Edited by
Walter Galenson. Madison, Wisconsin: University of Wisconsin Press,
1985, p. 301-32.
Taiwan, South Korea, Hong Kong, and Singapore, all of which are heavily
overpopulated and none of which is richly endowed with natural resources, have

managed during the past twenty years or so to escape the poverty trap and to launch themselves into continuous, self-sustained economic growth. The authors show the significance of the expansion of productive potential. They suggest that the necessary increase in productive capital must be financed through savings, either by creating the conditions permitting the rise of domestic savings or by attracting foreign sources of money. The rôle of foreign trade and investment is crucial in improving technology, management methods, marketing skills, and, particularly, in providing capital.

579   **A comparative study of foreign investment laws in Taiwan and China.**
      Timothy Haosen Wan.   *California Western International Law Journal,*
      vol. 11 (1981), p. 236-301.

Examines and compares the foreign investment law and investment climates of Taiwan and China within both historical and ideological contexts. The author concludes that the future of both economies is likely to be bilaterally harmonious and beneficial to the interests of foreign investment. Appendices include an unofficial translation of the full text of the law of the PRC on joint ventures using Chinese or foreign investment.

580   **Taiwan's trade flows: the underpinning of political legitimacy.**
      Roy A. Werner.   *Asian Survey,* vol. 25, no. 11 (1985), p. 1096-114.

Taiwan's economy relies upon international trade expansion and is vulnerable to external threats. The author reviews current economic trends and then assesses how economic vulnerability might affect reunification possibilities with the People's Republic of China.

581   **Beyond recrimination: perspectives on US-Taiwan trade tensions.**
      Jimmy W. Wheeler, contributions by Maurice C. Ernst, Merit E.
      Janow.   Indianapolis, Indiana: Hudson Institute, 1987. 218p.

Provides a comprehensive framework for analysing US-Taiwan trade tensions. Following the description of the development strategies of East Asian countries, the authors discuss Taiwan's trade and investment patterns with the US and Japan, including proposals to ameliorate tensions. On the question of trade relations, the authors argue that in dealing with the US, Japan and South Korea are in a better political position than Taiwan. The decline of Taiwan's political-strategic significance does limit its bargaining power. Taiwan is also more trade-dependent than the others; its economy is dominated by small businesses to a greater degree than is Japan's or Korea's; and US encouragement for Taiwan to open its market to foreign imports tends to benefit Japan more than the US because Japan is the biggest trader with Taiwan. The authors bring all these considerations to bear on their policy proposals. They have done a good deed for the US-Taiwan trade community by providing this masterful analysis of the issues affecting the US-Taiwan trade relationship.

Guide to international trade and investment law in the Republic of China.
See item no. 305.

Trade and investment in Taiwan: the legal and economic environment in the Republic of China.
See item no. 308.

Legal efforts of the United States and the Republic of China at controlling the transnational flow of commercial counterfeit goods.
See item no. 316

The Taiwan economy in transition.
See item no. 524.

Guerrilla capitalism: export oriented firms and the economic miracle in Taiwan (1973-87).
See item no. 527.

Agricultural trade in the economic development in Taiwan.
See item no. 624.

Taiwan buyers' guide, 1986-87.
See item no. 806.

Taiwan trade directory.
See item no. 809

Taiwan exporters guide, 1988
See item no. 821.

Taiwan traders directory, Republic of China, 1986-88.
See item no. 822.

Energy

582 **Econometric analysis of interaction between energy utilization and industrial production for Taiwan, ROC.**
Ssu-li Chang. PhD thesis, University of Pennsylvania, Philadelphia, Pennsylvania, 1986. 152p. (Available from University Microfilms, Ann Arbor, Michigan, order no. 8623979).
Investigates the relationship between energy and economy in Taiwan. The results of this study indicate that high energy prices affect the structure of the energy market, which in turn affects the rest of the economy, including industrial output, capital accumulation, labour requirements, and import and export situations.

583 **The outlook for energy in Taiwan.**
David S. L. Chu. *Economic Review* (Taipei), no. 222 (1984), p. 1-6.
Predicting that energy will be in short supply in Taiwan by the end of this century, Chu emphasizes the need for conservation and careful utilization of energy in Taiwan.

584 **The research and development of renewable energy and effective energy utilization in Taiwan, Republic of China.**
Kuo-yu Kang. *Economic Review*, no. 221 (1984), p. 10-19.
Describes research and development in renewable energy sources: solar energy, wind energy, biomass energy, geothermal energy, small hydropower, and ocean energy. The author also discusses effective systems of energy utilization in the industrial, residential, commercial, and transportation sectors.

585 **Energy demand management in the Republic of China.**
Chi-yuan Liang. Taipei: The Institute of Economics, Academia
Sinica, 1987. 153p. (The Institute of Economics, Monograph Series,
no. 32).

This work is a revised version of the report on Taiwan undertaken by the Energy
Demand Management Technical Assistance Project, sponsored by the Asian
Development Bank. The author discusses various topics relevant to energy, including
energy resources, supply and demand in Taiwan, energy pricing policy, and the
institutional and legal arrangements in energy planning and demand management. The
final chapter focuses on the implications of future energy situations on international
relations between Taiwan and the rest of the world. Many illustrations and generous
statistical information are provided.

586 **Energy supply and the viability of the economy of Taiwan, Republic of
China.**
Chi-yuan Liang. In: *Energy, security and economic development in
East Asia.* Edited by Ronald C. Keith. New York: St. Martin's, 1986,
p. 109-37.

Reviews the energy supply and demand situation in Taiwan during the period 1965-83.
The author also examines the impact of the two oil crises of 1973-74 and 1979-80 on the
economy, and considers policy options for coping with the energy challenge in the
future. Liang points out that Taiwan is eighty-eight per cent dependent on external
commercial energy supplies.

Industry

587 **The division of labour is limited by the rate of growth of the market: the Taiwan machine tool industry in the 1970s.**
Alice H. Amsden. *Cambridge Journal of Economics*, vol. 9, no. 3 (1985), p. 271-84.
Analyses the processes of capital accumulation in the machine tool industry in Taiwan, in order to gain a better understanding of the nation's industrial development.

588 **Industrialization and employment in Hong Kong, Korea, Singapore, and Taiwan.**
Gary S. Fields. In: *Foreign trade and investment.* Edited by Walter Galenson. Madison, Wisconsin: University of Wisconsin Press, 1985, p. 333-75.
Identifies a number of similarities in industrialization and employment among the Asian newly industrialized countries (NICs). These similarities include large increases in employment and reductions in unemployment rates, the shift of the labour force from the agricultural to the manufacturing sector, and real wage increases for workers, with a decrease in inequality.

589 **International competitiveness, technical change and the state: the machine tool industry in Taiwan and Japan.**
Martin Fransman. *World Development*, vol. 14, no. 12 (1986), p. 1375-96.
One reason for the economic growth of East Asian countries is that they have become internationally competitive in a number of export industries. The author examines the case of the machine tool industry in Taiwan and Japan, showing the importance of several factors affecting international competition: the rôle of the state, the rôle of technical and productivity changes, social relations within the factory, and others. Fransman ends with a discussion of policy dilemmas relating to international competitiveness in the Taiwanese machine tool industry.

590 **Decentralized industrialization and rural development: evidence from Taiwan.**
Samuel P. S. Ho. *Economic Development and Cultural Change*, vol. 28, no. 1 (1979), p. 77-96.

Uses evidence from Taiwan to show that the level of rural non-farming activity depends significantly on the spatial pattern of industrialization. By allowing rural industry and agriculture to grow in a mutually reinforcing manner, decentralized industrialization has created rural employment opportunities and enabled a greater part of Taiwan's rural population to participate in industry without having to leave the countryside. The consequence of this decentralized industrialization is a reduction in the need for urban housing and infrastructure, and a smooth transition from agricultural to non-agricultural activity. This is a key article for anyone interested in rural Taiwan.

591 **Technical change and industrial policy: the case of computer numerically controlled lathes in Argentina, Korea, and Taiwan.**
Staffan Jacobsson. *World Development*, vol. 13, no. 3 (1985), p. 353-70.

Analyses how the substitution of computer numerically controlled (CNC) lathes for conventional lathes affects the conditions under which lathe producers in the newly industrialized countries can successfully compete in the international market. Taiwan and other countries are examined, with particular attention given to the rôle of government policies.

592 **Industrialization in Taiwan, 1946-72. Trade and import-substitution policies for developing countries.**
Ching-yuan Lin. New York: Praeger, 1973. 244p.

Examines the ways in which, after World War Two, Taiwan's economy moved to an import substitution based industry, and its export promotion programme was strengthened. The author offers an excellent review of the events that brought about all these changes of policy and demonstrates how the new policy stimulated industrialization in Taiwan in the 1960s. Moreover, he provides some useful information about economic institutions which developed in Taiwan during the post-war period.

593 **The villager as industrialist: ideologies of household manufacturing in rural Taiwan.**
Justin D. Niehoff. *Modern China*, vol. 13, no. 3 (1987), p. 278-309.

Traces Taiwan's transformation over the last twenty-five years from an agriculturally based country to an industrially based one. Because of this change in economic structure, there has been an increase in the number, and importance, of small manufacturers. This phenomenon is examined both historically and in the context of modern Taiwan. Niehoff's study helps to illustrate how the dramatic expansion of industrial capitalism in Taiwan has influenced the economic activities of individuals and social groups in rural areas.

Industry

594 **Networks of Taiwanese big business: a preliminary analysis.**
Ichiro Numazaki. *Modern China*, vol. 12, no. 4 (1986), p. 487-534.
The author gives evidence for the existence of an intensive network of corporate links among members of the Taiwanese business élite. The Taiwanese élite in big business form a distinct and dominant class whose members transcend their immediate family concerns to form a tightly organized corporate community above the mass of small-scale enterprises.

595 **Direct foreign investment and Taiwan's TV industry.**
Chi Schive, Ryh-song Yeh. *Economic Essays* (Taipei), vol. 9, no. 2 (1980), p. 261-91.
Examines the rapid growth of the television industry during the 1960s and 1970s, considering the differences between the technology of foreign companies and that of national firms and the changes in their performance over time. The study concludes that Taiwan's TV industry demonstrates how direct foreign investment can contribute to a developing country's industrialization.

596 **Original accumulation, equality, and late industrialization: the case of socialist China and capitalist Taiwan.**
Mark Selden, Chih-ming Ka. In: *The political economy of Chinese socialism*. Mark Selden. Armonk, New York: M. E. Sharpe, 1988, p. 101-28.
Although the authors focus principally on the socialist development in the PRC, they devote one chapter to a comparative study between mainland China and Taiwan. They attempt to identity whether there are any substantial differences between capitalist and socialist industrialization in late-developing countries. Socialist China (1953-57) and capitalist Taiwan (1953-60) are examined in terms of the rôle of land reform and the use of such extractive measures and control mechanisms as taxation and compulsory purchase, market controls, and wage, price and income policies. This study gives insight into the possibilities and costs associated with socialist and capitalist industrialization. A similar essay written by the authors appeared earlier in *World Development*, vol. 14 (1986), p. 1293-310.

597 **Location orientation of foreign owned industry in Taiwan.**
Roger Mark Selya. *Asian Profile*, vol. 11, no. 6 (1983), p. 535-52.
Taiwan attracted a lot of foreign investors between 1952 and 1980. Selya reviews the mechanisms and arguments used by the Nationalist government to foster foreign investment, examines the patterns of industrial investments, and considers the location orientations of the investments compared to the location of industry in Taiwan.

598 **Small-scale industry in Yingge, Taiwan.**
Richard Stites. *Modern China*, vol. 8, no. 2 (1982), p. 247-79.
Examines one factor in Taiwan's economic development that has often been overlooked – small-scale industries. 'Small-scale' is used to describe factories requiring relatively little capital and employing 100 or fewer workers.

Family structure and industrialization in Taiwan.
See item no. 205.

160

Entrepreneurs, multinationals, and the State.
See item no. 514.

Contending forces in Taiwan's economic policy making: the case of Hua Tung Heavy Trucks.
See item no. 536.

Intersectoral capital flows in the economic development of Taiwan, 1895-1960.
See item no. 611.

Industrial employment expansion under alternative trade strategies: case of India and Taiwan, 1950-1970.
See item no. 630.

Women and industry.
See item no. 633.

Chinese working-class lives: getting by in Taiwan.
See item no. 637.

Agriculture and Rural Development

599 **Share tenancy and fixed rent in Taiwan.**
Richard E. Barnett. *Economic Development and Cultural Change*,
vol. 32, no. 2 (1984), p. 413-22.
By examining the land reform programme in Taiwan, Barnett debates the issue of
whether or not share contracts in agriculture (sharecropping) lead to the inefficient
allocation of resources.

600 **The myth of two Chinas: an agricultural perspective.**
Peter H. Calkins. *Asian Profile*, vol. 9, no. 3 (1981), p. 203-11.
Demonstrates how, from the agricultural perspective, both China and Taiwan manage
the production and trade of rice and other staple grains through cooperative
organizations in order to achieve the strategic goal of self-sufficiency in food supply.
Moreover, both have been successful in accomplishing rapid economic development.
Therefore, the author argues, the statement that there are two Chinas with different
economic systems and political ethos is primarily a myth. Although he may be right in
saying that if the Communists had gained control of Taiwan, they would surely have
valued the infrastructure put in place by the Japanese, one still questions the likelihood
of economic success under the Communist system in Taiwan.

601 **Development of irrigation infrastructures and management in Taiwan,
1900-1940.**
Han-yu Chang. *Economic Essays* (National Taiwan University,
Taipei), vol. 9, no. 1 (1980),p. 133-57.
Describes how the framework of the modern irrigation system was introduced, how the
innovations of irrigation management were developed, and what effects irrigation and
flood control had on rice farming in pre-war Taiwan. The historical analysis in this
study may have some applications for the present and future development of irrigation
systems in other Asian countries.

602   **Land reform in Taiwan.**
Cheng Chen.   Taipei: China Publishing, 1961. 332p.
The author was appointed Governor of Taiwan Province in 1949, when the Nationalist government decided to safeguard the island as a base for national recovery. Chen was the major figure in charge of the land reform programmes undertaken in order to maintain social stability and achieve economic progress. In this book, Chen explains the rent reduction programmes and the land-to-the-tiller policy, and then compares Taiwan's land reform with the Communist land reform programmes. Relevant laws and regulations comprise half of the book (p. 131-302). This volume is a must for readers who are interested in land reforms in Taiwan or in developing countries in general.

603   **Rural poverty and the structure of farm household income in developing countries: evidence from Taiwan.**
Dennis L. Chinn.   *Economic Development and Cultural Change,*
vol. 27, no. 2 (1979), p. 283-301.
Presents a detailed analysis of changes in the structure of net farm income during the 1960s and 1970s in Taiwan. The author also discusses the contribution of non-farm income sources both to rising income levels and to declining inequality in Taiwan's rural area.

604   **A stochastic control approach to buffer stock management in the Taiwan rice market.**
Bruce L. Dixon, Wu-hsiung Chen.   *Journal of Development Economics,* vol. 10, no. 2 (1982), p. 187-207.
The authors consider government strategies to control the rice market in Taiwan. The policy of the Taiwanese government is to set targets for the farm price of rice. In 1976 an unusually large rice crop and a government pledge to support rice prices at the farm level resulted in an unacceptably high cost to the government. Dixon and Chen develop a new approach to efficient stock management which sets target trajectories for retail and farm prices over forty-eight months and then determines the optimal government stock operations.

605   **Socioeconomic life in rural Taiwan: twenty years of development and change.**
Bernard Gallin, Rita S. Gallin.   *Modern China,* vol. 8, no. 2 (1982),
p. 205-46.
Discusses the rural economic transformation in Taiwan and explores the continuities and discontinuities in social and community organization that accompany these changes.

606   **Effects of economic change on two Taiwanese villages.**
Stevan Harrell.   *Modern China,* vol. 7, no. 1 (1981), p. 31-54.
Considers what the economic growth pattern has meant for people in two very different rural settings: places which are part of the same local economic system but which have reacted in quite different ways to the economic changes. These two villages are Ploughshare, in the industrial core, and Wood, in the non-industrial periphery. Both are located in the southern Taipei basin.

Agriculture and Rural Development

607 **Agricultural development of Taiwan, 1903-60.**
Yhi-min Ho.   Nashville, Tennessee: Vanderbilt University Press,
1966. 172p. bibliog.
This econometric study measures the increase in farm output and the extent to which
this increase should be attributed to land, labour, capital, and technology. The findings
show that a little over one-third of farm output growth can be attributed to technology
and new knowledge. The implication is that technology holds great promise for
transforming traditional agriculture. However, the author fails to explore extensively
how technology should be introduced, diffused, and assimilated by the peasantry and
does not consider adequately the rôle of institutional reforms in agricultural
development.

608 **Government agricultural strategies in Taiwan and South Korea: a
macrosociological assessment.**
Hsin-huang Michael Hsiao.   Taipei: Institute of Ethnology, Academia
Sinica, 1981. 319p. bibliog. (Institute of Ethnology, Monograph Series
B, no. 9).
Shows that in both South Korea and Taiwan there has been a pro-industrial and anti-
agricultural tilt to economic development. Hsiao argues that successful rural
development programmes in Taiwan were due to the government's fear of the
revolutionary potential of the Taiwanese peasantry and a weak rural gentry. He adopts
several theoretical perspectives employed within the social sciences, for example, the
dependency/world-systems approach, as guides to his comparative analysis.

609 **Agricultural degradation: changing community systems in rural Taiwan.**
Shu-min Huang.   Washington, DC: University Press of America,
1981. 236p.
Studies the effects of industrialization and economic development on agriculture and
rural life in San-lin, a village in central Taiwan, and, by extension, in Taiwan as a
whole. Huang argues that village life and cohesion have been affected by ill-advised
economic development programmes. For instance, the younger generation is now more
oriented towards the towns, no longer forms close village friendships, and feels no
strong ties to the village. Huang paints a negative picture of Taiwan's economy and
adopts a nostalgic tone toward the traditional way of life. This book is worth reading
because of its different perspective on Taiwan's economic development.

610 **Agricultural growth against a land-resource constraint: Japan, Taiwan,
Korea, and the Philippines.**
Masao Kikuchi, Yujiro Hayami.   In: *Japan and the developing
countries*. Edited by Kazushi Ohkawa, Gustav Ranis, Larry Meissner.
New York: Basil Blackwell, 1985, p. 67-90.
Analyses how Japan, Taiwan, Korea, and the Philippines have responded to
population pressure on arable land. For these four countries, improvements in
irrigation systems have been the key to the development and diffusion of a land-saving
technology, characterized by seed development and increased use of fertilizers, which
has allowed agricultural productivity to increase markedly. The authors offer the
hypothesis that population pressure, while causing deterioration in the land-labour
ratio, has induced increases in land productivity.

611 **Intersectoral capital flows in the economic development of Taiwan, 1895-1960.**
Teng-hui Lee. Ithaca, New York: Cornell University Press, 1971. 197p.

In this primarily empirical study, Lee identifies the commodity and financial flows between agricultural and non-agricultural sectors in Taiwan. Although his survey is based on small samples, usually selected in a non-random manner, and thus considered questionable, Lee's attempt to measure Taiwan's intersectoral capital flows during the period 1895-1960 is a welcome addition to our understanding of the potential contribution of agriculture to economic development.

612 **Farm information for modernizing agriculture: the Taiwan system.**
Herbert F. Lionberger, H. C. Chang. New York: Praeger, 1970. 454p.

This valuable reference source describes how the government in Taiwan has created a system for distributing information related to improved farming techniques and examines how agricultural advisers and farmers perceive their rôles within the system. This study shows that farmers are willing to accept innovations in farming and agricultural advisers are very optimistic about advances in traditional agriculture. The system apparently operates satisfactorily.

613 **The effect of off-farm employment on farm incomes and production: Taiwan contrasted with southern Africa.**
A. R. C. Low. *Economic Development and Cultural Change*, vol. 29, no. 4 (1981), p. 741-47.

Although scholars argue that off-farm earnings in Taiwan provide an important complement to rural income, Low cautions that the reduction of rural poverty through increasing off-farm employment opportunities in southern Africa may involve additional costs not evident in the Taiwanese experience.

614 **Agrarian policy in the Republic of China and the People's Republic of China: the first decade.**
Noel R. Miner. *The Rocky Mountain Social Science Journal*, vol. 11, no. 2 (1974), p. 45-53.

Examines agrarian policies employed by the Chinese Communist Party in mainland China and by the Nationalist Party in Taiwan. Miner argues that both the Communist and the Nationalist ruling élites have failed to satisfy the agrarian needs in their societies.

615 **Economic growth and the rise of civil society: agriculture in Taiwan and South Korea.**
Mick Moore. In: *Developmental states in East Asia*. Edited by Gordon White. New York: St. Martin's Press, 1988, p. 113-52.

Focuses on the contributions, both positive and negative, of state regulation for agricultural growth by examining the Taiwanese and South Korean experiences.

Agriculture and Rural Development

616 **Rural institutions and their influence upon agricultural development in modern China and Taiwan.**
Ramon H. Myers. *Journal of the Institute of Chinese Studies of the Chinese University of Hong Kong*, vol. 2, no. 2 (1969), p. 349-70.

Discusses land inheritance, rural credit, and land tenure in both mainland China and Taiwan. The author concludes with an evaluation of the ways in which rural institutions relate to agricultural development in both regions.

617 **Doing the work of two generations: the impact of out-migration on the elderly in rural Taiwan.**
Ruth Ann Sando. *Journal of Cross-Cultural Gerontology*, vol. 1, no. 2 (1986), p. 163-75.

The author points out that young people dominate the pattern of rural-to-urban migration in Taiwan. Yet, it is older cohorts who direct 'outmigration'. They provide the necessary education and training for their children from the income generated by their farm work, and they also subsidize the new migrants. The outmigration leads to the depopulation of many villages, and older villagers are left to absorb the economic consequences of this depopulation.

618 **Food for the cities of Taiwan.**
Roger Mark Selya. *China Geographer*, no. 11 (1981), p. 73-87.

Where does the food for the cities of Taiwan come from? Are there limits to food procurement for the cities? These are the main questions pursued by Selya in this essay.

619 **Agricultural development on Taiwan since World War II.**
T. H. Shen. Ithaca, New York: Comstock, 1964. 399p.

One effective way to achieve remarkable increases in agricultural production is by the use of modern agricultural technology. Shen describes what has been done in Taiwan to make the most of its natural resources through all kinds of scientific production practices. He also shows that agricultural improvement was and is a sound base for the economic growth in Taiwan because farm products provide the major share of exports to help finance industrial development. This excellent study is well written and contains valuable statistical information and data.

620 **Taiwan's family farm during transitional economic growth.**
T. H. Shen. Ithaca, New York: New York State College of Agriculture and Life Science, Cornell University, 1976. 14p.

In historical perspective, the period 1950-75 was a transitional stage in Taiwan's economic growth. During this period, instead of maintaining an isolated self-sufficiency, the agricultural sector interacted with the industrial sector and became an integral part of the national economy. The Joint Commission on Rural Reconstruction acted as a catalyst in promoting both technological and organizational development within Taiwan's modernization effort. This paper describes how the Commission worked with the Taiwan Provincial Government in transforming Taiwan's family farm structure, management and mechanization.

621 **The functions and development of the farmers' associations in the Republic of China.**
Chyuan-jeng Shiau. *Journal of Social Science* (Taipei), vol. 34 (1986), p. 465-87.
Farmers' associations are among the most important organizations in Taiwan. Their operation and business are related to the livelihood of many inhabitants of rural areas. The author reviews the development of farmers' associations since 1949. The findings indicate that their function was shaped and changed by the relationships and interactions among several related groups, including the Taiwanese government, the US aid mission, the landlords, and the small farmers.

622 **External incorporation and internal reform.**
Denis Fred Simon. In: *Contending approaches to the political economy of Taiwan.* Edited by Edwin A. Winckler, Susan Greenhalgh. Armonk, New York: M. E. Sharpe, 1988, p. 138-50.
Deals with negotiations between the US and the Taiwanese Nationalist government over the implementation of land reform in the early 1950s. The main thesis is that the incorporation of Taiwan into the American defence network required the endowment of the ROC with 'free world' attributes, particularly a private sector with a broad distribution of economic assets and economic opportunities. The issues involved in the negotiation process included the rôle of the private versus the public sector and the degree of concentration of industrial capital in Taiwan.

623 **Rural local governance and agricultural development in Taiwan.**
Benedict Stavis. Ithaca, New York: Rural Development Committee, Center for International Studies, Cornell University, 1974. 122p.
This book is part of a broader project undertaken by Cornell University which seeks to understand how and under what circumstances rural political and administrative institutions influence the patterns of agricultural and rural development. Because of Taiwan's sustained growth in agricultural productivity, it serves as a model for other developing countries in their search for economic and institutional policies for development. This study is also useful to readers trying to understand the problems of Asian agricultural development.

624 **Agricultural trade in the economic development in Taiwan.**
Anthony M. Tang, Kuo-shu Liang. In: *Trade, agriculture and development.* Edited by George S. Tolley, Peter A. Zadrozny. Cambridge, Massachusetts: Ballinger, 1975, p. 115-46.
The authors consider the contribution of agricultural exports to Taiwan's successful development: gains in agricultural productivity were achieved in order to increase exports of agricultural staples in accordance with import requirements for industrialization. It was agriculture, as well as US economic aid, that financed industrialization in the early stage of Taiwan's post-war economic development. By the late 1960s, however, there was a transformation in economic structure and a change in the products designed for export. Taiwan's trade patterns changed, as manufactured exports displaced traditional exports, and the surplus in agricultural exports turned into a deficit.

625 **Taiwan: rural society.**
Stuart E. Thompson. *China Quarterly*, no. 99 (1984), p. 553-68.
Illustrates how Taiwan's economic miracle, distinguished by its rural industrialization, has resulted both in an improvement in average living standards and in a greater equalization of incomes.

626 **Farm plot dispersal, Lu-liao village, Taiwan, 1967.**
Paul Vandermeer. Taipei: Chinese Materials Center, 1982. 295p.
Through an examination of Lu-liao village, a wet-rice-growing farm community of around 130 households in southern Changhua county, Vandermeer presents an excellent case study of farm plot dispersal, including its causes and effects. Because of its clearly stated arguments and conclusions, as well as its tables, figures, and maps, this is an essential text for the study of Taiwan.

627 **Rice farming in Taiwan, three village studies.**
Sung-hsing Wang, Raymond Apthorpe. Taipei: Institute of Ethnology, Academia Sinica, 1974. 247p.
Provides remarkable material about peasant life in Taiwan. The authors examine the subtle interaction between kinship and other social systems, income distribution, and productivity. They discuss inheritance practices, informal rural credit, and labour hiring systems. This book is particularly valuable because it includes information about the farmers' associations which is seldom available in other published materials.

628 **Transforming agriculture in Taiwan: the experience of the Joint Commission on Rural Reconstruction.**
Joseph A. Yager. Ithaca, New York: Cornell University Press, 1988. 301p.
It is well known that the Sino-American Joint Commission on Rural Reconstruction, usually called the JCRR, played a crucial rôle in Taiwan's agricultural development from 1948 to 1979. First using US aid funds and later relying on money provided by the Chinese government, the JCRR helped to revive Taiwan's agriculture in the post-war period, stimulating a rapid increase in agricultural production that paved the way for later successful industrialization. This is the first comprehensive description of the JCRR's experience in Taiwan. It explores the reasons for the JCRR's success and provides lessons for economic growth in other developing countries. Each chapter includes a brief summary at the end. No selected bibliography for additional reading and research is provided, although footnotes on every page offer some documentation.

629 **Socioeconomic results of land reform in Taiwan.**
Martin M. C. Yang. Honolulu, Hawaii: East-West Center Press, 1970. 576p.
Based mostly upon questionnaires addressed to more than 3,000 people, Yang's book analyses the effects of land reform beyond those of reduction of farm rental rates, the transfer of land ownership from landlord to tenant-cultivator, and the increase in the number of owner-farmers. His findings show that a majority of farmers feel economically better off since the land reform. This book should be of great interest to students of rural sociology or agricultural economics.

Labour and
Employment

630 **Industrial employment expansion under alternative trade strategies: case of India and Taiwan, 1950-1970.**
Ranadev Banerji, James Riedel. *Journal of Development Economics*, vol. 7, no. 4 (1980), p. 567-77.
Provides quantitative estimates of the effects of alternative trade strategies on industrial employment expansion. In Taiwan, the industrial structure shifted towards labour-intensive sectors, while, in India, it moved toward capital-intensive industries. This difference explains in part the faster rate of employment expansion in Taiwan.

631 **American and Chinese managers in U.S. companies in Taiwan: a comparison.**
Samuel K. C. Chang. *California Management Review*, vol. 27, no. 4 (1985), p. 144-56.
This article is based on a survey of 200 top-level American and Chinese managers of US-owned companies and joint ventures in Taiwan regarding their attitudes towards their work. Where there are strong differences in basic value systems, as with American 'issue-orientation' or 'individual-orientation' versus Chinese 'person-orientation' or 'family-orientation', cross-cultural or inter-racial interaction and understanding among management personnel becomes important for harmony and efficiency in the multinational corporations and joint ventures that employ both Chinese and American managers.

632 **Managerial attitudes and leadership power in United States companies in Taiwan, ROC.**
Samuel K. C. Chang. *International Journal of Comparative Sociology*, vol. 28, nos. 1-2 (1987), p. 14-29.
Studies differences in managerial attitudes between top-level Chinese and American managers of US-related companies in Taiwan. About two hundred Chinese and American executives were surveyed. The findings show that Chinese and American managers do not show significant differences in general job attitudes. However, Chinese managers have a greater interest in company paternalism, which is probably attributable to cultural differences.

633 **Women and industry in Taiwan.**
Norma Diamond. *Modern China*, vol. 5, no. 3 (1979), p. 317-40.
Examines the experience of one segment of the working class, adolescent female factory workers, during the process of Taiwan's industrial growth. The article examines the effect of outside employment on women's status, autonomy, and control over their present and future lives.

634 **The labour force, wages and living standards.**
Walter Galenson. In: *Economic growth and structural change in Taiwan*. Edited by Walter Galenson. Ithaca, New York: Cornell University Press, 1979, p. 384-447.
According to Galenson's observations, working men and women in Taiwan do not earn an income sufficient to buy what would be considered minimum necessities in the US. In comparison with workers in other developing countries, however, they have made great progress in improving their living standards. The experience of Taiwan confirms the view that creation of a sufficient volume of economically productive employment is a key factor in the attainment of adequate levels of welfare for all groups in society.

635 **The entry of Chinese women into the rural labour force: a case study from Taiwan.**
Rita S. Gallin. *Signs*, vol. 9, no. 3 (1984), p. 383-98.
Examines women from a Taiwanese village that has changed over the past twenty years from an economic system based almost entirely on agriculture to one founded predominantly on non-farm employment. Gallin finds, however, that women's participation in work outside the home has not been accompanied by a significant redefinition of their status in the society.

636 **Women, wages, and discrimination: some evidence from Taiwan.**
Kenneth Gannicott. *Economic Development and Cultural Change*, vol. 34, no. 4 (1986), p. 721-30.
Presents empirical results and notes to show that discrimination seems to be a feature of the labour market in Taiwan. Gannicott also suggests that the government needs to look carefully at legislation to limit wage discrimination as a means of encouraging female participation in highly-skilled jobs.

637 **Chinese working-class lives: getting by in Taiwan.**
Hill Gates.   Ithaca, New York: Cornell University Press, 1987. 256p.
bibliog.

By studying the life stories of nine, mainly elderly, working-class people in present day Taiwan, Gates offers the readers a comprehensive glimpse of Taiwanese society. First, Gates introduces his field-work methods and discusses the history and economic development of Taiwan. The life histories are then grouped in chapters that include discussions of the individual's financial position, family, age, sex, folk religion, and education. This life history method is valuable because the reader learns about the structure of society from the bottom up, as it is seen and experienced by its participants.

638 **Changes in intersectoral terms of trade and their effects on labour transfer.**
Susumu Hondai.   In: *Japan and the developing countries*. Edited by Kazushi Ohkawa, Gustav Ranis, Larry Meissner. New York: Basil Blackwell, 1985, p. 249-65.

Modern economic growth involves the flow of capital and labour between the agricultural and non-agricultural sectors. Drawing on the economic experiences of Japan and Taiwan, Hondai analyses how terms of trade between the two sectors affect that flow.

639 **Measurement of potential labour reserve in Taiwan.**
Dave Y. C. Hsu.   *Economic Development and Cultural Change*, vol. 30, no. 4 (1982), p. 843-61.

Shows that the human-resource base that has enabled Taiwan to develop rapidly in the past has not yet been depleted. The existence of unutilized labour reserves along with shortages of certain types of labour needed by Taiwanese industries in recent years reflects the malfunctioning of the labour market.

640 **Leadership and values: the organization of large scale Taiwanese enterprises.**
Robert H. Silin.   Cambridge, Massachusetts: East Asian Research Center University, 1976. 226p. (Harvard East Asian Monographs, no. 62).

Offers an overview of the management of large enterprises in Taiwan and examines the relationship between government and industry. The author also reviews how traditional Chinese values and attitudes toward interpersonal relations affect management practices in these enterprises. This interesting and stimulating study may inspire future research on the ways in which Taiwanese enterprises have changed in the 1980s as both the economy and business have become more complex.

641   **Structural change and intergenerational occupational mobility.**
Charles T. Stewart, Jr.   *Journal of Developing Areas*, vol. 2, no. 2
(1987), p. 141-57.
Countries experiencing rapid structural change must also achieve a rapid increase in
their supply of professional and technical workers. Yet because this increase is
concentrated on younger age groups, who remain employed for decades, occupational
opportunities for later generations may be more limited. Drawing on official data,
the author examines occupational opportunity in Japan, Taiwan and South Korea. The
study shows that occupational opportunity has fallen dramatically in Taiwan.

**Economic and political control of women workers in multinational electronics
factories in Taiwan: martial law coercion and world market uncertainty.**
See item no. 228.

Factory women in Taiwan.
See item no. 236.

Female employment and reproductive behavior in Taiwan, 1980.
See item no. 255.

The politics of national development and education in Taiwan.
See item no. 279.

**There are no strikes in Taiwan: an analysis of labor law in the Republic of
China on Taiwan.**
See item no. 312.

**The Taiwan success story: rapid growth with improved distribution in the
Republic of China, 1952-1979.**
See item no. 525.

Transport

642 **Monthly Statistical Report on Taiwan Transportation.**
Department of Communications.   Nan-tou, Taiwan: Department of
Communications, Taiwan Provincial Government, Republic of China.
monthly.

Gives a comprehensive account of the present status of transportation in Taiwan
Province, excluding the city of Taipei. Data are divided into five chapters for: railway,
highway, harbour, shipping business, and tourism. For easy comparison the metric
system is adopted. In keeping with international practice, the report still employs the
British system of tonnage for vessel measurement.

643 **Applications of computerization to Taiwan transportation system.**
Ching-chien Kiang.   In: *Proceedings of IMC's 1985 Asia-Pacific
regional information and micrographic management congress*. Taipei,
1985, p. 693-714.

Kiang suggests that the administrative management and business operation of Taiwan's
transportation system should be computerized. The author discusses the general
applicability of computer technology for several transportation agencies, for example,
the Taiwan Highway Bureau and the Keelung Harbor Bureau.

644 **Monthly Statistics of Transportation and Communications, Republic of
China.**
Ministry of Communications.   Taipei: Ministry of Communications.
monthly.

Contains information about railway activities, highway systems, postal services,
telecommunications, waterway transportation, civil aviation, harbour activities,
tourism, and meteorology. These topics are presented in more than fifty tables with
brief explanations in both Chinese and English.

The Environment

645　A personal look at Taiwan's air pollution problems.
Thomas J. Bierma.　*Illinois Geographical Society Bulletin*, vol. 27,
no. 2 (1985), p. 18-27.
In the summer of 1984 the author had an opportunity to work with the Air Pollution
Control Division of Taiwan's Bureau of Environmental Protection. This essay
describes his observations and reflections concerning the pollution problem in Taiwan.
Maps showing the pollution situation are included.

646　Protecting the Republic of China from oil pollution in the sea:
accounting for damages from oil spills.
Joseph W. Dellapenna, Ar-young Wang.　*Texas International Law
Journal*, vol. 19 (1984), p. 115-38.
Oil pollution is of particular concern to Taiwan, which has a long and exposed
coastline. One major oil spill occurred in the waters off Taiwan when the oil tanker
Borag ran aground near Keelung. In retelling this incident, the authors consider the
possibilities for preventing such spills under existing or proposed international
regulations and assess the feasibility of recovering damages.

647　The institutional problems of land-use and environmental planning in
Taiwan.
Chien Han.　*Urban Law and Policy*, vol. 8, no. 5 (1987), p. 455-63.
Population growth along with economic development in Taiwan have created
tremendous pressures on land and other related natural resources. The author
examines the institutional mechanisms for dealing with environmental problems in
Taiwan. Han notes that governmental fragmentation is a major problem which must be
resolved if real progress in environmental protection is to be achieved.

648 **Water and air pollution in Taiwan.**
Roger Mark Selya. *Journal of Developing Areas*, vol. 9, no. 2 (1975), p. 177-202.

Points out that the Taiwanese government's emphasis on economic modernization has resulted in neglect of the necessity for environmental protection. Water contamination and air pollution are quite obvious in Taiwan. Funds are limited for anti-pollution projects and remedial costs are extremely high. Citizens are reluctant to agitate for pollution control, either through indifference or from reliance on governmental initiatives.

649 **Industrial pollution and the regional variations of life expectancy at birth in Taiwan.**
Tin-yu Ting, Susyan Jou. *Sociological Inquiry*, vol. 58, no. 1 (1988), p. 87-100.

Examines variables influencing the regional variations of life expectancy at birth in Taiwan. After controlling other independent variables, findings show a negative and significant relationship between the total number of factories in the area and the level of life expectancy at birth.

Science and Technology

650 **ROC-US cooperative relations in the development of science and technology.**
Ho-ching Lee Liu. *Issues and Studies*, vol. 24, no. 11 (1988), p. 117-42.
Reviews past developments and the current state of cooperative relations between Taiwan and the US in the fields of science and technology. Liu places considerable emphasis on the strategic direction of future efforts and the pace of such programmes.

651 **Taiwan, technology transfer, and transnationalism: the political management of dependency.**
Denis Fred Simon. PhD thesis, University of California, Berkeley, California, 1980. 632p. (Available from University Microfilms, Ann Arbor, Michigan, order no. 8113191).
Advocates of the 'dependency' approach contend that the world capitalist system has benefitted the development of industrialized countries but, at the same time, has generated underdevelopment within the Third World countries. Taiwan's experience suggests that a reassessment of the dependency theory is necessary. While in many important ways Taiwan does remain technologically dependent on external sources, for example, transnational corporations from the US, it has been able to secure desired resources without seriously distorting social, economic, and political development patterns. Through his examination of Taiwan's development experience, Simon evaluates the rôle of the State in the development process and examines Taiwan's strategy of using the island's links with transnational corporations to serve both political and economic goals. Finally, Simon contends, the discussion of technology transfer in Taiwan suggests that continued interaction with transnational corporations has permitted Taiwan to upgrade the technical capacity of its economy.

652 **Technology transfer and national autonomy.**
Denis Fred Simon.   In: *Contending approaches to the political economy of Taiwan*. Edited by Edwin A. Winckler, Susan Greenhalgh. Armonk, New York: M. E. Sharpe, 1988, p. 206-23.

Explores the rôle of internal and external factors in facilitating or impeding the progress of technology in Taiwan. This study shows the extent of Taiwan's success in securing and absorbing advanced technology. Both external and indigenous factors that have affected Taiwan's overall technological development are investigated. Finally, the issue of Taiwan's upward mobility in the international division of labour is examined in order to deduce what concrete policy steps a state can take to improve its technological position in the world economy.

Statistics

653 **Financial Statistics, Taiwan District, the Republic of China.**
Central Bank of China. Taipei: The Bank. monthly.
The *International Financial Statistics* (IFS) published by the Interational Monetary Fund (IMF) contained data for Taiwan until 1980. When this service ceased, the Central Bank of China, in response to repeated requests, decided to take upon itself the responsibility for publishing this monthly report. The Central Bank uses the IMF format and methodology to facilitate comparison with corresponding figures for other countries, as published in the IFS. The reports provide up-to-date information on financial conditions in Taiwan and analyse changes in money supply, interest rates, and foreign exchange rates.

654 **Taiwan Statistical Data Book.**
Council for Economic Planning and Development. Taipei: The Council, Republic of China. annual.
This handy reference book includes a range of statistical data compiled from materials collected from various agencies covering both the municipalities of Taipei and Kaohsiung and Taiwan province. Seventeen chapters cover: area and population, national income, science and technology, money and banking, public finance, US aid, foreign investment, and international statistics. The international statistics are used to draw comparisons between Taiwan and other countries.

655 **Statistical Yearbook of Education, Taiwan Province, Republic of China.**
Department of Education.   Nan-tou, Taiwan: The Department, Taiwan Provincial Government, Republic of China. annual.
Covers all aspects of the education system, including higher education, secondary education, elementary education, special education, practical skill training, educational expenditures, and organization. Data are presented primarily by the school year. The term 'school year' denotes a period which begins in August of the current year and ends in July of the following year. A chart outlining the present day school system is printed for reference.

656 **Health Statistics.**
Department of Health. Taipei; Kaohsiung, Taiwan: Department of
Health, Executive Yuan, Taiwan Provincial Health Department, Taipei
City Health Department, & Kaohsiung City Health Department. 2 vols.
annual.

Volume one is entitled 'General health statistics'. It contains seven sections covering:
health organization and administration, health indices, medical affairs, public health,
communicable disease control, drug control and food sanitation, and environmental
sanitation. Volume two, 'Vital statistics', contains analyses of population, causes of
death, and neonatal and infant mortality. Although the figures presented are for the
current year, other annual figures are also given for comparison.

657 **Social base maps of Taipei City.**
Department of Sociology, National Taiwan University. Taipei: The
Department, 1965. 98p.

Consists of forty-nine maps which are classified into six groups: general ecological
features; population; industry and commerce; public health; educational and cultural
institutions and civic organizations; and poor households, crimes, and traffic accidents.
Accompanying each map is a brief explanation or statistical table which indicates the
facts incorporated in the map.

658 **Industrial Production Statistics Monthly, Taiwan Area, the Republic of
China.**
Department of Statistics, Ministry of Economic Affairs. Taipei: The
Department. monthly.

This monthly began in 1953 when a mining and industrial data reporting system was
established. The series of industrial production indexes is revised once every five years
in order to keep the indexes representative of rapid changes of Taiwan's industry. They
are designed to measure the ongoing trends of monthly industrial production, sales,
and inventory, as well as economic achievements. These statistics can provide a handy
reference work for both scholars and businesspeople in reviewing Taiwan's industrial
production and trade activities.

659 **Monthly Statistics of Exports and Imports, Taiwan Area, the Republic
of China.**
Department of Statistics, Ministry of Finance. Taipei: The
Department. monthly.

Covers only goods exported to and imported from foreign countries. Exports are not
considered exported until the carrying vessel (or aircraft) leaves the port. Imports are
recorded only upon completion of all customs formalities. All statistics are supplied by
the Inspectorate-General of Customs, which also issues *Monthly Statistics of Imports*
and *Monthly Statistics of Exports*.

660 **Commodity-price Statistics Monthly in Taiwan area of the Republic of China.**
Directorate-General of Budget, Accounting, and Statistics, Executive Yuan. Taipei: The Directorate-General. monthly.
Contains indexes of the wholesale price, consumer price, urban consumer price, import price, and export price for commodities. In addition to tables and figures presented for reference, brief analyses on price fluctuations are offered for the edification of the users.

661 **Monthly Bulletin of Earnings and Productivity Statistics, Taiwan Area, Republic of China.**
Directorate-General of Budget, Accounting, and Statistics, Executive Yuan. Taipei: The Directorate-General. monthly.
Based on sample surveys, the statistics cover eight major areas of industry: mining and quarrying; manufacturing; construction; commerce; transport, storage and communication; financing, insurance and real estate; and community, social and personal services. Figures for employees' earnings, working hours, turnover rate, and productivity are presented.

662 **Monthly Bulletin of Manpower Statistics, Taiwan Area, Republic of China.**
Directorate-General of Budget, Accounting, and Statistics, Executive Yuan. Taipei: The Directorate-General. monthly.
Provides basic information for economic planning, manpower development, employment service and labour policy by presenting the current conditions of manpower, employment, and unemployment on Taiwan. The information reported is based on a sample of 18,000 households surveyed every month.

663 **Monthly Bulletin of Statistics of the Republic of China.**
Directorate-General of Budget, Accounting and Statistics, Executive Yuan. Taipei: The Directorate-General. monthly.
The contents and format used in this monthly report match those of the *Monthly Bulletin of Statistics* of the United Nations and are intended to facilitate comparative studies of the data on Taiwan with those of other countries given in the UN publication. The reader is therefore requested to consult the UN *Monthly Bulletin* for the general note on international statistical terms and for definitions in current use.

664 **Monthly Key Social Indicators in Taiwan Area of the Republic of China.**
Directorate-General of Budget, Accounting and Statistics, Executive Yuan. Taipei: The Directorate-General. monthly.
Includes monthly information on population and the family, the consumer price index, employment, transportation, communication, air pollution, traffic and fire accidents, health insurance, and family income and expenditure. Data are presented in tables and figures.

665 **Monthly Statistics of the Republic of China.**
Directorate-General of Budget, Accounting and Statistics, Executive
Yuan. Taipei: The Directorate-General. monthly.

These reports are designed to give a comprehensive picture of present economic and
social conditions on Taiwan, and to provide the latest figures which incorporate all the
important statistical series published in the country. The data collected are submitted
by statistical units from government agencies and the sources of data are shown under
each table. Coverage includes a variety of topics, such as climate, population, land,
labour, industry, commerce, foreign trade, transportation, communications, money
and credit, and prices. The report presents its statistics in both Chinese and English.

666 **Quarterly National Economic Trends, Taiwan Area, the Republic of
China.**
Directorate-General of Budget, Accounting and Statistics, Executive
Yuan. Taipei: The Directorate-General. quarterly.

There are three parts to this report. Part one summarizes the fluctuations of gross
national product, economic growth, national income, money supply, prices, wages,
savings, investment, consumption, foreign trade, public finance, employment, and
unemployment. Part two contains important annual and quarterly national income
statistics, designed to facilitate time series analyses. In view of the close relationship
between domestic economic development and international economic fluctuations, key
economic indicators of major countries are shown in part three, serving to provide
comparisons with domestic economic activities.

667 **Standard classification of commodities of the Republic of China.**
Directorate-General of Budget, Accounting and Statistics, Executive
Yuan. Taipei: The Directorate-General, 1989. 4th ed. 1,820p.

The commodity standard classification described in this report is designed to match the
international commodity classification. It provides a unified base for use in preparation
of commodity statistics, collection of import duties, and management of trade.
Commodities are coded according to stages of the manufacturing process. As this
revision introduces a new classification system, a cross-reference table between old and
new systems is provided in order to facilitate conversion of data.

668 **Statistics on Overseas Chinese and Foreign Investment, Technical
Cooperation, Outward Investment, Outward Technical Cooperation, the
Republic of China.**
Investment Commission, Ministry of Economic Affairs. Taipei: The
Commission. monthly.

Measures the status of and significant changes in overseas Chinese and foreign
investment, technical cooperation, outward investment and outward technical
cooperation. Statistical data are based on cases approved by the Investment
Commission.

669 **Taiwan-Fukien Demographic Fact Book, Republic of China.**
Ministry of Interior.   Taipei: The Ministry. annual.

Contains population information such as age-sex composition, educational level, marital status, occupational classification, and figures for birth, death, divorce, marriage, and migration. All demographic data are based on the records of household registration and year-end household registration checks. Most of the statistical tables are tabulated for different levels of administrative unit. A companion volume is *Taiwan Demography Quarterly, Republic of China*, which is issued by the the same ministry.

670 **Urban and regional development statistics, Republic of China.**
Urban and Housing Development Department, Council for Economic Planning and Development, Executive Yuan.   Taipei: The Department, 1987. 178p.

Contains thirteen categories of urban and regional development statistics: planning and development; public health; transportation and communications; public utilities; housing; environmental quality; public order; education and culture; public finance; regional economy; family income expenditure and equipment; employment; and population.

Social statistics of Taiwan Province for forty years.
See item no. 217.

Statistics relating to maternal and child death in Taiwan.
See item no. 223.

Monthly Statistical Report on Taiwan Transportation.
See item no. 642.

Monthly Statistics of Transportation and Communications, Republic of China.
See item no. 644.

Language

671 **Borrowing and internal development in lexical change – a comparison of Taiwanese words and their Mandarin equivalents.**
Robert L. Cheng. *Journal of Chinese Linguistics*, vol. 15, no. 1 (1987), p. 105-31.
Cheng presents an etymological comparison of words found in Taiwanese texts and their Mandarin equivalents, and attempts to explain why content words in the two varieties of Chinese are more likely than function words to share etymons (or have a common ancestry).

672 **A comparison of Taiwanese, Taiwan Mandarin, and Peking Mandarin.**
Robert L. Cheng. *Language*, vol. 61, no. 2 (1985), p. 352-77.
Taiwan Mandarin is the variety of Chinese which is learned and used, primarily as a second language, by the people of Taiwan, eighty per cent of whom speak Taiwanese, a variety of Min-nan, as a native language. Taking Peking Mandarin as the designated standard, this paper identifies those Peking Mandarin features which are not common in Taiwan Mandarin, and those that are shared by Taiwan Mandarin.

673 **Group interest in treating words borrowed into Mandarin and Taiwanése.**
Robert L. Cheng. *Anthropological Linguistics*, vol. 27, no. 2 (1985), p. 177-89.
Discusses the borrowing of Western words into Mandarin and of Sino-Japanese words into Mandarin and Taiwanese. After examining structural factors that may explain the meagreness of English loan words in Chinese, the study explores how different groups of Chinese treat English and Sino-Japanese loan words.

674 **Language unification in Taiwan: present and future.**
Robert L. Cheng. In: *Language and society*. Edited by William
McCormack, Stephen A. Wurm. The Hague: Mouton, 1979, p. 541-78.
Mandarin Chinese has been promoted in Taiwan because of the two assumptions that
Taiwan is a province of China, and that Mandarin is the national language of China.
This paper examines the Nationalist language policy in Taiwan and shows that the
policy neglects proper planning for other vernaculars and, in practice, seeks language
unification through monolingualism rather than bilingualism. The thesis of this study is
that unification through bilingualism will achieve the government's goals of national
harmony, political unity, democracy, and social progress much better than will
unification through monolingualism.

675 **Sub-syllabic morphemes in Taiwanese.**
Robert L. Cheng. *Journal of Chinese Linguistics*, vol. 13, no. 1 (1985),
p. 12-43.
It is a well-known fact that Chinese morphemes are usually monosyllabic. As a variety
of Chinese, Taiwanese also shares this characteristic. Yet there are exceptions to this
general rule. Cheng investigates one of the exceptions: morphemes that are sub-
syllabic.

676 **A study of Taiwanese adjectives.**
Susie S. Cheng. Taipei: Student Book, 1981. 184p. bibliog.
This is a revised version of the author's master's degree thesis. It identifies and
presents the commonly used adjectives in Taiwanese and categorizes them in terms of
how they are formed. Lists of commonly used Taiwanese adjectives are appended.
Chinese summaries of every chapter are included.

677 **The concepts of topic and subject in first language acquisition of
Mandarin Chinese.**
Yu-chin Chien, Barbara Lust. *Child Development*, vol. 56, no. 6
(1985), p. 1359-75.
It has been argued in first language acquisition research that the concept of topic
provides a basic principle for general sentence organization and that topic may also
underlie the development of the grammatical concept of subject. The evidence
presented here suggests that Chinese children in Taiwan acquiring Mandarin Chinese
differentiate the concept of subject from that of topic, even though Chinese is regarded
as a 'topic-prominent' language. The implication is that it is necessary to attribute to
young children some sensitivity to formal grammatical concepts.

678 **Language choice and interethnic relations in Taiwan.**
David K. Jordan. *La Monda Lingvo-Problemo*, vol. 5, no. 13 (1973),
p. 35-44.
Indicates that the availability of the neutral language of Mandarin in Taiwan has served
to alleviate conflicts between the Hakkas and the Hoklos that had hitherto existed. The
implication is that the use of newly imposed national languages in other areas will act
as catalysts in reducing inter-ethnic tensions.

Language

679 **Taiwan's romanized script for Mandarin Chinese.**
David K. Jordan. *Language Problems and Language Planning*, vol. 9, no. 2 (1985), p. 134-36.
Linguists in Taiwan devised a new romanization system for spelling Mandarin Chinese in 1984. Jordan discusses the new system from an historical perspective and compares it with other existing systems.

680 **The language situation in Taiwan (the Republic of China).**
Robert B. Kaplan, J. Kwock-ping Tse. *The Incorporated Linguist*, vol. 22, no. 2 (1983), p. 82-85.
Reviews the language situation in the ROC, which has promoted the National Language Movement since the 1950s. The movement is intended to standardize and popularize the use of the national language of Mandarin. At present, most Taiwanese are bilingual in Mandarin and the local dialect.

681 **The influence of Southern Min on the Mandarin of Taiwan.**
Cornelius C. Kubler. *Anthropological Linguistics*, vol. 27, no. 2 (1985), p. 156-76.
The Southern Min people, who emigrated to Taiwan from Southern Fu-chien several centuries ago and speak the Southern Min dialect of Chinese, account for approximately seventy-one per cent of the population. Kubler shows that due primarily to language contact with Southern Min, the Mandarin commonly spoken in Taiwan differs considerably from that of Peking in syntax, phonology, and lexicon.

682 **Some differences between Taiwan Mandarin and 'textbook Mandarin'.**
Cornelius C. Kubler. *Journal of the Chinese Language Teachers Association*, vol. 14, no. 3 (1979), p. 27-39.
The Mandarin commonly spoken in Taiwan differs considerably from the language presented in most modern US Chinese language texts. Although students need not have perfect command of Taiwan Mandarin structures, Kubler encourages teachers to provide training in understanding both Taiwan Mandarin and other varieties of the language such as Hong Kong and Shanghai Mandarin.

683 **A study of code-switching in Taiwan.**
Yen-ling Lee. *Studies in the Linguistic Sciences*, vol. 11, no. 1 (1981), p. 121-36.
Investigates the situational selection of codes in Mandarin versus Southern Min (Taiwanese). Lee's findings show that the use of Mandarin is predominant in areas of friendship, employment, religion, education, and administration. The choice of Southern Min (Taiwanese) is correspondingly predominant in the domain of family and neighbourhood.

684 **Problems and trends of standardization of Mandarin Chinese in Taiwan.**
David Chen-ching Li. *Anthropological Linguistics*, vol. 27, no. 2
(1985), p. 122-40.

Li Points out that Taiwan is a linguistically enriched geographical location. The so-
called standard Mandarin Chinese has been accepted by the great majority of the
people in Taiwan regardless of their ancestral origins. Differences in lexical, phonetic,
and even syntactic features have been reconciled by speakers at all levels to avoid
jeopardizing their efficiency of communication.

685 **Standardization of Chinese in Taiwan.**
John Kwock-ping Tse. *International Journal of the Sociology of
Language*, vol. 59 (1986), p. 25-32.

Examines the history of the National Language Movement in Taiwan, which began in
1946 and was intended to promote Mandarin Chinese as the national language. The
essay also describes efforts to develop qualified teaching personnel, and outlines
contributions made by the Taiwan Provincial Committee for the Promotion and
Propagation of the National Language.

686 **Language planning and language use in Taiwan: social identity,
language accommodation, and language choice behavior.**
M. E. van den Berg. *International Journal of the Sociology
of Language*, vol. 59 (1986), p. 97-115.

Examines language use in Taiwan on the basis of data collected through observation of
naturalistic conversations in a variety of settings, especially the interchange between
customers and salespersons in a business setting. Mandarin Chinese and local
vernacular show different degrees of prevalence in different commercial situations.

687 **Attitudinal and sociocultural factors influencing language maintenance,
language shift, and language usage among the Chinese on Taiwan.**
Russell Lesile Young. PhD thesis, Claremont Graduate School and
San Diego State University, San Diego, California, 1987. 214p.
(Available from University Microfilms, Ann Arbor, Michigan, order
no. 8722382).

Analyses the sociolinguistic environment and the influence of selected sociocultural
and attitudinal factors on language maintenance, shift, and usage among the Chinese in
Taiwan. The study is based on the results of 823 surveys completed in 1986.

Literature

688 Modern poetry from Taiwan: three poets.
John J. S. Balcom. *Concerning Poetry*, vol. 17, no. 2 (1984),
p. 167-76.

Introduces three representative Taiwanese poets with brief decriptions of their lives
and translation of their poems. The poets are Lo Fu, Ya Hsien, and Bai Chiu.

689 Literary Formosa.
Lucy H. Chen. *China Quarterly*, no. 15 (1963), p. 75-85.

Presents the literary scene of various eras: the May Fourth Movement and the
Japanese colonial period (1895-1945); the period from the Japanese surrender (1945)
until 1955; and the age of realism and modernism (1956-63). Chen claims that most
established literati are too afraid or too lazy to expose and analyse their inner selves or
the changing society around them.

690 The isle full of noises: modern Chinese poetry from Taiwan.
Edited and translated by Dominic Cheung. New York: Columbia
University Press, 1987. 265p.

This anthology of translations from the works of thirty-two poets offers a glimpse of
current trends and movements, including the recent uproar over the nihilistic and
Western nature of some Taiwanese poetry, and the demand for a return to social
commitment and nationalism. Cheung includes examples of many strains of modernist
poetry: narrative and lyrical poems; highly abstract and deeply concrete poems; poems
for the realist and the existentialist; and poems for children.

691 **An anthology of contemporary Chinese literature.**
Edited and compiled by Pang-yuan Chi, John L. Deeney, Hsin Ho,
Hsi-chen Wu, Kwang-chung Wu.   Taipei: National Institute for
Compilation and Translation, 1975. 2 vols.

Contemporary Taiwanese literature has not received much serious attention in
America. This anthology represents a change in this trend and provides the reader with
the opportunity to look at the island from a literary perspective. Writers in this
anthology are introduced by a brief sketch of their lives and literary accomplishments.
The anthology is divided into two volumes for 'Poems and essays' and 'Short stories'.
In total fifty-four writers are included, with 190 poems, thirty-one pieces of prose, and
twenty-three short stories. These works form an adequate introduction to each of the
three genres represented (poetry, prose and short stories), outlining the general
development and issues of each genre. The translations are fluent and accurate.

692 **China China: contemporary poetry from Taiwan, Republic of China.**
Edited by Germain Droogenbroodt, Peter Stinson. Ninove, Belgium:
Point Books, 1986. 50p.

Following a brief introduction and a note on selection and translation, the anthology
presents thirty-seven poems by ten authors. Major poets, such as Lo Fu, as well as
younger-generation poets such as Huan-chang Lin are included. One criterion of
selection is the degree to which the original poem lends itself to English rendition. The
bibliographical information is somewhat dated. However, this volume adds to the still
slim collection of English translations of modern Chinese poetry from Taiwan.

693 **Chinese fiction from Taiwan: critical perspectives.**
Edited by Jeannette L. Faurot.   Bloomington, Indiana: Indiana
University Press, 1980. 272p. bibliog.

This volume contains several stimulating and lucid essays reflecting solid scholarship: a
historical survey of 'modernism' and 'romanticism' in Taiwan's literature, by Leo Ou-
fan Lee; a discussion of '*hsiang-tu*' literature (literature of the soil) and the
government's response to it, by Jing Wang; an analysis of Huang Chun-ming's stories
by Howard Goldblatt; a view of images of suffering, by Cyril Birch; an appraisal of
Chen Jo-hsi's sense of history, by Kai-yu Hsu; and a study of realism in Taiwanese
fiction, by Shi-kuo Chang. In addition, Joseph S. M. Lau, Lucien Miller, James C. T.
Shu, Ou-yang Tzu, C. H. Wang, and Robert Yi Yang contribute essays on the skills
and world perceptions of several Taiwanese writers. As a whole, these essays reveal,
for the first time in English, the considerable strength as well as the limitations of
Chinese writers in Taiwan.

694 **Born of the same roots: stories of modern Chinese women.**
Edited by Vivian Ling Hsu.   Bloomington, Indiana: Indiana
University Press, 1981. 308p.

One of the most emotionally-charged sociopolitical issues of twentieth-century China
concerns one half of its people, the women. This volume consists of fiction about
women. Several stories in this collection depict women's experiences in Taiwan's
society. For example, 'Born of the same roots', the title story, is by Yang Ching-chu, a
prominent figure in the native Taiwanese literature of the 1970s. Other writers from
Taiwan include Wang To and Chen Ying-chen.

Literature

695 **Winter plum: contemporary Chinese fiction.**
Edited by Nancy Ing. San Francisco, California; Taipei: Chinese
Materials Center, 1982. 498p.

As vice-president and secretary general of the Chinese centre of the International PEN
organization, Ing has been instrumental in bringing to the notice of Western readers
translations of works by Chinese writers. The fifty-three stories in this volume were
produced by writers born between 1920 and 1960 and are intended to portray life in
China both past and present. The subject matter of these short entries includes the
Sino-Japanese wars of the 1930s; rural life in mainland China; and tensions between
modernity and tradition in Taiwanese society. The diversity of approach and literary
standard demonstrated here derives from the highly disparate experiences and
professions of the authors.

696 **Chinese stories from Taiwan: 1960-1970.**
Edited by Joseph S. M. Lau, Timothy A. Ross, foreword by C. T.
Hsai. New York: Columbia University Press, 1976. 359p.

Eleven short stories by writers of both mainland Chinese and Taiwanese origin are
included in this collection. It is fairly well-organized, with a brief biographical
introduction for the writer of each story. Information about the original Chinese text of
each story is also provided. In the foreword to the book, Hsia offers a very brief survey
of Taiwanese literature and a cursory analysis of these short stories.

697 **How much truth can a blade of grass carry: Chen Ying-chen and the
emergence of native Taiwan writers.**
Joseph S. M. Lau. *Journal of Asian Studies*, vol. 32, no. 4 (1973),
p. 623-38.

Chen Ying-chen was considered a 'non-person' by the Nationalist government because
of his supposed anti-government activities. Yet no survey of Taiwan fiction can be
complete without giving him due attention. Lau analyses Chen's literary style and
social and political message, as well as the overall development of Taiwanese literature
since 1949.

698 **The unbroken chain: an anthology of Taiwan fiction since 1926.**
Edited by Joseph S. M. Lau. Bloomington, Indiana: Indiana
University Press, 1983. 279p.

This collection illustrates all the major thematic and stylistic trends in Taiwanese
fiction, from the 'transit passenger' mentality of the mainland Chinese refugees in the
1950s to the 'native soil' movement of the 1970s. As an editor and well-known
authority on modern Chinese fiction, Lau provides a concise preface to the collection
and gives a brief biographical and literary introduction to each author and story in this
volume. The collection can be highly recommended to anyone interested in Taiwanese
literature.

699 **Exiles at home: short stories by Ch'en Ying-chen.**
Translated by Lucien Miller.   Ann Arbor, Michigan: Center for
Chinese Studies, University of Michigan, 1986. 195p. (Michigan
Monographs in Chinese Studies, no. 57).

Western readers should feel indebted to Miller for this translation of representative
works by one of Taiwan's best-known writers. Chen is a central figure in the native
Taiwanese literature movement. His fiction deals with the plight of those marked by
poverty or ethnic inequity as well as the bland existence of the pseudo-intellectual, who
is characterized by hypocrisy and non-commitment. Chen's passion for the underdog is
revealed by his mockery of an unprincipled, affluent middle class.

700 **The wandering Chinese: the theme of exile in Taiwan fiction.**
Hsien-yung Pai.   *Iowa Review*, vol. 7, nos. 2-3 (1976), p. 205-12.

Discusses why writers from Taiwan have a sense of desperation when they live abroad.
Pai argues that, given the uncertainty of the political future of Taiwan and the terror of
the anti-intellectual campaigns on mainland China, there is nothing left for these
writers to be optimistic about.

701 **Wandering in the garden, waking from a dream: tales of Taipei
characters.**
Hsien-yung Pai, translated by Hsien-yung Pai, Patia Yasin, edited by
George Kao.   Bloomington, Indiana: Indiana University Press, 1982.
199p.

Pai is perhaps one of the most accomplished contemporary writers of fiction in
Chinese. His short stories have established his reputation not only in Taiwan, but also
in the overseas Chinese community, and recently even on mainland China. This
volume is Pai's first collection in English translation. The fourteen stories included here
appeared in Chinese in 1971 in Pai's first collection of short stories, 'Taipei Jen' (Taipei
people, or Taipei characters). These stories reveal the internal struggles of those who
lived in Taipei as refugees from the civil war on the mainland (1945-49). Pai's
characters can neither adapt to their new surroundings in Taipei nor shed their
memories of past glories, real or imagined. Pai's stories are certainly a welcome
addition to Chinese fiction and to world literature as well.

702 **Modern verse from Taiwan.**
Edited and translated by Angela C. Y. Jung Palandri, Robert J.
Bertholf.   Berkeley, California: University of California Press, 1972.
207p.

Palandri translates work by ten poets whom she considers to be representative of
Taiwan's modern poetry. She provides a twenty-page introduction at the beginning of
the anthology and biographical information before each selection. This volume
deserves attention from anyone interested in the modern poetry of Taiwan.

Literature

703 **Taiwan fiction: a review of recent criticism.**
Timothy A. Ross. *Journal of the Chinese Language Teachers Association*, vol. 13, no. 1 (1978), p. 72-80.
Reviews recent criticism in both Chinese and English of fiction written in Chinese by Taiwanese writers currently living in Taiwan or residing abroad. Attention is called to several useful Chinese bibliographical-critical works intended for students of contemporary Chinese fiction in Taiwan.

704 **The evolution of the Taiwanese new literature movement from 1920 to 1937.**
Jane Parish Yang. PhD thesis, University of Wisconsin, Madison, Wisconsin, 1981. 275p. (Available from University Microfilms, Ann Arbor, Michigan, order no. 8203203).
Early twentieth-century Taiwanese literature, from the satirical parodies of classical texts published in the early 1920s to the realistic phase of the 1930s, was closely related to social and political movements against Japanese colonial rule. The study shows that as the political and social climate changed, a progression in fictional modes from romantic to mimetic to ironic became discernible.

705 **Modern Chinese fiction: a guide to its study and appreciation.**
Edited by Winston L. Y. Yang, Nathan K. Mao. Boston, Massachusetts: G. K. Hall, 1981. 288p.
This is a useful bibliographic guide to studies and translations of modern Chinese fiction available in English. It contains two parts. The first part consists of four survey essays: 'Modern Chinese fiction, 1917-1949', by Howard Goldblatt; 'Chinese Communist fiction since 1949', by Michael Gotz; and two short pieces on Taiwan's fiction since 1949, by Winston L. Y. Yang and Joseph S. M. Lau. These essays are primarily limited to fiction that is available in English translation. The second part of the volume is devoted to bibliographies of scholarly studies and translations of modern Chinese literature. Included is a listing of English translations of the works of twenty-seven writers who have published in Taiwan since 1949.

706 **Social realism in recent Chinese fiction in Taiwan.**
Yuan-shu Yen. In: *Thirty years of turmoil in Asian literature.* Compiled by the Taipei Chinese Center, International PEN. Taipei: The Center, 1976, p. 197-231.
By the term 'social realism' the author means literature that deals with social realities. Yen discusses the development of social realism in Chinese literature in Taiwan by examining several representative writers, including Jo-hsi Chen, Ying-chen Chen, Chen-ho Wang, and Chun-ming Huang.

The Arts

General

707 **Chinese art.**
Heng Hu, Fang Lo, Tsai-ping Liang, Te-chen Wang, Li-lian Chao.
Taipei: Youth Cultural Enterprises, 1985. 288p.
Covers major aspects of Chinese culture and art in Taiwan. Topics include calligraphy, painting, music, Chinese opera, and Chinese customs and traditions. The discussions, enhanced by illustrations, make informative and enjoyable reading.

708 **The native art of Taiwan.**
Richard Petterson. *Claremont Quarterly*, vol. 11, no. 3 (1964), p. 49-58.
Describes Taiwan's native arts as shown in temple buildings, during religious ceremonies, and in the course of other aspects of daily life.

709 **Research activities in the performing arts in the Republic of China: a bibliographical report.**
C. K. Wang. *Chinoperl Papers*, no. 13 (1984-85), p. 139-52.
Describes research activities in the performing arts in Taiwan during the 1970s and early 1980s. A bibliography of recent studies on the performing arts is enclosed.

Selection of masterworks in the collection of the National Palace Museum.
See item no. 794.

Great national treasures of China: masterworks in the National Palace Museum.
See item no. 795.

The National Palace Museum in photographs.
See item no. 798.

Architecture

710 **Domestic architecture in Taiwan: continuity and change.**
Emily M. Ahern.   In: *Value change in Chinese society*. Edited by
R. W. Wilson, A. A. Wilson, S. L. Greenblatt. New York: Praeger,
1979, p. 155-70.

The use of space has proved a popular topic for anthropologists working on theories of family structure and sex rôle division. By looking at Taiwanese architecture, the author argues that the Taiwanese have different attitudes towards different kinds of livelihood: farming on the one hand, and commerce and industry on the other. This paper shows how the spread of urban styles of housing into the countryside gives an unusually clear index of changes in occupation, and of concomitant changes in attitudes towards the ways in which households are connected to outside world. This is an interesting article on Taiwanese architecture from the anthropological perspective.

711 **China's traditional rural architecture: a cultural geography of the common house.**
Ronald G. Knapp.   Honolulu, Hawaii: University of Hawaii Press,
1986. 176p.

Researchers have long been concerned with the architectural principles and symbolism of Chinese monumental buildings, such as temples, mansions, palaces, walled cities, and imperial grave sites. To some extent, the author claims, Chinese architecture is a sculptured expression of the cosmos. However, the continuous migration into diverse natural environments that has taken place in Chinese history has shaped a variety of distinct cultural landscapes. Knapp points out that rural housing in China by and large has been built rather than designed, with tradition acting as the regulator. Practicality and economic capability have guided housing forms, just as the local environment has dictated building materials. In Taiwan, the structure and layout of the dwelling can be seen as humanized space that is symbolic of family unity and aspirations. Illustrations and photographs are presented alongside the text. A reference list is appended.

712 **Chinese rural dwellings in Taiwan.**
Ronald G. Knapp.   *Journal of Cultural Geography*, vol. 3, no. 1
(1982), p. 1-18.

Knapp examines rural dwellings in Taiwan in an attempt to support the proposition that these dwellings express Chinese sociocultural norms and communicate symbolic and structural elements of Chinese folk culture, in addition to being the products of a rich architectural tradition.

713   **The exotic pavilions of South Garden.**
      Jeffrey Simpson.   *Architectural Digest*, vol. 45, no. 1 (1988), p. 76-83.
South Garden is an elaborate set of two-storey tile-roofed buildings, open-air
pavilions, courtyards, and ponds and gardens situated in a valley near Taipei. It was
designed according to Taoist principles, with attention to 'feng-shui' ('wind and water'
or geomancy). Simpson points out various features of traditional Chinese architecture
that are reflected in the building of South Garden and includes several photographs.

714   **Taiwanese architecture and the supernatural.**
      Sung-hsing Wang.   In: *Religion and ritual in Chinese society*. Edited by
      Arthur P. Wolf. Stanford: Stanford University Press, 1974, p. 183-92.
The domestic architecture of Taiwan reflects the people's beliefs about the
supernatural as well as their need for shelter against cold, damp winters and hot,
humid summers. The author shows that these beliefs affect the choice of a building
site, the orientation of the house with respect to the landscape, and the number of
rooms and the uses to which they are put.

Music

715   **The collection of Chinese folk songs.**
      Compiled and edited by Government Information Office. Taipei: China
      Publishing Company, 1980. 2 vols.
Contains more than 800 folk songs from various provinces. The section on Taiwan
includes Fukien, Hakka and aborigine pieces. Pop songs which have prevailed in
Taiwan for more than thirty years are also included. These pop songs reflect the
sufferings of the Taiwanese under the Japanese occupation. An English interpretation
of each song is attached.

716   **Chinese music: an annotated bibliography.**
      Fredric Lieberman.   New York, London: Garland, 1979. 2nd ed. 257p.
      (Garland Reference Library of the Humanities, no. 75).
Provides exhaustive coverage of publications in Western languages as well as critical
annotations. Lieberman includes materials on Chinese music, dance, and drama, since
in Chinese society these are basically interrelated. Essays on the development of
Taiwan's music or on items published in Taiwan are not arranged in a specific
Taiwanese section, but appear along with other entries on the same subject.

717   **Music in Taiwan.**
      L. G. Thompson.   *Claremont Quarterly*, vol. 11, no. 3 (1964), p. 71-78.
Describes the development of music in Taiwan. Thompson notes that traditional music
faces the possibility of extinction in the face of competition form Western music.

718   **Popular music in Taiwan.**
       Georgette Wang.   *Critical Studies in Mass Communication*, vol. 3,
       no. 3 (1986), p. 366-68.
Wang uses Taiwan as a case study in her examination of the development of popular
music in a defined area, with special attention to Western influences.

Visual arts

719   **The folkware collection of the National Central Library, Taiwan
       Branch.**
       Edited by I-ting Chang, et al.   Taipei: National Central Library
       Taiwan Branch, 1980, 1984. 2 vols.
The first volume includes 208 illustrations of objects collected in the National Central
Library Taiwan Branch. The second volume consists of 180 illustrations. The
explanation which accompanies each item includes its date of origin, place of
production, style, special title, and size.

720   **Descriptive and illustrated catalogue of the paintings in the National
       Palace Museum.**
       Chao-shen Chiang, translated by Thomas Lawton.   Taipei: National
       Palace Museum, 1968. 125p.
Includes 342 paintings from the National Palace Museum, Taipei. Black and white
photos of the paintings are accompanied by short descriptions.

721   **The paintings of Chang Dai-chien.**
       Editorial Committee.   Taipei: National Museum of History, 1978.
       2nd ed. 134p.
Includes illustrations of some 100 paintings created by Dai-chien Chang (Ta-chi'en
Chang, 1899-1983), a famous contemporary Chinese painter who died in Taiwan. A
chronological record of Chang's life and work is appended.

722   **Essays on painting from the master Chang Dai-chien.**
       Edited by Edward H. Hsung.   Taipei: Chinese Art Gallery Publication
       Service, 1975. 159p.
Dai-chien Chang was an acknowledged master in the field of Chinese painting. This
volume consists of several short essays by the artist on various aspects of Chinese
painting and more than eighty marvellous illustrations.

723   **Arts and crafts from the Republic of China.**
       Edited by Tsai-lang Huang.   Taipei: Council for Cultural Planning and
       Development, Executive Yuan, 1986. 169p.
Popular art is valuable because it exists and evolves quite beyond the range of any
academic or outside influences. Without strict adherence to fixed rules or formalities,
popular art moves with the habits and customs of the people and the changing rhythms

of life in a particular place. The excellence and beauty of Chinese arts and crafts are presented in this collection, which includes enamel work, Chiao-chih pottery, bamboo handicrafts, Chinese knotting, casting, wood carvings, and ceramics. Each item is introduced by a colour illustration.

724 **Special exhibition: traditional woodblock prints of Taiwan.**
Edited by Tsai-lang Huang, et al. Taipei: Council for Cultural Planning and Development, Executive Yuan, 1985. 302p.

Owing to the pattern of Chinese migration to Taiwan from the provinces of Fukien and Kwangtung, the traditional woodblock prints of Taiwan tend to be closely associated with the districts in these two provinces. Since these two provinces were important southern Chinese centres of handicraft culture, it is hardly a surprise to find that the art of woodblock printing in Taiwan was highly developed. The scope of this volume embraces surviving woodblock prints of Fukienese and Kwangtung origin which arrived in Taiwan during the Ch'ing dynasty; woodblock prints produced locally in Taiwan; and early woodblock print production tools. In addition to illustrations of the prints, the volume includes several articles on the history of printmaking in China, the origin and development of traditional printmaking in Taiwan, and the relation between printmaking and popular culture in Taiwan.

725 **The reform of Peking opera in Taiwan.**
Irmgard Johnson. *China Quarterly*, no. 57 (1974). p. 140-45.

Describes the fate of traditional Peking opera in Taiwan. Johnson argues that aesthetic and theatrical aspects of the reforms taking place in Peking opera can in no way be disentangled from social and political forces on Taiwan.

726 **Chinese paintings in Chinese publications, 1956-1968: an annotated bibliography and an index to the paintings.**
E. J. Laing. Ann Arbor, Michigan: Center for Chinese Studies, University of Michigan, 1969. 308p. (Michigan Papers in Chinese Studies, no. 6).

This bibliography includes publications issued between 1856 and August 1968 which reproduce Chinese paintings that are held primarily in Chinese public and private collections. The great majority of these publications appeared in Taiwan, Hong Kong, and mainland China. Most have provided a tremendous wealth of illustrations for art historians and students of Chinese painting. In addition to the detailed publication information for each entry item, a general evaluation of the quality of the reproductions is included with qualifications whenever possible.

727 **Collection of woodcuts by Lee Kuo-chu.**
Kuo-chu Lee. Taipei: Li-ming Cultural Enterprise, 1984. 83p.

The woodcut is a familiar form of art to the Chinese. K. C. Lee, an artist who has dedicated himself to woodcuts for thirty years, is among the fine artisans practising this art form in Taiwan. This volume includes a brief introduction to his art and to sixty of his works.

728 **A selection of landscape sketches by Professor Liang Chung-ming.**
Chung-ming Liang. Taipei: Li-ming Cultural Enterprise, 1978. 74p.
Seventy pencil sketches are assembled in six major categories; scenes of the forest, charcoal drawings, construction scenes, fishing scenes, images of Quemoy-Matsu, and views of foreign countries. The sketches are based on Liang's tour of Taiwan, Taiwan's offshore islands, and the Philippines.

729 **The calligraphy of ten contemporary masters.**
Edited by Alice B. H. Lin. Taipei: Taipei Fine Arts Museum, 1987. 120p.
Ten artists from Taiwan are selected to show their artistic achievements in calligraphy, or the art of writing. These artists are: Chih-pan Ting, Chiu-pu Tsao, Chiu-yin Chu, Ching-nung Tai, Yen-tao Liu, Kai-ho Wang, Tung-an Hsieh, Shao-chieh Tseng, Chuang-wei Wang, and Chuan-fu Fu.

730 **Fukienese wood carvings: a survival in Taiwan.**
Stephen Markbreiter. *Arts of Asia*, vol. 19, no. 3 (1989), p. 97-104.
Through a description of the skills of a Lu-kang carver, this article traces the development of crafts from the Fukien province of China as they evolved in Taiwan. The carver's family emigrated from Fukien province four generations ago. Excellent illustrations are included.

731 **The graphic art of Chinese folklore.**
National Museum of History. Taipei: National Museum of History, 1977. 140p.
This collection of Chinese folk prints from the National Museum of History, Taipei, is divided into seven categories: ancestral-sacrificial; Confucian sages and wise men; Taoist saints and masters; Buddhas; other folk deities (e.g., gods of the sun and medicine); amulets and Lunar New Year paintings. The artistic composition of these Chinese folk prints is of great value in the study of folklore, as well as Chinese history and society, including that of Taiwan. The collection, which contains ninety-seven prints with English titles, will enable readers to appreciate better the folk tradition of the Chinese people.

732 **Cloisonné of Kuo Ming-chiao, master artist of Taipei, China.**
Ursula Roberts. *Arts of Asia*, vol. 15, no. 5 (1985), p. 110-13.
Cloisonné is a method of enamelling upon a metal plate or form, with the coloured areas separated by thin metal strips fixed to the body either by soldering or by the enamel itself. This essay introduces Ming-chiao Kuo, who has become a cloisonné artist of international repute. His work rivals that of classical Chinese craftsmen.

733 **Shi Teh-chin memorial exhibition.**
Teh-chin Shi. Taipei: Taipei Fine Arts Museum, 1983. 60p.
Contains forty-nine of Teh-chin Shi's best works, including drawings, oil paintings, calligraphy, watercolours and ink paintings. Although Shi was born in mainland China, he set himself the task of painting the natural beauty of Taiwan. Readers will perceive something of the traditional Chinese spirit in his painting, although he uses Western techniques.

734   **Works of grace: Yang-tze Tong.**
      Yang-tze Tong.   Taipei: Hilt, 1987. 119p.
Presents a collection of recent art work by Tong, a famous calligrapher working in
Taiwan. Through more than fifty pieces demonstrating the calligrapher's artistry,
readers can appreciate the superb deployment of forms in Tong's calligraphy, whether
in a single character or in a whole scroll.

735   **An exhibition of contemporary Chinese sculpture in the Republic of
      China.**
      Edited by Tai-chi Wang.   Taipei: Taipei Fine Arts Museum, 1985.
      154p.
This exhibition includes thirty-four sculptures selected from among the 101 works
submitted for consideration. Some pieces, in the author's view, represent the pure
expression of form and space. A variety of materials, such as iron, steel, marble,
wood, and bronze are used. This book includes a brief introduction to each artist,
outlining his training, awards, and experiences.

Sports and Recreation

736 **Mountains and streams of inexhaustible splendor: Taiwan's favorite new scenic spots.**
Editorial committee. Taipei: Kwang-hwa, 1986. 235p.

Introduces Taiwan's newly popularized scenic spots, such as Tai-ping mountain, Yang-ming-shan National Park, and Tai-chi gorge, and some of the favourite recreation activities carried out on the island, like deep-sea fishing, and bird-watching. For each location or activity, readers will find useful information about transportation, food, and lodging. The final section contains a discussion of tourism in Taiwan and an analysis of 'what tourists love best in Taiwan'. The book is generously illustrated.

737 **The realm of jade mountain: the ten top scenic spots of Taiwan, the Republic of China.**
Kwang-hwa Magazine. Taipei: Kwang-hwa, 1985. 131p. map.

The proliferation of natural beauty in once secluded areas of Taiwan's northeast coast and the marine wonderlands off the south coast form the topics of this volume, which presents Taiwan's 'ten top scenic treasures'. The appendix includes an introduction to the National Palace Museum, and to the memorial halls of Sun Yat-sen and Chiang Kai-shek.

738 **The beauty of Yushan.**
Ministry of Interior. Taipei: Ministry of Interior, 1987. 167p.

More than sixty-two of Taiwan's peaks rise over 3,000 metres above sea level. The tallest (3,954 metres) and perhaps the most spectacular of these is Mount Morrison or Yushan (Jade Mountain). Because of recent government emphasis on the conservation of nature and natural resources, Yushan National Park was established in 1985. This richly illustrated photographic album captures the park's harmony, serenity, and grandeur.

739   **Tourism, hot spring resorts and sexual entertainment, observations from northern Taiwan: a study in social geography.**
Wolfgang Senftleben.   *Philippine Geographical Journal*, vol. 30, nos. 1-2 (1986), p. 21-41.
Examines the interaction betwcen two social groups: prostitutes or girls closely associated with sexual entertainment on one side, and male tourists or local clients on the other side. This is a case study undertaken in northern Taiwan. Differing patterns of 'sexual entertainment' are discussed.

740   **Beer houses: an indicator of cultural change in Taiwan.**
Christopher Sutherland, Jack Williams, Cotton Mather.   *Journal of Cultural Geography*, vol. 6, no. 2 (1986), p. 35-50.
An interesting phenomenon has commanded widespread public and official attention in Taipei. It is the sudden appearance of a type of drinking establishment known locally as a 'beer house.' The authors examine the causes and problems of beer houses and argues that they manifest the cultural stress caused by spectacular economic development within a traditionally conservative oriental society.

The 'two-Chinas' problem and the Olympic formula.
See item no. 399.

Mass Media

General

741 Content of Taiwan's English and Chinese press.
Robert L. Bishop, Judy Hansen. *Journalism Quarterly*, vol. 58, no. 3 (1981), p. 456-60.
Examines whether Taiwan's press comes under direct or indirect control of the government. The authors' findings show that press control exists on Taiwan. It is also probable that the papers closest to the masses – the Chinese language press – are far more closely controlled than the English press.

742 The growth and development plans for telecommunications in Taiwan.
P. C. Chen. *Telecommunications*, vol. 15, no. 6 (1981), p. 27-32.
Describes recent projects designed to modernize telecommunication networks in Taiwan, for instance, the introduction of a high-order digital transmission system and the establishment of a satellite communication system.

743 Press freedom on Taiwan: the mini hundred flowers period.
Judy P. Hansen, Robert L. Bishop. *Journalism Quarterly*, vol. 58, no. 1 (1981), p. 38-42.
For a brief period of eighteen months between 1956 and 1958, Taiwan relaxed its press control. The authors describe that period and explore the reasons for the final crackdown.

744 Television broadcasting in the Republic of China on Taiwan, 1962-1983: analysis from a dependency perspective.
Hsing-sheng Hwang. PhD thesis, Northwestern University, Evanston, Illinois, 1984. 281p. (Available from University Microfilms, Ann Arbor, Michigan, order no. 8411152).
In recent years, the dependency theory regarding Third World development and communication has been debated. This theory asserts that Third World countries are caught up in a dependency relationship with the capitalist world economy, and that their economic dependency relationship is then reproduced in the fields of culture and the mass media. This study examines and analyses the development of television

broadcasting in Taiwan during the period 1962-83 in the light of the assumptions of the dependency theory. The results indicate that economic dependency does induce dependency in the television industry.

745 A cross-national comparison of media uses and international political knowledge.

Yun Peng. *Journal of National Chengchi University*, vol. 51 (1985), p. 19-36.

Examines the media exposure, gratifications sought and avoidance behaviour considered relevant to international political knowledge for 225 American residents of Chicago and 234 Chinese living in Taipei, Taiwan. Peng shows that in both samples no relationship could be established between the respondents' newspaper exposure time and their knowledge of international affairs. But there was a positive relationship between Chinese respondents' television exposure time and their international political knowledge.

746 American TV and social stereotypes of Americans in Taiwan and Mexico.

Alexis S. Tan, Sarrina Li, Charles Simpson. *Journalism Quarterly*, vol. 63, no. 4 (1986), p. 809-14.

For many foreign audiences, American television is the major source of information about US culture and people. This study analyses the relationship between exposure to US television programmes and the social stereotypes of Americans held by adult audiences in Taiwan and Mexico, where these programmes are available.

747 A newspaper without news.

G. Wang. *Journalism Quarterly*, vol. 59, no. 2 (1982), p. 286-89.

Min Shun Bao (or *Ming Sheng Pao*) is the only paper of its kind in Taiwan. It has no editorial section and does not carry straight news reports except for unusually important events. Instead, it covers gossip, the entertainment world, health and medicine, art, modern living, and miscellaneous other items. Wang interviewed 160 subscribers and 142 former subscribers, and found out that without straight news to satisfy the common needs of newspaper readers, *Min Shun Bao* seemed to have a difficult time in pleasing the general population.

Newspapers

748 Asian Wall Street Journal.

Hong Kong, 1976- .

Provides extensive coverage of political and economic events in Asia, including Taiwan. It is published daily except weekends and designated legal holidays.

749 Capital Morning Post.

Taipei, 1988- .

The *Capital Morning Post* claims to be the paper that really belongs to the society of Taiwan and reports the news in good faith. Its publisher is Ning-hsiang Kang, a member of the recently formed Democratic Progressive Party. In consequence, it tends to present viewpoints different from the papers controlled by the Nationalist Party.

750 Central Daily News.

Taipei, 1928- .

This newspaper moved to Taiwan in 1949. It publishes a number of daily and weekly sections, covering news analysis, mainland affairs, literature and modern living. Children's and colour pictorial sections are also produced. Since 1950, *Central Daily News* has issued an overseas edition for circulation abroad. It is owned by the Nationalist Party (KMT), and thus tends to support government policies and to reflect the KMT's opinions.

751 China News.

Taipei, 1949- .

This is the oldest English-language daily in Taiwan. It features world news, local events and issues, as well as items on business and industry, entertainment and social events.

752 China Post.

Taipei, 1952- .

This is an English morning paper. Its wide coverage includes international events and issues, domestic affairs, business and industry, sports, and local community news.

753 China Times.

Taipei, 1950- .

Initially called *Cheng-hsin Hsin-wen Pao*, this newspaper now ranks as one of the top three newspapers, along with *Central Daily News* (q.v.) and *United Daily News* (q.v.). The newspaper also owns a weekly, *Shih-pao Chou-kan* ('*China Times Weekly*') and the *Commercial Times*. In 1975, it issued an overseas edition, but discontinued it in early 1985 for financial reasons. This paper covers political and social news, as well as financial and economic affairs.

754 Independence Evening Post.

Taipei, 1947- .

Recently, the *Independence Evening Post* began publishing a companion newspaper called the *Independence Morning Post*. This paper is known for its editorial opinions that are independent from any political party's control, as the newspaper's name indicates.

755 United Daily News.

Taipei, 1951- .

Through the years, this newspaper has been expanding into a publishing group with such affiliated newspapers and publishing companies as the *Economic Daily News*, *Min Sheng Pao*, *World Journal* (weekly) in New York, China Economic News Service, and the Linking Publishing Company. The *United Daily News* is privately owned and operated. It usually competes vigorously with the *China Times* (q.v.) for unique news reports as well as for readers' subscriptions.

Periodicals

756 **Arts of Asia.**
Kowloon, Hong Kong: Arts of Asia, 1971- . bimonthly.
Intended for a readership of well-educated people and connoisseurs, this magazine occasionally includes articles about art and antiques from Taiwan.

757 **Asian Perspectives.**
Honolulu, Hawaii: University of Hawaii Press, 1957- . semiannual.
A semiannual publication on Asian and Pacific archaeology and prehistory, it occasionally carries articles about Taiwan.

758 **Asian Profile.**
Hong Kong: Asian Research Service, 1973- . bimonthly.
This magazine is devoted exclusively to the multi-disciplinary study of Asian affairs. Articles on Taiwan and comparative studies of Taiwan with other societies appear frequently.

759 **Asian Survey.**
Berkeley, California: University of California, 1961- . monthly.
A monthly review of contemporary Asian affairs. Each issue contains six or more articles which deal with political, social, and economic developments in Asia. In addition, an in-depth analysis of every Asian country's development during the preceding year is provided in the first issues of each year.

Periodicals

760 **Asiaweek.**
Hong Kong: Asiaweek, 1975- . weekly.
This magazine is a valuable resource for educational institutions, scholars, and general readers interested in gaining a knowledge of current Asian developments. Every part of Asia, including Taiwan, is covered. Editorials and reviews reflect Asian points of view, which should prove particularly interesting to Western readers.

761 **Bulletin of the Institute of Ethnology, Academia Sinica.**
Taipei: Institute of Ethnology, 1956- . semiannual.
Occasionally this bulletin carries articles in English concerning Taiwan's history, social changes, and other related matters. Readers interested in Taiwan's prehistory, archaeology, history in the Ch'ing period, and social development will find this periodical very helpful.

762 **China and Pacific Rim Letter.**
Washington, DC: Global Strategy Council, 1989- . bimonthly.
This publication strives to provide a balanced survey of the important events that take place not only in the People's Republic of China, but also in Hong Kong, Tibet, and the Republic of China on Taiwan.

763 **China Quarterly.**
London: School of Oriental and Asian Studies, 1960- . quarterly.
One of the most substantial and well-known scholarly periodicals on China, *China Quarterly* contains essays, written by specialists on all aspects of China. International developments, foreign relations, political meetings, and economic and social topics are all covered. Although most articles deal with mainland China, articles on Taiwan are occasionally included.

764 **Chinese Pen.**
Taipei: Taipei Chinese Center, International PEN. 1972- . quarterly.
The goal of this publication is to help readers understand and appreciate the literature, poetry, and art of Taiwan. Includes a list of cultural activities that take place in Taiwan.

765 **Chinese Yearbook of International Law and Affairs.**
Taipei: Chinese Society of International Law – Chinese (Taiwan) Branch of the International Law Association, 1981- . annual.
This periodical serves as a forum for scholarly discussion on problems of international law or affairs concerning the Republic of China. Each yearly volume contains articles, book reviews, a record of contemporary practices of the ROC relating to international law, a list of bilateral agreements concluded by the ROC, lists of ROC diplomatic and consular missions abroad and of foreign diplomatic missions in the ROC, and statistics of the ROC in brief. Readers interested in the ROC's practice of international law will find this periodical very useful.

766 **Current Contents of Foreign Periodicals in Chinese Studies.**
Taipei: Center for Chinese Studies, 1984- . quarterly.
Presents a compilation of articles and book reviews in Chinese studies, including Taiwan studies, that have appeared in foreign periodicals. Items are arranged by periodical title. Information concerning author, title, and volume number is provided. Most well-known journals in Chinese studies are included.

767 **Economic Review.**
Taipei: International Commercial Bank of China, 1950- . bimonthly.
This periodical contains current news of banking, trade and other matters related to Taiwan's economy. Tables and statistical data are provided.

768 **Far Eastern Economic Review.**
Hong Kong: Review Publishing, 1946- . weekly.
In addition to its excellent reports and reviews of Asian economies, the stock market situation, and industrial developments, this magazine provides valuable information concerning political and social development in Asian societies. Much scholarly research depends on this magazine for up-to-date information.

769 **Foreign Broadcast Information Service (FBIS). Daily Report, China.**
Springfield, Virginia: National Technical Information Service.
This report is published daily, excepting Saturday and Sunday, and contains current news and information on China. Materials included are obtained from foreign radio, news agency transmissions, television broadcasts and newspapers. Items are generally processed from the first or best available source. One section in the volume on China deals with Taiwan. For readers unable to read or understand Chinese, the FBIS provides excellent English translations of Chinese materials. Since the FBIS is a US government publication, readers can usually locate copies in the government document section of US libraries or directly from the publisher.

770 **Free China Review.**
Taipei: Kwang-hwa, 1951- . monthly.
This periodical is published in English, French, Spanish, and German. Essays touch upon every aspect of Taiwanese society and are generally unrelated to politics. One of the recent issues of *Free China Review*, in 1989, for example, provides comment and discussion on the movement for ecological conservation in Taiwan. A very enjoyable magazine not only because of its topic selection but also because of the excellent photographs supplementing the text, this journal is getting better and better.

771 **Industry of Free China.**
Taipei: Council for Economic Planning and Development, Executive Yuan, Republic of China, 1954- . monthly.
This publication carries articles on Taiwan's economic development as well as economic statistics for the ROC. Chinese and English essays are grouped together. For researchers on Taiwan's economy and industrial development, this is an important periodical for consultation and reference.

Periodicals

772 **Issues and Studies.**
Taipei: Institute of International Relations, 1964- . monthly.
This publication's primary focus is Chinese communism. The articles, reviews, and short comments on the Communist Party, Chinese social policies, foreign affairs and other pertinent topics make this a worthwhile selection for specialists as well as general readers. Taiwan is covered, especially in studies comparing mainland China and Taiwan, and in articles dealing with Sino-US relations.

773 **Joint Publication Research Service (JPRS).**
Springfield, Virginia: National Technical Information Service. irregular.
Numerous articles and books are translated by the JPRS each year. All of the publications translated and abstracted are done at the request of at least one US government agency. These publications consist of: books, newspapers, and journal articles; science abstracts; medical and technical journals; conference proceedings; economic and industrial reports; and military documents. The JPRS occasionally carries reports or articles from Taiwan. Currently issued on microfiche, the information collected by the JPRS tends to be less time-sensitive and appears less frequently than that of many other publications. Any serious research library should have JPRS translations, which can be located by using the TRANSDEX Index.

774 **Journal of Asian Studies.**
Ann Arbor, Michigan: Association for Asian Studies, 1941- . quarterly.
With articles concentrating on social and historical studies, this is one of the most important journals for the study of Asian affairs. Its reviews often make up half of each issue and provide detailed and critical comments on new books about Asia. The *Journal's* reviews of books about Taiwan can provide an excellent source of reference.

775 **Journal of Chinese Linguistics.**
Berkeley, California: Project on Linguistic Analysis, 1973- . semiannual.
Publishes essays on topics related to Chinese languages and their various dialects. Essays can be historical, descriptive, theoretical, applied, or literary.

776 **Journal of Educational Media and Library Sciences.**
Taipei: Tamkang University, 1970- . quarterly.
This publication was formerly the *Bulletin of Educational Media Science* (1970-80) and the *Journal of Educational Media Science* (1980-82). It is devoted to studies in the fields of library science, audio-visual media, and educational technology.

777 **Journal of Library and Information Science.**
Taipei: Department of Social Education, National Taiwan Normal University and Chinese American Librarian Association of the United States, 1975- . semiannual.
This publication strives to promote the development of Chinese library and information services in Taiwan.

778 **Kuo-li Cheng-chih Ta-hsüeh Hsüeh-pao** (Journal of National Cheng-chih University).
Taipei: National Cheng-chih University, 1960- . semiannual.
This journal occasionally carries articles in English dealing with various aspects of Taiwan's economy, education, society, domestic politics, and foreign affairs.

779 **Journal of Sunology: a Social Science Quarterly.**
Kaohsiung, Taiwan: Sun Yat-sen Institute for Interdisciplinary Studies, National Sun Yat-sen University, 1985- . quarterly.
This journal carries articles related to political science, economics, sociology, history, philosophy, and other fields of social science. Each issue covers one specific topic. Articles may be either previously unpublished works or translations of published essays.

780 **Journal of the Institute of Chinese Studies of the Chinese University of Hong Kong.**
Hong Kong: Chinese University of Hong Kong, 1968- . annual.
This journal occasionally includes articles on Taiwan's economy and society.

781 **Modern China.**
Beverly Hills, California: Sage, 1975- . quarterly.
Articles concerning Taiwan's economic development, society, rural changes, folk religions and state-market relations occasionally appear in this publication.

782 **National Central Library Newsletter.**
Taipei: National Central Library, 1969- . quarterly.
This periodical carries short essays or news briefs regarding library management and activities in the National Central Library as well as in regional libraries of Taiwan.

783 **Pacific Review.**
Oxford, England: Oxford University Press, 1988- . quarterly.
Provides a forum for broad and in-depth analysis of the prospects and problems of the Pacific. Articles on Taiwan occasionally appear. Although it is intended for the academic community, the information in this journal is accessible to the business community and non-specialists as well.

784 **Taiwan Communiqué.**
Seattle, Washington; The Hague: International Committee for Human Rights in Taiwan, 1980- . bimonthly.
The stated purpose of this journal is to campaign for the release of political prisoners in Taiwan and to support the establishment of a free and democratic society in the ROC.

Periodicals

785 **Taiwan Culture.**
Long Island City, New York: Taiwan-US Culture Exchange Center,
1985- . bimonthly.

Carries articles in Chinese and English on Taiwan's social, economic, and political
development. The purpose of this periodical is to promote Taiwan's independence
movement and to denounce the rule of the Nationalist Party.

786 **Taiwan Studies Newsletter.**
East Lansing, Michigan: The Committee on Taiwan Studies, China and
Inner Asia Council of the Association for Asian Studies, 1982- .
quarterly.

This newsletter carries conference details, publication news, information on research
resources, and project announcements. This is an invaluable resource for students of
Taiwan studies.

Chinese periodicals in the Library of Congress.
See item no. 808.

An annotated guide to Taiwan periodical literature.
See item no. 810.

**National Taiwan University list of serials in Chinese, Japanese and Korean
languages.**
See item no. 817.

Libraries, Museums, and Research Collections

787 **Proceedings of international Ch'ing archives symposium, July 2, 1978-July 6, 1978, Taipei, China.**
Edited by Chieh-hsien Ch'en.   Taipei: National Palace Museum, 1982. 427p.

In 1978, more than one hundred scholars participated in an international symposium in Taipei to discuss the materials for the study of Ch'ing history and other related matters. This volume contains papers selected from this symposium. Several authors discuss sources for Ch'ing history in the archives of the National Palace Museum, the Institute of Modern History, the Academia Sinica, and the Institute of History and Philology. In one article, the records of the Government-General (Sotokufu), the highest Japanese government authority in Taiwan, are introduced and a guide is provided to the land report surveys conducted during the Japanese colonial period. The author describes the location of materials and their condition. Readers interested in studying Chinese history and the colonial history of Taiwan may find this volume helpful in planning their research.

788 **Chinese Communist materials at the Bureau of Investigation Archives, Taiwan.**
Peter Donovan, Carl E. Dorris, Lawrence R. Sullivan.   Ann Arbor, Michigan: Center for Chinese Studies, University of Michigan. 1976. 105p. (Michigan Papers in Chinese Studies, no. 24).

One excellent repository open for research into the Chinese Communist movement is the Bureau of Investigation Collection (BIC), which is located in Hsin-tien, Taipei County. The BIC holds over 300,000 volumes of primary documents on Chinese Communist activities dating from before 1949. Some were supplied by Nationalist agents or Communist defectors. Others were seized in the arrest of Communist cadres and the exposure of their political organizations. These documents are generally unavailable in libraries and archives outside mainland China. The problem of using the BIC is the absence of a comprehensive guide to the collection and the purpose of this book is to give scholars a general description of the BIC. The authors also point out the usefulness of the BIC for research on some of the important issues in the history of the Chinese Communist movement.

789 **Library education in the Republic of China.**
James S. C. Hu.   In: *Library and information science education*.
Edited by James S. C. Hu. Taipei: Department and Graduate Institute
of Library Science, National Taiwan University, 1986, p. 37-64.

Provides an overview of the current status of the six library science programmes in Taiwan. Information and statistics included in this study are based primarily on a survey conducted in 1985.

790 **Continuing education and staff development for librarians in the Republic of China.**
Shih-hsion Huang.   In: *Library and information science education*.
Edited by James S. C. Hu. Taipei: Department and Graduate Institute
of Library Science, National Taiwan University, 1986, p. 205-15.

Describes programmes and opportunities for the continuing education of librarians and discusses the problems involved. For example, the author maintains that curriculum planning should correspond with developing global trends and practical needs.

791 **Design of the curriculum for a 2-year Library Technical Assistant Program in the recruitment plan of the Republic of China.**
Chien-chang Lan.   In: *Library and information science education*.
Edited by James S. C. Hu. Taipei: Department and Graduate Institute
of Library Science, National Taiwan University, 1986, p. 169-79.

Describes the present nature of library technical assistant programme available in the West and the East. The author proposes a curriculum for the programme in Taiwan.

792 **Education and training for online use of databases in the Republic of China.**
Lucy Te-chu Lee.   In: *Library and information science education*.
Edited by James S. C. Hu. Taipei: Department and Graduate Institute
of Library Science, National Taiwan University, 1986, p. 181-203.

Describes the current state of education and training for the use of online databases in Taiwan. Lee discusses the background development which will be required, the organizations that can provide education and training, and the persons to be trained. She outlines problems involved and suggests possible solutions.

793 **Notes: recent publication in Taiwan.**
Frederick W. Mote.   *Journal of Asian Studies*, vol. 17, no. 4 (1958),
p. 595-606.

Although this brief survey is somewhat outdated, Mote's remarks and observations offer a general outline of publishing activities in Taiwan, as well as a guide to sources available for scholars who want to find materials published in Taiwan during the 1950s.

794 **Selection of masterworks in the collection of the National Palace Museum.**
Compiled by Chih-liang Na.   Taipei: National Palace Museum, 1972. 213p.

The objects in the National Palace Museum collection are so numerous and so varied that no catalogue could ever do them justice. It is certainly impossible to include all of them (an estimated 240,000 objects) in one book. This volume, however, manages to give readers a general impression of the collection. The contents are arranged under seventeen headings: bronzes; pottery and porcelain; jade; lacquer ware; enamel ware; carving; apparel; miniatures; writing materials; Tibetan Buddhist ritual implements; calligraphy; silk textiles; calligraphy rubbings from stone tablets; paintings; portraiture; books; and documents. The book contains one hundred fifty illustrations. The broad contours of China's cultural history can be easily detected and appreciated by browsing through this selection of objects from the Museum collection.

795 **Great national treasures of China: masterworks in the National Palace Museum.**
National Palace Museum.   Taipei: National Palace Museum, 1988. 327p.

Selects representative national treasures from the National Palace Museum to allow readers to gain a more accurate impression of the broad range of the Museum's holdings. Categories include bronzes, ceramics, jades, lacquer ware, enamel ware, miniature carvings, costume and personal ornament, religious articles, writing materials, calligraphy, stone-inscription rubbings, paintings, portraits, embroideries and tapestries, books and documents. All illustrations are in full colour. The explanatory text is presented in Chinese and English.

796 **Problems confronting library science education in the Republic of China.**
Harris B. H. Seng.   In: *Library and Information Science Education.* Edited by James S. C. Hu. Taipei: Department and Graduate Institute of Library Science, National Taiwan University, 1986, p. 65-79.

Discusses the problems of education for librarianship in Taiwan. At the end of his study, the author names certain skills and qualities needed by prospective librarians.

797 **T'ai-wan yen chiu ti chi kou chi tzu liao.** (Institutions and materials for Taiwan historical studies.)
Shih-ching Wang.   Taipei: National Book, 1976. 41p. (Committee for Taiwan Historical Studies, Association for Asian Studies, Working Paper Series, no. 1).

Provides an important reference source for students of Taiwan's history who can read Chinese. This volume describes institutions and materials relevant to the study of this island's history. Although the text is written in Chinese only, this entry is included because of its invaluable information about research materials available in various institutions in Taiwan.

798 **The National Palace Museum in photographs.**
Edited by Teh-hsing Yuan.   Taipei: National Palace Museum, 1987.
191p.

After the National Palace Museum moved to Taipei, it underwent numerous changes
in its buildings and grounds, its facilities and its presentation of exhibits. This book
gives readers a historical and illustrated overview of those changes.

Directory of the cultural organizations of the Republic of China.
See item no. 816.

Bibliographies and Directories

799 Yearbook of 1986 Chinese composers of ROC.
Asian Composers League, ROC National Committee.   Taipei: Asian
Composers League, 1987. 159p.

Chronicles and describes the works of Taiwanese composers in an attempt to delineate
the concrete achievements of their musical creations. This book covers the period
1946-84. Only members of the ROC National Committee of Asian Composers are
included in this compilation.

800 Bibliography of Asian studies.
Association for Asian Studies.   Ann Arbor, Michigan: Association for
Asian Studies, 1946- . annual.

This volume attempts to cover the extensive literature in the field of Asian studies as
exhaustively as possible. It is arranged firstly by geographical area, and secondly by a
classified list of subject headings, and an index is provided for personal names of
authors, editors, and translators. This is one of the most comprehensive lists of
publications written in Western languages related to Taiwan. Since it is printed using
the Apple Macintosh microcomputer and laser printer, its annual volumes should
appear eighteen to twenty-four months after the end of the year in which entries are
compiled.

801 Contemporary China: a research guide.
Peter Berton, Eugene Wu.   Stanford, California: Stanford University
Press, 1967. 695p.

This guide covers materials on post-1949 mainland China and post-1945 Taiwan, which
originated in mainland China, Taiwan, Hong Kong, Japan, the United States, Great
Britain, and the Soviet Union. With emphasis on the humanities and social sciences,
especially on primary sources in those fields, the guide includes bibliographies,
reference books, directories, handbooks, atlases, documentary sources, and serial
publications. It is essentially a reference work keyed to those materials providing
access to sources on contemporary China and, to a lesser extent, to the sources

themselves. More than 200 items are organized according to category of material and by subject, usually without distinction as to language or place of publication. This book is of great service to academic communities. Scholars in China studies and comparative studies will find new suggestions for locating the information that they need.

802   **Major companies of Taiwan.**
      Edited by Jennifer L. Carr.   In: *Major companies of the Far East, 1986*. London: Graham and Trotman, 1986, vol. 2, p. 339-88.

Companies are arranged alphabetically and indexes are provided on coloured paper at the back of the book. Most of the information in this volume is submitted by the companies themselves and is updated regularly. Each entry lists names of senior executives, addresses, principal activities, and financial situation.

803   **Economic development in Taiwan: a selected bibliography.**
      Center for Quality of Life Studies. Taipei: The Center, Ming-teh Foundation, 1984. 88p.

This book contains 646 references, published in English, and pertinent to Taiwan's economic development. The bibliography covers monographs, journal articles, and PhD dissertations. Entries are arranged in alphabetical order by author's name. Regrettably, no subject index is available.

804   **Top 500: the Largest Corporations in the Republic of China, 1988.**
      China Credit Information Service.   Taipei: China Credit Information Service. annual.

Ranks manufacturing and non-manufacturing corporations by sales. Also included are the leading 100 corporations in export and domestic sales respectively, and a section on the performance of government enterprises. There is a general discussion of large companies in Taiwan at the beginning of this book. This is an invaluable source for readers interested in Taiwan's economy and foreign trade.

805   **Who's who of the Republic of China.**
      Compiled by the Chinese Who's Who Publishing Center, edited by Jau-wei Chang.   Taipei: Asian Pacific International, 1982. 1,731p.

Collects biographical sketches for 3,500 persons. This volume is published in both Chinese and English.

806   **Taiwan Buyers' Guide, 1986-87.**
      Corporate Culture Promotion Department, China Productivity and Trade Center.   Taipei: China Productivity and Trade Center. biennial.

In its sixteenth edition since 1958, this is the most useful and comprehensive business directory published in Taiwan. It contains more than 12,000 entries and consists of four parts, namely: manufacturers, exporters/importers, services, and an appendix.

807 **Taiwan politics.**
Compiled by Anthony Ferguson. In: *East Asian politics: China, Japan, Korea, 1950-1975*. Paris: International Political Science Association, 1977, p. 117-26.

Those who have long appreciated the utility of the International Political Science Abstracts (IPSA) will find this compilation of abstracts of articles on Taiwan convenient. However, scholars who want to find original titles in languages other than English or summaries of the articles will still need to check full bibliographic references in IPSA. Subjects include: the Kuomintang Party, foreign relations, economy, youth and students, law, the military, political opposition, and the unification issue.

808 **Chinese periodicals in the Library of Congress.**
Compiled by Han Chu Huang. Washington, DC: Library of Congress, 1978. 521p.

Chinese language serials in the Chinese collection of the Library of Congress's Orientalia Collection are listed in this bibliography. More than 6,400 titles from the period 1868-1975 published in mainland China, Hong Kong, and Taiwan are included in this compilation. It covers every conceivable subject, from the social sciences and the humanities to the natural sciences, excluding only Chinese legal serials, which are in the custody of the Far East Law Division of the Law Library of the Library of Congress. This publication is a significant advance toward the development of new and broader research possibilities in Taiwan studies.

809 **Taiwan Trade Directory.**
Importers and Exporters Association. Taipei: Importers and Exporters Association of Taipei, 1963- . annual.

Contains vital background information about the Importers and Exporters Association of Taipei and the structure of Taiwan's economy. This directory also describes government plans for the future and the effect that those plans are likely to have on industry. A list of Taiwan's import/export commodities and the businesses and financial institutions in Taipei is arranged alphabetically in English.

810 **An annotated guide to Taiwan periodical literature.**
Edited by Robert L. Irick, revised and enlarged by K. M. Ho. Taipei: Chinese Materials and Research Aids Service Center, 1972. 174p.

This revised edition lists 1,070 periodicals, including some English and bilingual publications. Entries are arranged alphabetically, followed by a stroke count index (for Chinese periodical titles) and a general subject index. The editor warns that the latter is not cross-referenced. For each entry, publication information and a brief annotation are provided.

811 **Taiwan: a comprehensive bibliography of English-language publications.**
Compiled by J. Bruce Jacobs, Jean Hagger, Ann Sedgley, with an
introduction by J. Bruce Jacobs. Bundoora, Australia: Borchardt
Library, La Trobe University; New York: East Asian Institute,
Columbia University, 1984. 214p. (Occasional Papers of the East
Asia Institute).

This volume is arranged by subject and includes publications in the social sciences and
humanities that appeared between 1945 and 1980. Its index includes individual authors,
corporate authors, and the titles of edited collections included in this bibliography as
well as the editors of those volumes. Although unannotated, this is an important
reference tool for anyone interested in Taiwan studies.

812 **China watching by the Japanese: reports and investigations from the
first Sino-Japanese War to the unification of China under the
Communist Party: a checklist of holdings in the East Asian collection,
Hoover Institution.**
Compiled by Michiko Kiyohara. Stanford, California: Hoover
Institution Press, 1987. 387p. (Hoover Press Bibliography, no. 66).

Recently Western scholars have recognized the enormous value of Japanese field
research in China during the first half of the twentieth century. While some Japanese
'China watching' activities consisted of translating official documents and special
Chinese works, most research was highly original and extensive in its analysis of the
elements of Chinese society. Scientific surveys of soils, rivers, forests, and minerals
were also conducted. Items compiled here cover the period 1895-1949, and include
works about colonial Taiwan produced by many Japanese government-sponsored
agencies for strategic, economic, and political purposes. This volume forms a
particularly convenient checklist.

813 **An annotated bibliography of selected works about Republic of China.**
Compiled by Karen Siu-chu Lee, Anna Choung-mei Tai. Taipei:
Kwang-hwa, 1981. 105p.

Lists 200 publications introducing various aspects of Taiwan, including agriculture and
fishery, communications and transportation, economics, industry, engineering, education, public health, politics, science, religion, and others. There are twenty-six
categories in total. The appendix contains addresses of publishers, as well as an author
index and title index.

814 **Chinese law past and present: a bibliography of enactments and
commentaries in English text.**
Compiled and edited by Fu-shun Lin. New York: East Asian
Institute, Columbia University, 1966. 419p.

This bibliography, which concentrates on English language materials, puts its emphasis
on studies of the law of communist China. Materials on traditional China and the ROC
– from its beginnings to the present day in Taiwan – are also included in the 3,500
entry items. Administrative ordinances, however, are excluded. Subjects cover the
judicial system, public law, commercial law, finance and taxation, labour law, civil
procedure, criminal law and procedures, conflict of laws, and other areas.

815 **Taiwan studies on *Dream of the Red Chamber*: a selected and classified bibliography.**
Tsung-shun Na. Taipei: Shin Wen Feng, 1982. 210p.
The *Dream of the Red Chamber* is probably one of the most famous, and controversial, Chinese novels. This bibliography of materials on the novel contains 925 titles of articles and books published in Taiwan from 1950 to 1982. This volume uses Wade-Giles romanization and carries two indexes and an appendix. All titles also appear in Chinese characters.

816 **Directory of the cultural organizations of the Republic of China.**
National Central Library. Taipei: The Library, 1987. 6th ed. 1,102p.
Designed to strengthen services to domestic and overseas scholars and to promote international exchange among cultural organizations both in Taiwan and abroad, this volume lists 980 organizations. Entries are in Chinese and English, with an alphabetical title index in English.

817 **National Taiwan University list of serials in Chinese, Japanese and Korean languages.**
Compiled by the National Taiwan University Library. Taipei: The Library, 1985. 3rd ed. 569p.
Contains serials in the Chinese, Japanese, and Korean languages held in the main library and its forty-four branches. In total 6,833 titles are collected, 4,007 in Chinese, 2,557 in Japanese, and 269 in Korean. In addition, seventy-five newspapers are included. For each entry, the volume includes the location of the item as well as publication information.

818 **Business groups in Taiwan, 1983-84.**
Publication Department, China Credit Information Service. Taipei: China Credit Information Service, 1983. 828p.
The term 'business group' is defined in this book as three or more firms that fit the following requirements: (1) they have minimum total assets of 200 million New Taiwan Dollars; (2) one person, a group of persons or one of the companies is able to control or significantly influence all the other companies of the group; (3) all the companies acknowledge they are of the same group. In accordance with this definition, 100 groups (or 713 companies) are covered in this volume, including most of the influential groups in Taiwan. Each group is described in terms of its size, leading character, management, financial condition, and industrial standing and perspective. A profile of the group's member companies is supplied, along with a diagram which indicates the relationships between companies within the same group. A brief introductory chapter deals with general trends and changes in Taiwan's business groups.

819 **Research institutions and current research in the Republic of China.**
Science, Technology Information Center. Taipei: The Center, National Science Council, 1987. 713p.
Contains information on eighty institutions engaged in fundamental and applied research. Institutions are arranged in alphabetical order and grouped into four categories according to fields of endeavour: agricultural, biological and medical sciences; applied sciences and engineering; humanities and social sciences; and physical

219

sciences. This publication provides an invaluable guide to research and development activities conducted by government and non-academically supported organizations.

820 **Businessman's Directory of the Republic of China, 1988.**
Edited by Taiwan Enterprise Press. Taipei: Tong-hsing Culture Press. annual.

Contains the addresses and phone numbers of government organizations, foreign embassies and consulates, religious centres and hospitals. The book is then divided into three main sections: services, manufacturers/suppliers, and importers/exporters. This is a useful handbook for both businessmen and tourists.

821 **Taiwan Exporters Guide, 1988.**
Edited by Taiwan Enterprise Press. Taipei: Tong-hsing Culture Press. annual.

Consists of a brief survey of Taiwan's export industry, with lists of products, manufacturers, and exporters. Company entries are organized alphabetically.

822 **Taiwan traders directory, Republic of China, 1986-88.**
Taiwan Importers and Exporters Association. Taipei: The Association, 1986. 611p.

A manufacturers' index and a commodity classification index are both listed in Chinese and in English. The appendices cover overseas offices of government agencies and local foreign banks in Taiwan.

823 **Women in China: a selected and annotated bibliography.**
Karen T. Wei. Westport, Connecticut: Greenwood, 1984. 250p.

Covers mainland China and Taiwan from the late nineteenth century to 1982, with emphasis on the economic conditions, status, and liberation of Chinese women. The volume includes books, journal articles, dissertations, theses, conference papers, book chapters, and non-print media. This bibliography provides a very much needed reference tool for any serious student of women in Chinese history and culture.

824 **Bibliography of Taiwan archaeology from 1950-1968.**
Wei-lan Wu. *Asian Perspectives*, vol. 15, no. 2 (1973), p. 177-85.

This bibliography of Taiwanese archaeology is presented with an introductory note describing the development of organized archaeological research in Taiwan.

825 **Bibliography of Taiwan geology: 1973 through 1985.**
Tzen-fu Yui. Taipei: Institute of Earth Sciences, 1986. 88p.

Covers English-language publications which appeared during the period 1973-85. More than 1,000 items on Taiwan's geology are included. An author index and subject index are provided.

Bibliography of studies of the Chinese family.
See item no. 200.

Studies on Taiwan plains aborigines: a classified bibliography.
See item no. 265.

Research activities in the performing arts in the Republic of China: a bibliographical report.
See item no. 709.

Chinese music: an annotated bibliography.
See item no. 716.

Chinese paintings in Chinese publications, 1956-1968: an annotated bibliography and an index to the paintings.
See item no. 726.

Indexes

There follow three separate indexes: authors (personal and corporate); titles of publications; and subjects. Title entries are italicized and refer either to the main titles, or to other works cited in the annotations. The numbers refer to bibliographic entries rather than pages. Individual index entries are arranged in alphabetical sequence.

Index of Authors

224

Index of Titles

China Quarterly 763
China question: essays on current relations between mainland China and Taiwan 421
China, seventy years after the 1911 Hsin-hai revolution 67
China, Taiwan, and the offshore islands 488
China Times 753
China watching by the Japanese: reports and investigations from the first Sino-Japanese War to the unification of China under the Communist Party: a checklist of holdings in the East Asian, Hoover Institution 812
China's global presence 334
China's island frontier: studies in the historical geography of Taiwan 69
China's military modernization: international implications 481
China's practice of international law: some case studies 298
China's traditional rural architecture:a cultural geography of the common house 711
Chinese art 707
Chinese city between two worlds 127, 162, 184
Chinese communist materials at the Bureau of Investigation Archives, Taiwan 788
Chinese family and its ritual behavior 199
Chinese family law and social change 300
Chinese fiction from Taiwan: critical perspectives 693
Chinese law past and present: a bibliography of enactments and

commentaries in English text 814
Chinese medical herbs of Taiwan 37
Chinese music: an annotated bibliography 716
Chinese paintings in Chinese publications, 1956-1968: an annotated bibliography and an index to the paintings 726
Chinese Pen 764
Chinese periodicals in the Library of Congress 808
Chinese pioneer family: the Lins of Wu-feng, Taiwan 1729-1985 89
Chinese stories from Taiwan: 1960-1970 696
Chinese women: past and present 240
Chinese working-class lives: getting by in Taiwan 637
Chinese Yearbook of International Law and Affairs 765
Christianity and animism in Taiwan 154
Christianity in Taiwan 157
City in late imperial China 77, 84, 144
Coastal fishes of Taiwan 45
Collection of Chinese folk songs 715
Collection of woodcuts by Lee Kuo-chu 727
Colleges and universities in the ROC: a pictorial introduction 297
Colonial development and population in Taiwan 95
Committee of One Million: 'China lobby' politics, 1953-1971 424
Commodity-price Statistics Monthly in Taiwan area of the Republic of China 660
Compilation of the laws of

the Republic of China 304
Conference on economic development and social welfare in Taiwan 218
Confucianism and economic development 174, 543, 547
Contemporary China: a research guide 801
Contemporary Republic of China: the Taiwan experience 1950-1980 170
Contending approaches to the political economy of Taiwan 198, 358, 360, 425, 513, 514, 516, 622, 652
Contest for the South China Sea 500
Court-martial of the Kaohsiung defendants 367
Cult of the dead in a Chinese village 124
Current Contents of Foreign Periodicals in Chinese Studies 766

D

Demographic anthropology 261
Descriptive and illustrated catalogue of the paintings in the National Palace Museum 720
Development and cultural change: cross-cultural perspectives 510
Developmental states in East Asia 542, 615
Developmental strategies in semi-industrial economies 529
Digest of commercial laws of the world 310
Directory of the cultural organizations of the Republic of China 816

Index of Subjects

Map of Taiwan

This map shows the more important towns and other features.

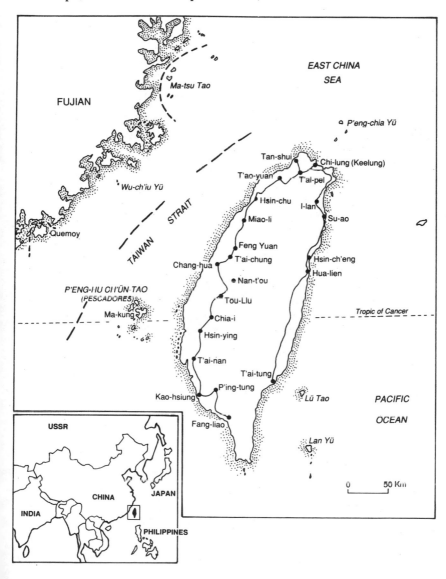